Encounters
Ten Appointments With History

Encounters
Ten Appointments With History

Richard L. Hermann

Persimmon Alley Press
Arlington, VA

Cover design by David E. Manuel

All images and cover photographs from
Wiki Commons and Public Domain

Library of Congress Control Number:
2017946335

ISBN-13: 978-0-9991366-0-7
ISBN-10: 0-9991366-0-7

Acknowledgements

If there is a better editor around than David Manuel, I have yet to encounter him or her. His knowledge of and facility with both language and the subject matter of this book is remarkable and unique in my writing experience. He took an unwieldy set of topics and rendered them much more interesting, resonant, and relevant than my original draft. I thank him for that.

This book owes much to the authors of the books listed in the Bibliography, especially the ancient chroniclers. I am especially indebted to Herodotus for his history of the Greek-Persian conflict that is the subject of Chapter One, Aeschylus who was actually present at the epic Battle of Marathon where he fought in the hoplite ranks of the Athenian phalanx, and to the Roman historian Livy, whose account of the meeting of the aged, forcibly retired and exiled generals, the Carthaginian Hannibal and the Roman Scipio, laid the groundwork for Chapter Two of this book. Their stories of these encounters enthused and energized me to tackle the eight additional chapters that comprise this book.

To Anne, who is always the first line of editorial defense.

Contents

Prologue

Confession: I am not a professional historian. I just enjoy reading history and marveling about the past—how we got to where we are, and are there any lessons there that can tell us where we might be heading. There is nothing more exciting or interesting. It is with good reason that "story" is the root word of history.

Beyond devouring history, I have had the good fortune to visit many places where some of history's most momentous events took place. Whenever I am in such a locale—Gettysburg, Poitiers, Canterbury, Passchendaele, Nuremberg, Pompeii—I am beside myself with excitement. Magic places where great events took place move me like nothing else. They are hallowed—and haunted—grounds. Often, these have been out-of-body experiences.

I wrote this book in order to share some of this wonder, and also to try to show that a subject that is ruined for many of us by numbing school texts as we grow up, does not have to be that way. History, recited properly and enthusiastically, is the most vibrant, exciting, and entertaining "read" there is, with unlimited possibilities for both pleasure and good lessons.

While history is fascinating and fun, footnotes are not. They are too disruptive in a "popular" history, interrupting an otherwise interesting account. Hence, you won't find any here. You will, however, find a bibliography at the end of the book. If you would like to know more about the historical figures and events in this labor of love, I commend it to you.

Introduction

History is made by men and women. Without human interaction, there is no history.

I am fascinated by the interactions of the great men, women, and events of history. Were the giants of an age destined to meet? Were their encounters inevitable? Was their time together pre-ordained by a higher power? Did rockets go off when they met? What did two powerful personalities say to each other? What did they think of each other? Did anyone bother taking notes?

In our time, it is commonplace for the great and famous to meet. So commonplace, in fact, that we take such encounters for granted. Often we don't even pay attention. The media has seen it all before, and wearily "ho-hums" such encounters. They don't always even merit the front page or the evening news.

We "moderns" are jaded. If Nixon can toast Mao in Beijing, Sadat embrace Begin at Camp David, Rabin shake hands with Arafat in the White House Rose Garden, and Mandela become the ally of de Klerk, then there can be little left to surprise us about subsequent encounters.

Even more astounding, we actually get to witness all these momentous meetings in "real time," thanks to the miracle of modern communications technology.

This is a recent development. Great encounters have happened throughout pre-history and recorded history. For most of time, it took days, weeks, and sometimes months for the paradigm-shifting nature of such events to become known, sink in and be recognized.

Nowadays, it is increasingly difficult, given the hype and buildup surrounding almost every event, to identify significant occurrences from what are really non-events. Consider, for example, how many sporting events are billed as the "Game of the Year," "Game of the Decade," or even "Game of the Century." The trivialization of made-for-television events extends so far that virtually every professional athlete at one time or another is deemed a "superstar," and everyone else even tangentially in the public eye is a "celebrity," no matter how little accomplished, vapid, or downright uninteresting s/he happens to be. What is it about them that we are celebrating, anyway?

Before "information-overload" became the norm, it was easy to spot true superstars and celebrities. Joe DiMaggio, Ted Williams, and Stan Musial were superstars and had the statistics to prove it. Jim Brown ran the football like no one else. Basketball honors its true superstars by foreshortening our references to them to a single name: Russell, Wilt, Oscar, Magic, Bird, Michael, Kobe, LeBron. Hollywood and its political counterpart, "Hollywood-on-the-Potomac" (a.k.a. Washington, DC), are just as prone to this silliness. Now every two-bit, so-called actor is a celebrity despite a meager resume and every back-bench politician aches for the title.

In a world where associations, societies, committees, and clubs dominate the social, intellectual, academic, artistic and every other scene, the coming together of the best and the brightest evoke few emotions or expressions of interest other than yawns. Celebrities have roasted each other so often that they have singed the genre.

Until recently, it was not at all customary for meetings between giants even to take place. Each person usually worked in splendid isolation from his or her peers, and that was that.

****

There is no common theme linking my selections other than how uncommon these encounters were. I have tried to inject an element of diversity, so that different worlds are depicted. Politics, music, art, and war are all represented. I present these encounters chronologically – earliest to latest – which seems as logical as any other organizing principle.

Human nature compels us, no matter where and in what era we live and write, to consider our own place and time far more significant than anything that has ever gone before. In researching and writing this book, I often found myself fighting this same tendency. I succeeded for the most part. Only two of the ten encounters in this book took place in the last 100 years.

My litmus test for including a great encounter in these pages was simply this:

1. Did the encounter change history? OR

2. Are we still affected today by what happened? OR

3. Were there only one or two encounters between the principals? OR

4. Did the encounter captivate me?

The answer to test question number 4, in all ten cases, was a resounding YES. I hope they captivate you as well.

****

We begin on an obscure spit of rock-strewn land on Greece's Aegean shore where, just over 2,500 years ago, a handful of peaceful citizens reluctantly took up arms and fought the greatest battle to date against the most formidable foe in history.

Fast-forward 250 years and cross the Hellespont to Asia Minor, where two of the greatest military adversaries of their or any other time met one afternoon to chew over their glory days.

Move down the Mediterranean coast to the great city of Alexandria and witness the meeting that changed a fallen woman into an empress who would save her country.

Fast-forward 600 years and traverse the Mediterranean to Rome and the day when the most influential saints of the Roman Church arrived together at the throne of St. Peter to be invested with their missions by the greatest of the medieval popes.

Move several hundred miles west to witness the meeting between two of the greatest seafarers of any era, and of the Discoverer and a rival king who finally realized his fatal mistake and plotted to reverse it.

Travel 350 more years and a few hundred miles Northeast, and you can be present as the two greatest composers of all time size each other up during their only brief encounter.

The time interval diminishes, but the distances increase, as we move into the early years of the nineteenth century and a meeting between the greatest man of action and greatest intellectual of that century.

Then we march thousands of miles to the south where, in the middle of equatorial Africa, the greatest explorer of his age confronts his arch-rival on the banks of the Congo River and settles the fate of a continent.

Ahead to the modern world. The year is 1945 and muscular new lands are emerging, shoving aside old regimes. The leader of the Free World meets the leader of an ancient tribe in an even more ancient land to seal a pact guaranteeing the free flow of the mother's milk of the twentieth century . . . oil.

Only 16 years later and back to Vienna to set the stage for Armageddon, where the leaders of the first two nations with the power to exterminate an entire planet and its inhabitants play fast and loose with billions of lives, proving that great encounters can also be very dangerous ones.

Greek Hoplites

Chapter 1 - Marathon

Freedom's First Stand

The mountains look on Marathon—
And Marathon looks on the sea,
And musing there an hour alone,
I dream'd that Greece might yet be free
For, standing on the Persians' grave,
I could not deem myself a slave.

George Gordon, Lord Byron, "The Isles of Greece"

Encounters between cultures, ideologies, and ways of life—not just individuals—are the most momentous and lasting ones of all. They capture the imagination of students of history and the public alike in a way nothing else can. Witness, for example, the clashes of this type that so afflicted and disrupted the twentieth century and all of the current new century to date, diverting and wasting lives, resources and energies. They dominate our daily news and, increasingly, our literature: the battles to the death between Fascism and Democracy, followed immediately by the deadly serious competition between Communism and Capitalism, and now Radical Islam and the West.

Historically, this brand of encounter has always carried with it sinister overtones of conquest and subjugation, "winner-take-all," and annihilation of the losing side and its values, as well as a "final conflict" flavor pitting East against

West. Inevitably, these clashes have typically been resolved on the battlefield or have harbored the threat of all-out war, although that has not always been the case. Invariably, these contests have changed the world.

There are a number of worthy candidates for scrutiny, including several of a (relatively) peaceful nature that, given the passage of time, were of tremendous import: Columbus landing in the New World; da Gama opening up the sea route between Europe and Asia; the opening of Japan, to name just a few that, with time, proved earthshaking in their own right, without "benefit" of total war. And among the more fractious, we could certainly include the several occasions when the West had to "stop" the East from overrunning it (or failed in that attempt, such as at Constantinople in 1453): the invasions of Western Europe by Alaric in 410 and Attila later in the fifth century; Charles Martel's defeat of advancing Islam at Poitiers in 732; the many Mongol incursions into Russia and Eastern Europe 500 years later; Count Niklas Graf Salm, helped by nature (torrential rains), halting the Turkish advance at the very gates of Vienna in 1529.

For our first encounter, I have selected the very first of these recorded "final conflicts," one that "set the scene" for all later East-West clashes to follow. One that was of such tremendous significance, so influential and epic, that it changed the course of history down to the present day. Had Darius the Persian and his successor Xerxes prevailed 2,500 years ago, would we even know of the "glory that was Greece" or of the tremulous flicker of two of the greatest ideas ever conceived by the mind of man: freedom and democracy?

The Run-Up

As the fifth century BC began, Persia stood atop the world, a colossus. For 50 years, Persian troops had overrun almost all of what today constitutes Iran, Iraq, Syria, Turkey, Lebanon, Israel, Jordan and the rest of the Middle East. Beginning with their imperial founder Cyrus, the Persians had created the world's first global empire.

By this time, Greece and Persia had developed a history. What is now western Turkey had been settled by Greeks centuries before. These small cities were considered part of the Persian Empire, and they paid dutiful obedience and tribute to the King of Kings and the regional satraps. However, every once in a while, one or more of them, often goaded by their countrymen back in Greece, defied the Great King in some small or even big way.

Irritated by two small Greek city-states in Asia Minor, aided by their parent cities in Greece, King Darius looked west over the Aegean Sea and became annoyed. Sparta sent emissaries warning him to keep his hands off the Greek cities of Asia Minor. Athens sent troops deep into Persia and burned the ancient city of Sardis to the ground before hastily retreating home.

Darius sent his own emissaries to Sparta and Athens demanding the traditional offerings of submission—earth and water. The Spartans threw the messengers into a well, shouting that there they would have all of the earth and water they wished. The Athenians simply murdered them, but did send earth and water. No matter, because following those mixed signals, the Athenians did everything they could to provoke a confrontation.

The bear baiting was led by the Athenian *Philaid* family, which traced its origins back to the legendary Trojan War hero, Ajax. They ruled in the *Chersonese*, a portion of the Crimean Peninsula settled by Greeks, and developed a reputation for good government. In 516 BC, Miltiades, who will loom very large later in this chapter, became the ruler of the Chersonese, but the expansion of the Persian empire made it politic for him to become Darius' vassal. In fact, in 513, he was ordered by Darius to help guard the Bosphorus crossing while Persia campaigned against the Scythians. While there, he unsuccessfully attempted to incite the Greeks to destroy the bridge and strand the Persian army on the European side of the straits.

Three years later, the Scythians overran the Chersonese and Miltiades fled. He was in exile from his lands for 14 years. When the Persians finally defeated the Scythians, Miltiades returned to the Chersonese, but found that Darius had not forgotten his treachery. Having dealt with the Ionian revolt, Darius now turned his attention to his disloyal vassal. In 493, Miltiades and his family escaped to Athens, where he was greeted as a Persian lackey. He was accused and tried for the capital charge of "repressive government," mainly (and counterintuitively) because he had stood up to the Persians. The intimidated Athenians feared that the Persians would punish them if they did not punish Miltiades. Nevertheless, he was acquitted after deftly arguing that his time in Persia made him an expert on Persian military tactics. His return to public legitimacy was swift. Three years later, he was elected one of Athens' ten *strategoi* (tribal leader). It was a remarkable turnaround and came none too soon...for Athens.

The cumulative effect of all of this Greek defiance was too much for Darius. The die was cast.

The Threat

The democratic idea might have been snuffed out in its infancy had not Athens, a small, unprepossessing and contentious city-state located on an inhospitable, rocky piece of turf thrusting south from the Balkan peninsula into the warm waters of the Mediterranean, decided to fight for its recently won liberties against the most powerful military force on Earth. Even at the time, this contest took on mythical proportions in the minds of both participants and observers. The Athenians were acutely aware of the implications of defeat, so defeat became impossible to countenance. The threat became THE THREAT. It got all of Greece's attention, although, with only one exception, the other 230-plus Greek city states were content either to knuckle under to Persian intimidation or sit on the sidelines and hedge their bets on the victor until they had a better feel for which way the wind would blow.

So why not Athens?

The Athenians who rose to the challenge inspire us to this day. They knew what was at stake and what they had to do. That in itself was a remarkable innovation in the advance of human and political development. For the first time, a people down to the humblest *hoplite* (citizen-soldier) in the Greek ranks, knew what the implications of defeat were, and was energized by them. Resistance was not futile. Defeat was not an option.

Whose heart does not beat a little quicker, and who does not experience a feeling of pleasure, upon first hearing about Marathon, Thermopylae, Plataea, and Salamis? The names are timeless, legendary, and still speak loudly to us across the millennia.

Moreover, this first epic encounter between civilizations strikes a very modern chord for we who keep alive the precious flames of democracy and freedom 2,500 years later. The analogies to our own time, when the free world was thrice threatened with extinction by totalitarian contempt for freedom—first Fascists, then Communists, now radical Islam— are very *apropos*:

- Each encounter pitted two civilizations on a collision course, a game of global chicken that went to the culture that did not blink.
- Each time the East attempted to impinge on the West, and lost.
- Each clash pitted a totalitarian invader against defenders who had a survival stake in their hard-won liberties.

- Each contest required the transformation of a peacetime economy into a war footing.
- Each was an ideological contest in which the positions of the parties were clearly delineated and unambiguous.
- Each was a battle to the death.
- Each time freedom and democracy were threatened, its defenders learned a great deal from their counterparts who fought the same desperate struggle in the fifth century BC.

One final preliminary word before relating this true tale of David against Goliath: In addition to the inspiration we still draw from Marathon, it did one more remarkable thing: it actually launched the *idea* of history, the events being so stimulating, exhilarating, riveting, and compelling, so all-consuming, not to mention being one hell of a story, that it made men like Herodotus (a contemporary) and Thucydides (a near-contemporary) take up their styluses and write it all down! *No one had ever done that before.* Marathon made Herodotus' career. Reading his account after the passage of 2,500 years does nothing to diminish the drama of his description.

In fact, it is Herodotus upon whom we must rely for virtually all of our information about Marathon. No other contemporaneous writing about the battle has survived. Absent Herodotus' innovation, there would have been no Marathon, Thermopylae or Salamis to inspire us today when faced with overwhelming odds.

And make no mistake, we are inspired. Every weekend somewhere there is a celebration of this first great awakening of the idea of freedom. It is captured not through a religious observance or a parade or flowery political speeches. Rather, it is in the form of a simple, long-distance footrace that tests the limits of man's endurance and pays homage at the same time to the epic events of 2,500 years ago, in the most fitting manner possible: one person persevering against the odds.

Significance

Marathon. The name itself is steeped in mystique.

Marathon and its successor battles ten years later were the first epic confrontation between East and West that would decide the fate of the "known" world, "known" at any rate to Europeans and Central Asians.

The story of Marathon is complex. By the fifth century BC, Greek culture, politics and international relations were highly developed and dispersed, and thus made of Marathon much more than a simple contest of East versus West.

The Ionian Greek cities located in Asia Minor (modern Turkey) were creatures of the *metropolis*—the "mother" city. Athens was the primary mother city for most of the Ionian outposts, and it was to her that they looked for direction and instruction. It was their actions that set Darius of Persia on his collision course with Greek civilization.

At the same time, events back in Greece contributed. The balance of power was shifting, thanks to the undisputed authority of muscular, young Sparta in the Peloponnese, the almost half of Greece that dangles like a cow's udder below the Isthmus of Corinth, and its new mode of muscle-flexing among its neighbors. Something of a "cold war" had been going on for years, with the Spartan warrior philosophy competing for intellectual dominance of the Balkan Peninsula with the Athenian espousal of democracy. In 510 BC, Sparta escalated this competition to new levels by intervening to thwart Athens' adoption of democratic principles. The competition between the two cities, both political and military, lasted a full century, constantly interrupted by disturbing distractions from across the Hellespont—the narrow strait now known as the Dardenelles—that separates Europe from Asia, namely the emerging power of autocratic Persia.

The Persians were also flexing their new muscles, and doing so in a manner designed to provoke the Greeks. Attacks on Greek Ionian outposts increased in frequency and intensity, and pleas for assistance from the beleaguered cities barraged Athens. In 499 BC, urged on by the mother city, the Ionian settlements rebelled against Darius, launching a five-year conflagration that was eventually crushed.

The difficulties and expense involved in suppressing this revolt made Darius conclude that it was crucial to deal with the root cause of the Ionian uprising. In short, the Mediterranean world was not big enough for both despotic Persia and semi-democratic Greece. Something had to give.

Thus, in the summer of 490 BC, Darius outfitted a highly-trained and battle-hardened army of 50,000 men. He then assembled the greatest armada in history at Samos, just off the Ionian coast, loaded on the army, and took ship for mainland Greece. His intention was nothing less than the complete subjugation of Athens and the "Athenian Way of Life," which had in a short time established itself as the world's very first bulwark of liberty, democracy and cultural refinement of the highest order, a remarkable achievement for a small city no bigger than a modern rural town.

Persia was a land, not a naval, power, and the boldness of a stroke at central Greece from the sea was radical. Darius intent was to establish a bridgehead, sever Attica (the region in which Athens is situated) from the Peloponnese, and then subjugate Sparta and its sister cities in the south. The only other alternative would have been a long, overland campaign moving down the peninsula from the north, during which many men would undoubtedly have been lost and provisioning a distant army would become a problem.

Despite the alien nature of seafaring to the Persians, they possessed one singular advantage when it came to sea power and navigation: their navy was manned by Phoenicians, a subject people who happened to be the greatest sailors in the world.

The triremes that launched from Samos island-hopped across the Aegean, never remaining at sea for more than 30 miles or about eight hours. The first stop was Naxos, where the Persians got in some raping, pillaging, and burning, just to keep their skills sharp. Next came Delos, which escaped unscathed. From Delos, the fleet steered northwest through the Cyclades, making for the long island of Euboea, just across the Gulf of Petaloi from Athens itself. Refusing to provide hostages or troops, the Euboeans suffered the same fate as Naxos.

As the Persian fleet crossed the Aegean, it was being monitored by Athenian intelligence. The closer the ships came to Athens, the more inevitable it became that battle would be necessary. After several days in Euboea, the Persian fleet pushed off across the Gulf toward an Athenian ally, the island of Eretria. The island held out for several days, but was then betrayed by a fifth column. After ransacking its temples, the Persians rounded up and incarcerated most of the citizens, eventually selling them into slavery in the east.

Eretria subdued, the triremes set forth on the final leg of the invasion. The forces of darkness were now poised on freedom's frontier. The plain of Marathon, with its placid bay and fine beach, lay inviting.

Back Story

The Athenians had striven long and hard for their precious gift of liberty and were not about to relinquish it without a fight. However, they knew that they would be facing the greatest fighting force in the world, and also knew that they were woefully outnumbered. If they were to survive, it would only be with assistance, so they set out to transform the dispute with Persia beyond one with just Athens, and make it into a wider conflict of Persia and all of Greece.

As with so many other innovations that emerged in these centuries from this remarkable city-state, the idea of an alliance for politico-military purposes among many disparate communities was a completely new one. But what else could one expect from this tiny enclave that, in a span of only one hundred years, harbored the greatest collection of geniuses until Florence almost 2,000 years later? Herodotus, the world's first historian; Thucydides, who followed him; Socrates, the founder of philosophy; Plato, his disciple and scribe; Aeschylus, the father of dramatic art; Pindar the poet; Phidias, the world's greatest sculptor; Sophocles, the greatest tragedian, unmatched until Shakespeare; philosophers

Anaxagoras and Protagoras; playwrights Euripides and Aristophanes; mathematicians like Euclid and Pythagoras; and many others.

Anticipating the Persian onslaught and its own feeble counterforce—Athens could raise only 9,000 men from among its citizens and slaves who were of fighting age (20-60)—the city sought help first from its arch-rival Sparta, the foremost military power in Greece. The city fathers sent forth their finest long distance runner, Philippides (a.k.a. Pheidippides), to traverse the seacoast and crags comprising the 150-mile stretch between the two rival cities, in order to urge the Spartans to help defend against the Persian threat. Philippides left early one summer morning on this first of his epic runs, toward Sparta and immortality.

Homo sapiens are the greatest long distance runners in the animal kingdom. They had to be in order to eat and survive during their formative evolutionary years in the African Savanna. They could not match the speed bursts of their natural prey or easily avoid becoming prey themselves to lions and cheetahs who could easily run them down as long as they did not have to run very far. Anaerobic weaklings, humans were constructed to become aerobic champions, able to persist in running down prey until their four-legged meals on wheels tired and gave up. Philippides was the natural result of millions of years of evolutionary fine-tuning of this remarkable talent.

As he ran up-country, he could look back and, in clear weather, see the Persian armada off to the east, the greatest fleet ever assembled to that time. The shock of that sight firmed up his resolve and pushed him to overcome his fatigue and soreness. He pressed on to Sparta.

The Persian Empire was the predominant military and political power of the ancient world, stretching from the Bosphorus, Dardanelles, and Sea of Marmara in the west to the Indian subcontinent in the east and from beyond the Caucasus in the north to Upper Egypt in the south. Emperor Darius counted among his troops Ethiopians, Afghans, and horsemen from beyond the Hindu Kush.

He could also count on the perfidy of the exiled Hippias, the ousted tyrant of Athens, as well as Hippias' followers still in the city who were suspicious of the fledgling democracy and all too willing to subvert it and turn Athens over to Oriental satraps. By the beginning of the fifth century, BC, the great democratic legacy of the Mediator Solon had taken firm root, but still needed a great deal of watering, nurturing, and watching over in order to survive and thrive.

Athens was the first corporation and first bureaucracy in the modern sense. It was governed by committee. There was a board for everything—roads, harbors, military affairs, magistrates, finances, temples, etc. Responsibility was dispersed among an array of democratic participants. Consequently, it was not easy to arrive at decisions, much like in a modern state.

The "upside," however, was a very salutary one: everyone in the *polis* developed a participatory sense of involvement in decisions once arrived at. And participation was the name of the game in democratic Athens. The citizenry met formally *40 times a year*, and nary a year went by without additional calls to meeting in special session. Attendance at governmental sessions was considered a mandatory civic duty and shirkers were labeled *idiotes*, which term has come down to us and is often used to describe the modern manifestation of similar studied ignorance.

Civic passion in Athens was high, and that is the best basis upon which to build a defense of one's community.

The Odds

Athens' gross domestic product in 490 BC was approximately 250 talents. Persia's amounted to 12,500 talents, 50 times more than Athens.

The Athenians were a peaceful people, devoting themselves principally to agriculture, trade and fishing. The Persians, in contrast, were a militant people, honed by fifty years of continuous, triumphant war.

Persia was an empire. Athens was a tiny town.

Persia had a standing army of indeterminate size, but decidedly larger by far than anything the Athenians could possibly muster from their paucity of farmers turned *hoplites*.

A betting man would have been insane to put his money on Athens.

Topography

The plain of Marathon lies 25 miles northeast of Athens, where it reveals itself as a broad, pebbled beach. From Marathon to Athens, the Persians would have two alternate routes, one along the coast adjacent to the Saronic Gulf, the other across a series of hills. Regardless, unless they were stopped at the point of debarkation, Athens would lie open to them, as vulnerable as a delicate flower. Sure, the Acropolis was a natural defensive redoubt, but no longer. In the time of their Achaean ancestors, this natural crag, suddenly thrusting more than 200 feet above the surrounding Attic plain, contributed significantly to the selection of the place as the site for the city. But Athens, in the intervening 700 years, had abandoned the Acropolis to legend and myth and established itself on the low ground below. There were no city walls to speak of. The city was defenseless.

The Alliance

Philippides ran on. On the ninth of *Boedromion* (approximately equivalent to our month of August), two days after leaving Athens, one day after crossing the Isthmus of Corinth that separates northern Greece from the Peloponnese, he descended from the rock-strewn mountain passes of the eastern Peloponnese into the valley of *Eurotas*, littered with fig trees and olive groves, to Sparta, called *Lacedaemon*.

Like Athens, Sparta had no walls or other fortifications. It relied, instead, on its constant readiness and legendary military prowess. Also like Athens, the capital of the Peloponnese was little more than a small town, able to muster a fighting force of only 10,000 men. Sparta, too, was governed by a minority population of free citizens, with the majority being slaves. But there the similarities ended.

Sparta was constructed around military principles. It was the only place, according to one contemporary wag, where "war constituted the only respite from training for it." Sparta was an armed camp. The warriors of Sparta regarded their Athenian arch-rivals as soft and looked with contempt upon their unruly democratic ways. Athens thought little more of Sparta; to Athenian eyes, it was a humorless, repressive, totalitarian state.

The Athenian perception, however, was not wholly accurate. Sparta was governed by its own version of participatory politics. Every warrior over the age of thirty had the right to vote for a board of five magistrates (*ephors*) in whom the real power reposed. It was to this board that Philippides carried his petition. He, like his countrymen, knew that if you had to fight to defend yourself, your hearth, and your family from annihilation, you wanted Sparta on your side.

Regardless of their stark differences, Athens and Sparta were both Greek cities and had much more in common with one another than either shared with the Persian invaders. Nevertheless, Philippides well understood the daunting task he faced in trying to persuade Sparta to come to the aid of its ancient enemy. He prepared his arguments while he ran on: He would invoke Athens' membership in the Spartan League, a vestige of the recent wars between the two cities; and he would draw a graphic illustration of the Persian hordes, reminding Sparta that, if Athens fell, Sparta would almost certainly become the next target. Herodotus quotes Philippides plea to the Spartan Ephors:

> "Men of Lacedaemon. The Athenians pray you come to their assistance and not allow our most ancient Hellenic city to be reduced to servitude by the barbarians."

The Ephors' reply was ambiguous. Sparta agreed to come to Athens' aid, but not until the end of the festival of *Carnea*, six days hence. Disappointed, Philippides turned around and ran back up the valley toward the mountains and home.

The run back to Athens took one day longer, during which time the exhausted runner arrived at a shrewd decision. He would not temper his comments with the disappointing equivocation he had received from the Spartans so as not to demoralize them. Instead, he told the Athenians that Sparta had agreed to come to the aid of their countrymen. Technically the truth. And a big morale booster at a moment when such a lift was sorely needed.

Mobilization

The day Philippides arrived back in Athens, the Persian fleet landed at Marathon, hundreds of transports escorted by warships, debouching tens of thousands of men onto the beach, led by Darius' nephew Artaphernes and the great Persian general Datis. Tagging along came the treasonous Hippias, who had been chief navigator on the last leg from Eretria, dripping with perfidy and thirsting for revenge against the city that had exiled him.

With the Persians now only 25 miles away, Athens was consumed by a crisis atmosphere. Mobilization was in full swing. If there was any hesitancy before, there was none now, thanks to the terrifying reports of Persian atrocities as the fleet made its way across the Aegean Sea. Athens stood united, ready to fight, ready to die. On confirmation of the landing, the Athenian assembly gathered and made one of the most important decisions in the history of democratic government, then or now: to advance quickly and meet the Persian army at the invasion point, rather than to wait and attempt to fend them off when they attacked the city.

It is difficult to appreciate the momentous implications of this audacious decision without some context: Greek cities *never* marched their troops out to meet opposing forces. And this particular Persian force was not only larger than any a Greek army had ever faced, but had also never been defeated in the field. Finally, where is the logic in an undermanned army aggressively seeking out a juggernaut? Truly David versus Goliath!

Miltiades, the Athenian with the up-and-down political career that would have made Richard Nixon proud, was a leading proponent of this innovative strategy. He was an expert on Persian military tactics and so commanded a great deal of respect in the high councils of the city. Moreover, his personality was one most conducive to the audacious. The assembly went along and voted for going on offense. The ten traditional tribes of Athens marshaled their paltry 9,000-citizen force and marched out of the city onto the Attic Plain, at the end of which 50,000 highly experienced, battle-hardened, professional Persian troops waited. Athenian generals and hoplites marched in a column across the dusty plain that August, each man responsible for his own provisioning, each thinking his own thoughts of life and death and family. Nine thousand bronze helmets gleamed brilliantly in the hot sun as the column made its way toward the coast.

Drawing close, the Athenians took to the foothills above the plain for concealment purposes. They were stunned to find that the Persians had not moved from their landing site. The other sight that amazed them was the sheer size of the invasion force, with hundreds of triremes and transports lying offshore in the bay, and tens of thousands of troops swarming along the beach and plain. If they had second thoughts about what they were poised to do, Herodotus does not mention them.

One note of caution before we proceed: There is no confirming record of the size of the Persian invasion force. Herodotus had a tendency to exaggerate such numbers in his histories, so I have discounted his wild reports of hundreds of thousands of soldiers. After examining various secondary sources, I decided on a conservative "compromise" figure ... 50,000 Persian fighters. Suffice it to say that the enemy outnumbered the Athenians by at least 5:1. Moreover, the Persian troops were highly trained and experienced professionals, while their Athenian opponents were citizen volunteers.

Strategies

Herodotus notes that the Persians were more lightly armed than the Greeks, probably because so many Persian engagements were decided by bow and arrow, i.e., at long distance. Each archer stood behind a large shield made of wicker, set up on the ground to protect him against arrows from the other side. The Persian army was divided into units of ten thousand ("myriads"), which were in turn subdivided into units of thousands, hundreds, and tens. It is critical to note that the archers had only minimal experience fighting man-to-man against an enemy.

In addition, there were expert cavalrymen skilled at shooting arrows from horseback. However, due to the difficulties of transporting horses by sea, there were only a handful of small cavalry units at Marathon. Thus, the Persians went into battle without one of their most effective—and feared—advantages.

Traditional Persian battle strategy, dating back to the days of Cyrus, was to attempt to win battles *before* coming face-to-face with the enemy. Should it come to pass, however, that they had to fight hand-to-hand, the Persian soldier was armed with a dagger and short spear. Since the possibility that hand-to-hand combat would ever be determinative in a Persian engagement—or even necessary—was remote, the Persians were willing to sacrifice defense for speed and flexibility. Thus, the reliance on *wicker* shields and light weaponry.

The Greeks, in contrast, had some advantages when it came to armaments, although it was deemed highly doubtful that they would ever be in a position to profit from them. The overwhelming firepower of the Persian archers would see to that long before the Athenian shock troops ever came close enough to maximize their advantage in close-in, hand-to-hand combat.

The Greek hoplite was far more heavily armed than his Persian counterpart. In addition to a bronze helmet and large bronze shield, he wielded a long spear and a heavy, two-edged sword suitable for hacking off limbs at close quarters. While these heavy weapons inhibited speed and maneuverability, woe to the enemy who came close enough for them to be deployed!

And so the issue was about to be joined. Less than a mile separated the main bodies of both opposing forces. For several days, the two sides just watched each other, neither venturing to move. For the Athenians, delay was of overwhelming importance, since every day brought new hope that the Spartan expeditionary force would arrive to bolster the Greek forces. Every morning, as the ten Athenian generals awoke on the slopes of Mount Agrelika overlooking Marathon, the hope was renewed. As the days wore on, it was dashed. The Spartans never came. All that the rest of Greece could muster in Athens' defense was a tiny contingent of Plataeans from Boeotia. Plataea came to Marathon out of obligation. It owed its freedom and continued protection to Athens, and in one of the most honorable manifestations of the exercise of such responsibilities in history, sent its entire armed force to Marathon to fight alongside its benefactor. Despite being able to contribute only 600 hoplites, Plataea's noble gesture energized the Athenians and elevated their spirits.

On approximately August 11, the Athenian council of generals held a decisive meeting. They included among their number three soon-to-be legendary commanders: Miltiades, whose force of personality and knowledge of Persian tactics persuaded Athens to attempt to stop the Persians at their landing zone; Themistocles, destined to become one of the greatest leaders of the fledgling Athenian state; and Aristides, known to his fellow Athenians as "The Just" for his impartial adjudications. Overall command was in the hands of the *polemarch*, a.k.a., the "War *Archon*," Callimachus, whose turn to command happened to coincide with the year 490 BC.

The fundamental question before the council was whether to fight or continue to wait in the waning hope that the Spartans would appear. Debate was spirited. Miltiades wanted to take the battle to the Persians on the plain immediately. Half the council supported him. The other half was for waiting, arguing that they had stymied the Persians thus far without suffering any losses. The "X" factor was how long they could expect to continue without the Persian "fifth column" in Athens (an eternal Athenian affliction) attempting a *coup d'etat*. They knew that Hippias had agents in the city, talking up just such a coup. Any further delay might encourage the traitors to act, what with the army 25 miles away, unable to respond. Miltiades argued that delay would cause Athenian spirits to decline from their fragile heights, and that this would greatly influence the ultimate outcome when it eventually came to a fight:

> "Fight before the rot sets in and, if the gods are willing, we can get the better of them. It therefore rests with you, Callimachus. Support my view, and Athens shall not only be free, but the foremost city in Hellas. Support those who decline to fight, and the reverse will become true."
>
> *Herodotus*

Callimachus was persuaded and sided with Miltiades. The next morning at dawn, it was decided, the Greeks would attack.

That evening the soothsayers delved into their mysteries. An altar was constructed on the mountainside, and a sacrificial animal was led to the slaughter. The sources do not tell us if it was a sheep, pig, or something else. The patterns of the flames and smoke were interpreted, the entrails were read, and the priests announced that the omens were positive.

The Battle Is Joined

The Athenian generals woke their troops early the next morning. After prayers and sustenance, the hoplites donned their heavy crested helmets, breastplates, and shields and formed up. At approximately 5:30 AM, just before sunrise, the 9,000 Greek citizen-soldiers—merchants, farmers, potters, etc.—moved down the slope to face at least 50,000 hardened professionals who had, to this point, defeated both Croesus and Nebuchadnezzar and themselves never tasted defeat. The War Archon and Polemarch Callimachus led the way. The playwright Aeschylus was in the ranks that morning, his immortal destiny interrupted.

Athens' army moved in units of its ten tribes: Aeantis, the tribe of Callimachus, followed by Erechtheis, Aegis, Pandionis, Leontis, Acamantis, Oeneis, Cecropis, Hippothontis, and Antiochis.

As the defenders of the small city-state marched down the mountain toward the ranks of the best soldiers of an empire that was master of 90 percent of the known world, they must have been preoccupied by the hallowed nature of the ground on which they would make their stand. Myths of the gods' doings in the area abounded, and the Greeks knew that they were treading over ground sacred to Heracles, son of Zeus, as well as the Athenian hero, Theseus. It heartened them to follow in those illustrious footsteps.

By this time, the Greeks knew that the Persians had brought along relatively little cavalry, so one major anxiety was somewhat allayed. However, they still feared the devastation that the Persians invariably wrought with their archers. Particularly given the plodding way in which Greek armies fought, relying on the eight-rank, hard-on each-others'-heels, shoulder-to-shoulder *phalanx*. Hence, the need for as much surprise as possible. Thus too, the motivation for launching the initial attack under cover of darkness (a two-edged sword in any such conflict). But even that was not enough for Miltiades, the general who knew the most about Persian battle tactics.

Miltiades was troubled by the ponderous nature of the phalanx, of necessity a slow-moving, slow-turning, rather predictable tortoise-like mass of men. He had personally witnessed the speed and flexibility of the Persian forces, who relied upon bowmen, cavalry, and quite unconventional small units and individuals to act as harassers. While the phalanx was a powerful shock troop at close quarters, maneuverability was non-existent and its very density made it highly vulnerable to Persian battle tactics.

Arriving at the edge of the plain, the Greeks formed up into phalanxes, with Callimachus commanding the right wing, the traditional place of honor reserved for the polemarch. The Plataeans were assigned the extreme left wing, and the tribes of Leontis and Antiochis formed up side-by-side in the center, led by their generals, Themistocles and Aristides.

It was at this moment that the commanding influence of Miltiades prevailed over 300 years of Greek fighting tradition (the phalanx had emerged in the eighth century BC). For the first time in Greek military history, the phalanx was abandoned in order to neutralize the enemy advantage. Instead of bunching up, eight-deep, the phalanx was greatly extended to thwart the anticipated Persian flanking maneuver that Miltiades had observed so often before. The Greek line now was stretched to cover the whole distance between the foothills and the sea, rather than the less than half of this ground that would have been covered by the traditional phalanx formation. This was accomplished by reducing the depth of the phalanx from eight rows down to three or four.

As the Greeks deployed, Datis and his Persian commanders scurried to take up positions about a mile away, near the beach. There was little time to extend the *myriads* to counter the stunning Athenian maneuver.

Suddenly, there was a great clamor, as the Greek forces began closing the distance between them and their Persian adversary. Later, Aeschylus reported the exhortations of the generals in the front rank:

> "On, sons of Hellas! Strike for the freedom of
> your land! Strike for the liberty of your children
> and of your wives! for the shrines of the ancestral
> gods and the tombs of your fathers!"

For the first time ever, a Persian commander faced an *advancing* Greek force. Datis was momentarily confused, befuddled by the lumbering mass of men who walked slowly toward him.

Tempted by the thin ranks in the middle of the formation, Datis set up his archers to decimate the Greek center. Behind the archers, he massed a huge force, poised to strike the death blow once the bowmen had softened up the thin middle ranks of the Greeks.

Deeply ingrained in the Greek DNA was the principle that honor required man-to-man, face-to-face combat. They regarded war at long distance as dishonorable and beneath them. Thus, their contempt for Persian reliance on archers was intense, and served to further enflame their resolve.

While the Persians stood still and waited behind their wicker shields, the Greeks continued to advance. At 400 meters, the Persian archers were ordered to prepare their bows with arrows. Datis waited. At 200 meters, the bowmen flexed their weapons and took aim. The mile-long Greek line was almost upon them. Motionless, they waited for the curious, snail-like Greek advance to close the gap between the armies.

At approximately 100 meters, Datis gave the order to fire. Throughout the more than 50-year Persian advance through Asia, this had always been the moment of truth when enemy forces would crumble under the terrible onslaught of Persian arrows from above. Not this time.

The very instant that Datis gave his order, the Greeks suddenly leveled their long spears and broke into a run, charging the Persian line. This sudden, inspired, and unprecedented tactic saved Athenian democracy and the western world.

The baffled Persian archers overshot their mark and, by the time they realized what had happened, it was too late for a second volley. The Greeks were upon them. They had no choice but to draw their lightweight, usually idle side arms.

The thinned-out phalanx, with its heavy weapons and fearsome spears, was far superior to the light Persian swords and made a mockery of their wicker shields. In no time, the Persian archers were decimated.

It was not only Datis and the Persian troops who were stunned and shocked by what had happened. The Greeks, nurtured on a lifetime of terrifying stories of Persian invincibility, could not believe that they had so easily annihilated the legendary archers, the pride of the Persian military. Abruptly, the psychology of the battle reversed itself.

Bursting with new confidence, the Greeks grabbed the momentum.

The Persian army reeled, recoiling at the shuddering shock of the phalanx. The only thing that stopped the charge was the mounting dead weight of the pile of Persian bodies rapidly building up in front of the Athenian ranks.

The fighting in the center now evolved to the push of shield against shield and hand-to-hand combat. It was no contest. The Persian wicker shields were no match for Greek metal. Similarly, Persian scimitars and war axes were pale shadows of the much sturdier Greek broadswords and bronze shields. In short order, the invaders were methodically hacked to pieces. The carnage was terrible.

The Persian ground troops, who had maintained positions behind the archers (and in many battles never even had to be used), now were ordered forward to join the battle. Faced with this heavily manned force, the thin ranks of the phalanx in the center fell back, no match for the overwhelming manpower pitted against them. But the Greeks fought with a fury and passion that comes of defending freedom and homeland against an external invader. The phalanx bent, but did not break.

The Greek center retreated, drawing the Persian horde deeper into the plain. Meanwhile, on the wings, the now reformed, eight-deep rank of the phalanxes, with their superior weapons, beat back the Persians, driving them toward the sea. Eventually, the thin Persian forces on the flanks broke and ran for their ships.

Simultaneously, however, the concentrated Persian *myriads* in the middle of the plain pressed relentlessly forward, making of the Greek line a concavity. The trap was sprung.

The two Greek wings allowed the routed Persians in front of them to escape. Now they turned their attention to their own beleaguered center. From two sides, they converged on the Persian forces, an astounding reversal of the usual tactic that had resulted in so many Persian victories.

Nervously, the Persian commanders in the center of the plain eyed the two-sided Greek pincer. They turned their attention to the flanks as quickly as possible, forgetting about the center. Soon, after closing on the now-trapped Persians, the soil of Marathon ran red with Medic blood. The slaughter was even more terrible than the annihilation of the archers.

Aftermath

Datis had no choice but to order a general retreat to the line of ships in the bay. The surviving Persians made for their vessels as fast as they could, with the Greeks hot on their heels, hacking away. Many Persians drowned or were trampled in the marshy waters.

The Greeks pursued relentlessly, but the Persians were largely able to get to their ships and hasten away. Only seven triremes and transports of the hundreds that had landed at Marathon fell to the Greeks.

At the edge of the marsh, the victorious Callimachus was struck down and killed. Another general, Stesilaus, also lost his life near the end of the engagement.

The triremes pulled away from the beach. The battle was over. It was time to take stock of the situation. Exhausted, the Greeks at first could not believe that they had won. Perhaps there have been greater military "upsets" in the long history of battles, but I cannot think of any.

Herodotus tells us that 6,400 Persians lost their lives that day on the plain of Marathon. Only 192 Athenians died. He does not give us any figures for the estimable Plataeans, nor does he indicate the number of wounded. It is likely that few of the wounded Greeks survived. Exanguination (blood loss) and resulting shock was—and still is—what kills the overwhelming majority of wounded soldiers. From long before Marathon until very recently, battlefield medicine was incapable of saving the wounded. It is a safe bet that warriors who suffered severe blade wounds from pikes, arrows, javelins, spears and swords did not survive. Although exhausted, there was no time for the Athenians to rest. The great fear of the Greek generals, as they watched the Persian ships move away to the south towards Cape Sunium, was that they would make for vulnerable Athens, now without any army whatsoever to defend it.

Before moving out their troops, the commanders ordered the great runner Philippides to make one last run, a relatively short one this time—25 miles—compared to his Herculean feats of the week before, in order to carry the news of victory to Athens. The tired athlete, who had fought in the phalanx all day long, took off immediately for the city.

Even the intrepid Philippides, however, could not tax his endurance beyond human limits. During the run, he hallucinated. Nevertheless, his euphoria over the great victory impelled him onward. He staggered into the city precincts and stumbled to the agora where, legend tells us, he cried out: "Nike!" (victory). Then he collapsed and died, an immortal.

As evening fell on the once more placid Aegean coast, the Athenian generals ordered a forced march to their city in hopes of thwarting the invader. It proved a wise and propitious move.

The Persians were, in fact, intent on precisely what the Athenian generals feared: an attack on Athens. As the Greeks marched along the coast, the Persian fleet made for Phalerum, the Athenian port only three miles from the Acropolis. However, seeing the setting sun glint off the helmets of the victors marching home proved a sufficient deterrent, and the Persian fleet gave up and sailed back to Asia, its commander pondering how to explain the defeat to the autocrat Darius. It could not have been a pleasant contemplation.

Meanwhile, the Spartans, who had marched on the full moon, arrived at Marathon several days after the battle. They looked around, marveled at what they saw, and left impressed with their Athenian rivals. They also left "softened up" for the next round of Athenian advocacy, ten years later, when Spartan participation in the defense of Greece against Xerxes, Darius' successor, would prove vital to victory. The Athenian victory at Marathon made possible the Spartan Leonidas' and his Three Hundred's epic stand at Thermopylae a decade hence. Its example also, arguably, made possible every later struggle against impossible odds where the stakes were survival: Plataea, Poitiers, Vienna, the Battle of Britain, El

Alamein, and Stalingrad.

Within only weeks, Marathon moved from fact into the rarified realm of myth and legend. Monuments were raised on the site of the great victory to the heroes of the battle. These no longer exist, having crumbled into the sands of the plain. The 192 Athenians who perished defending freedom and democracy were buried in a great mound of earth, which still can be seen today.

****

Although it is not far-fetched to assert that Marathon was the most significant military engagement in history, the battle itself did not really solve much of anything. The immediate problem of the Persian threat was still there. In fact, if it did anything at all, the embarrassment of the rout aroused the ire of the Persian emperor, Darius, and his successor, Xerxes, to a frenzy and rendered the subjugation of the Greeks and of Europe an obsession that would not permit them any rest until realized.

Marathon gave Athens and Greece a ten-year reprieve, during which both city and "nation" were able to prepare themselves for the next assault, which they did successfully. But the greater import of Marathon was on men's minds.

First, the Athenian victory instilled confidence in the Athenians, of course, but also more broadly in the Greeks. A Greek city state of modest size and no military renown defeated the armed might of the Persian Empire, thereby proving to themselves and to the Greeks that the myth of autocratic, barbarian invincibility was just that—a myth, unable to withstand the precious, flickering flames of freedom and democracy that, on occasion, have fired men's souls and enabled them to perform incredible feats of heroism in the name of something somewhat abstract, but tremendously important.

Second, although only one other Greek city joined Athens in its fight, the victory sparked for the first time the idea of *Hellas*, the Greek nation, a concept much larger than any individual city-state. The next time the Persians invaded, there was no question about the identity of the defenders. They were Greeks and thought of themselves as such.

Third, the idea that a free people and a democracy with a citizen army could prevail over a totalitarian state whose armies and navies were comprised principally of slaves impressed into service was completely new and exciting. The inspirational Athenian example lives on even today.

We owe the victors of Marathon a great debt.

Scipio Africanus

If the contest between Greece and Persia was the focal event of the fifth century BC, the contest between Rome and Carthage was certainly its third and second centuries BC counterpart. Looking back at our Occidental heritage from today's vantage point, we say it derives from "Greece-and-Rome." That is because history is written by the victors.

But for a few subtle turns of fate, we might instead be saying: "Persia-and-Carthage."

Chapter 2 - Ephesus

Hannibal and Scipio Debate the Vaunted Days of Yore

Delenda est Carthago (Carthage must be destroyed)

Cato the Censor

The next encounter is one of the most intriguing: the two greatest military commanders of their time, and perhaps of any time, generals whose place in history fed upon—and depended upon—each other as adversarial point-counterpoint, got together one afternoon long after they both retired. In their few hours together, they reviewed their epic rivalry, one upon which the fate of the world turned.

Their meeting took place in Asia Minor, in modern-day Turkey, and comes down to us over a span of more than two millennia, thanks to one of great historians of the classical era.

Livy's *History of Rome* contains a superb, concise account of the Second Punic War between Rome and Carthage, arch rivals for domination of the Mediterranean basin for over 200 years. Livy is a quick read and, once past all of the major battles between the two great ancient powers—Trebia River, Lake Trasimene, Cannae, Zama—he abruptly switches gears and takes us into something totally new to historical writing at the time, and quite astonishing: the post-war lives of the two principal antagonists, Hannibal Barca of Carthage and Publius Cornelius Scipio "Africanus," the Roman commander-in-chief.

Livy relates that, almost ten years after the end of the war, they met at the court of Antiochus at Ephesus. They sat and talked with one another, retirees reflecting about their clashes and the historical context of their generalship.

Here is how they got there.

Hannibal Barca and
The Rise of Carthage

To understand the remarkable personality and career of Hannibal Barca, you first have to know something about his country, Carthage.

Kart-Hadasht, "new city" in the ancient Phoenician language, was founded on the most propitious and agreeable promontory on the North African coast by exiles from Tyre, the principal city-state of Phoenicia, in the ninth century BC. Like their progenitors, the Carthaginians became superb seafarers and traders, and made the Western Mediterranean a Carthaginian lake. Also like their Phoenician forebears, who sacrificed infants to the god Moloch, they were a rather cruel and harsh race. It was, for example, a powerful incentive to Carthaginian generals and admirals to go undefeated in military confrontations. One loss usually meant crucifixion upon returning home.

Two other Carthaginian traits worthy of note:

1. First, their ruthlessness translated into severe treatment of conquered peoples, which in turn meant that any enemy of Carthage could count on a lot of support from any North African locals the Carthaginians subjugated. The Romans were shrewd enough to treat defeated foes quite differently. As a result, no invaders of Italy ever profited from turncoat vassals of Rome despite numerous attempts at bringing that off. When Hannibal marched through six hundred miles of Roman territory on his way to Italy, followed by marching hundreds more miles up and down the Italian peninsula, he had almost no success enlisting subject peoples despite offering substantial bribe money and other lucre.

2. Second, most Carthaginians did not have surnames, which makes for a historian's nightmare, especially when combined with the fact that they were downright unimaginative when it came to naming their children. The history of Carthage is littered with Hannos, Hasdrubals, Magos, and Maharbals, all running around getting themselves chronicled at the same time as others with the same names. Historians find this peculiarity impossibly difficult to sort out. Fortunately, one of the few Carthaginians to be blessed with a surname was Hamilcar Barca, the father of the great Hannibal. That makes tracing the history of this remarkable family much easier.

The Trouble with Rome

Carthaginians over many years developed something of a siege mentality, perhaps because they were often under siege. Their insularity brought them difficulty. As did the examples of early attackers of the city, whose campaigns were studied and refined by all of their successors until Carthage was ultimately destroyed.

As the centuries went by, Carthage and Rome both grew more powerful and prosperous. Separated by only 300 miles of water, it was inevitable that they would become arch rivals, each growing too big to share the same (Mediterranean) pond.

The trouble began quite predictably at the halfway point between Carthage and Rome, the bountiful and strategic island of Sicily. Carthage had lusted after Sicily for years, fighting first against the Greeks who colonized the island, then against their Syracusan successors. In 280 BC, the Greek king Pyrrhus of Epirus landed in Italy to battle Rome, but then became interested in Sicily, thus threatening Carthaginian commercial interests on the island. In its defense, Carthage formed an alliance with Rome and together they exhausted Pyrrhus, who ultimately withdrew after heavy losses. Pyrrhus, much respected by his contemporaries, was certainly one who did not learn well the lessons of history and repeated them to his detriment again and again. The attrition of his forces at the hands of the Rome-Carthage alliance was not by any means his first "Pyrrhic" victory. The story goes that, as he stood at the stern of the ship carrying him across the narrow strait of Messina from Sicily to Italy, he remarked, gazing back at the island: "My friends, what a wrestling match for Carthaginians and Romans we are leaving behind us."

More prophetic words were never spoken.

The First Punic War

The inevitable conflict between the two great powers erupted in 264 BC. It was to last a generation before it ended (temporarily), and it marked the beginning of the end for Carthage.

At the beginning of the First Punic War, Rome, a garrison state, was the greatest land power in the world and Carthage, like most mercantile states in history, was a naval power, the greatest sea power on the planet.

By 264, the Roman Republic had conquered the entire Italian peninsula. For the moment, there was nothing left to do militarily. For the first time in its long history, the Roman Republic, finding itself master of a domain surrounded on three sides by water, became interested in ocean commerce. Rhegium, the present-day Reggio di Calabria and a Roman ally, looked eight miles across the strait at Messina, which had the misfortune to be under the domination of a bunch of criminal murderers called Mamertines, the "sons of Mars."

Syracuse, the principal power on Sicily, decided that the Mamertines were a potential threat and sent an expedition to destroy them. Whereupon a minority Mamertine faction invited Carthage to come to its assistance. Unfortunately for Carthage, the majority faction among the Mamertines simultaneously sent emissaries to Rome to ask for help.

That year's Roman Consul, Appius Claudius, marched his troops down the Italian boot to Rhegium where they boarded the handful of sad-looking and barely seaworthy ships that comprised the nascent Roman navy for the trip across the strait dividing the mythical Scylla from Charybdis. Waiting for them in the middle of the passage was a Carthaginian naval task force. In short order, the greatest navy in the world overwhelmed the Roman ships, sinking a few triremes and capturing the rest.

Both sides were a bit shocked at the skirmish. After all, Carthage and Rome had, according to the historian Polybius, first signed a friendship treaty in 508 BC and had renewed it regularly since.

Carthaginian Admiral Hanno (one of the many with that name) immediately proposed a peace conference in an attempt to restore normalcy before things got further out of hand. Tactlessly, he used the occasion to boast of his navy's prowess and, by contrast, the sorry state of its Roman counterpart. The more he bragged, the more Appius Claudius seethed in silence. Finally, Appius could not stand it any longer and said, in words as prophetic as those earlier uttered by Pyrrhus: "If you ... compel us to learn naval warfare, you will soon see that the pupils have become superior to their teachers."

A few moonless nights later, the powerful Roman army snuck into Sicily in an armada of little boats, put Messina under siege, and forced Hanno to retreat, whereupon he was forthwith "dispatched" according to the Carthaginian custom. Worse for Carthage, once on the ground in Sicily, the Romans realized the implications of the island's strategic and commercial position vis-a-vis the Western Mediterranean.

Within only four years of its Sicilian success, Rome constructed a huge navy consisting of 120 ships with which to challenge Carthage. The same year, 260 BC, Rome's very green admirals devised a brilliant and revolutionary plan to turn naval warfare inside out and give themselves a tremendous advantage.

For a millennium, naval warfare was all about ramming, a complex maneuver that took tremendous navigational skill on the part of both leaders and men. The consul Duilius, hardly a seafaring man, set forth to devise a means of employing Rome's exceptional land-based capabilities afloat. His innovation: swinging gangways near the bows of each of his ships to enable them to sidle up to enemy vessels, ensnare them, and allow them to be boarded by the Roman army.

The litmus test of the Duilius' idea came at the battle of Mylae, just off the northern coast of Sicily, in that same year. The gangways worked magnificently and, once on board the Carthaginian ships, the superior Roman troops decimated the Carthaginian mercenaries. Carthage lost 50 ships.

While one of the greatest advances ever in warfare, it was by no means the endgame. The war dragged on, with both sides having their good and bad days. The Romans were great fighters, but nature was even greater. In 255 BC, for example, a single storm destroyed 284 Roman ships, 80 percent of its entire fleet. Polybius says that the First Punic War witnessed the loss of over 700 Roman ships in total, and that more than 200,000 men drowned. (*Note*: Early historians almost always exaggerated both the size of armies and navies and their losses. We can discount these figures somewhat.)

Finally, in 241 BC, the last great Carthaginian fleet ever to sail the Mediterranean was lost during the battle of the Aegates Islands, west of Sicily, and the war of attrition was finally over. Roman hegemony now reached its apex. The threat to Carthage was enormous.

The next time Rome and Carthage locked horns over world domination 20 years later, the tables were turned. Now the greatest sea power in the world reposed on the banks of the Tiber, while the greatest land power lay 300 miles southwest on the North African coast.

Interlude: The Numberless Punic War

The First Punic War exhausted Carthage. its coffers were depleted, its manpower reduced to tired mercenaries returned from Sicily, angry and embittered by broken promises of pay not received. To top it off, Rome demanded staggering reparations.

Within weeks the mercenaries mutinied. A bitter internal war followed, lasting 40 months, and became a struggle of survival for Carthage. At the beginning, Carthage had no standing army now that its mercenaries were in revolt, and its navy, as we have just seen, had been destroyed by Rome. All that was left to defend her was the "Sacred Band," an aristocratic, elite bodyguard of 2,500 soldiers from whose ranks the Carthaginian military leadership historically had been drawn.

But the Sacred Band was a paltry force when pitted against 100,000 rebels. Something more was needed.

The threat of national annihilation often produces great leaders who step forward to save the nation. This is not just a Hollywood construct. It really happens, and has been repeated many times throughout history, from Judah Maccabee to George Washington to Winston Churchill. Roman lore is replete with commanding figures who came to the fore when all appeared lost and proceeded to save the day: Cincinnatus. Decius. Camillus. Horatius-at-the-bridge. And the greatest of them all, Publius Cornelius Scipio. We will get to know him later.

For Carthage, the rebellion of the mercenaries was such a defining moment, when a hero was desperately needed to save the empire. His name was Hamilcar Barca (Barca meant "lightning") and his generalship is exceeded in Carthaginian annals only by that of his son, the great Hannibal.

Hamilcar raised an army of 10,000 men and promptly won a stunning victory against overwhelming counterforce. He employed brilliant military strategies and won battle after battle. But no matter. A generation of war had depleted Carthage, both economically and psychologically. Rome, as shrewd and selective as always, waited and watched, once again carefully picking its spot and its timing, and profited greatly.

This time the Roman objective was the Tyrhennian island of Sardinia, Phoenician and by inheritance Carthaginian for 700 years, a vast source of timber, minerals, and men. Rome contrived an "invitation" from the indigenous population and sent an occupation force. Carthage formally protested and the Roman Senate promptly declared war.

By this time, Carthage had nothing left with which to fight. Sardinia was lost. Moreover, Carthage had to agree to pay Rome additional reparations. All it had left were bitter memories. Ones that, like those that afflicted Weimar Germany in the 1920s, festered, were exaggerated, and were not forgotten.

Hamilcar in Spain

The interwar period saw Hamilcar alone abandon revenge as the motivating force behind Carthage's geopolitical policy. Which intelligent attitude, of course, made him many times more dangerous to Roman interests than his more single-minded—and narrow-minded—colleagues.

Hamilcar devised a brilliant plan for the revival of his city: Developing Carthage's Spanish colonies, until now confined to a few coastal outposts. Accompanied by a small force and his young sons, Hannibal (who was ten) and Hasdrubal, he sailed to Spain in 237 BC. Over the next eight years, he systematically expanded the Carthaginian base in Spain by both military and diplomatic means, and in the process developed an immensely valuable province for his homeland.

When he died in battle against a local warlord in 229 BC, he was succeeded by his son-in-law, another Hasdrubal, who continued his work, founding New Carthage (now Cartagena) and making it the capital of the Spanish possessions, and generally solidifying Hamilcar's plan for Spain. Unfortunately, he too was cut down in his prime, murdered by an assassin in 221 BC.

Hannibal Takes Command

Hannibal Barca was 28 years old when the Carthaginian Senate appointed him commanding general in Spain. The choice was a natural. He already was something of a legend back home, noteworthy for his bravery, military skill, and diplomacy. An extremely intelligent and unusual child, he had grown up not only next to his charismatic father's side, even when in battle, but spent every spare moment studying the campaigns of his hero, Alexander the Great, who had lived only 100 years earlier.

Hannibal spent the next three years clashing with Roman interests in Spain, for Rome had always found Spain a tempting target. The Roman Senate deemed him so dangerous to Rome's Western interests that, in the fateful year of 218 BC, it sent a delegation to Carthage to boldly demand that Hannibal be declared a hostage and sent to Rome. Carthage's refusal meant war.

The Second Punic War

At the beginning of the Second Punic War, Rome was military mistress of all she surveyed. She immediately sent two naval expeditions to Spain and North Africa respectively, in order to end things quickly. However, to Rome's astonishment, when the Spanish fleet arrived, Hannibal was gone.

Where had he gone and to what purpose? That was the overriding question in Rome's councils. The answer was soon in coming. Rome was about to experience 16 years of sheer terror. From New Carthage, Hannibal headed north with a massive army consisting of 90,000 foot soldiers and 12,000 cavalry, plus 37 elephants designed to terrify the enemy. During his famous trek, he traversed three mountain ranges (the Pyrenees, the Alps, and the Apennines) with his horde. First the Pyrenees, where he recruited more troops in southern Gaul, adding modestly to his strength, forded the Rhone, and proceeded up the valleys leading to Mount Blanc and the high Alps.

It took him five months to march the 800 miles between New Carthage and the Po Valley in Northern Italy, and not only the terrain, but also the cost, was steep. Weather, topography, and hostile forces all tried to stop him. While historians (the only historians we have to rely upon are Hannibal's Roman enemies) differ on the numbers, suffice it to say the attrition to Hannibal's army was huge. When he came down the Alpine valleys into Italy from the Dolomites, his strength was reduced by at least half. Among the elephants, the devastation was even worse. Only one survived the march.

Nevertheless, the best-trained and most battle-hardened army in the world was now in Rome's backyard. The threat was palpable on the streets and in the Senate, unaccustomed as the Republic was to being invaded. Despite the undercurrent of panic, Rome confidently sent out the Consul Sempronius with 44,000 legionnaires to make a hasty end of the upstart Carthaginian before he could march closer to Rome.

The Battle of the Trebia River

Sempronius force-marched his troops north. By the time they reached the Trebia River, just south of the Po near present-day Piacenza, in the darkening winter days of 218 BC, they were tired, chilled and exhausted.

Hannibal, his forces rested and fed, did not hesitate. In the middle of the night, while the exhausted Roman army rested, he sent a small band of Numidian horse screaming through Sempronius' camp, designed both to scare the Romans and to dangle some interesting bait. As the Numidians retreated across the river, Sempronius bit at the bait like a voracious trout.

The Consul roused his weary soldiers and made them ford the shoulder-depth, ice-cold Trebia in darkness. Hannibal's army waited on the other side. Emerging dripping and frozen from the river, Sempronius attacked Hannibal's line unsuccessfully. Simultaneously, Hannibal's brother Mago, at the head of 2,000 hand-picked men, charged down from a low ridge behind Sempronius and closed the circle.

The slaughter was terrible, a gruesome precursor of future Roman encounters with the great Carthaginian general. By dawn, Sempronius had lost three quarters of his troops. Thirty-four thousand legionnaires died in the battle. Only 10,000 Romans made it back to Rome to tell the tale of the Roman rout.

The road to Rome was now clear. And Hannibal took it, although obliquely. Instead of marching down the Tyrrhenian coastal lowland, he kept to the ridge of the Apennines in the center of the Italian peninsula for 200 hard miles. Three-and-a-half months later, he took up positions in the steep hills rising from Lake Trasimene, which lies in a valley in the Apennines in Northern Umbria, just south of Tuscany. He also positioned a contingent parallel to the lakeshore road, which led after only 70 more miles, to Rome. Now the Carthaginians waited.

Lake Trasimene: History's Greatest Ambush

Rome had no choice but to fight, although a strong contingent of appeasers thought otherwise. The Republic could not sit idle after the shocking defeat at the Trebia River and permit Hannibal to march and maraud, unobstructed, throughout Italy and ultimately, on Rome itself. Someone had to *do* something.

The chosen someone was the Consul Flaminius, hardly an appeaser. Rather, he was eager for battle and vigorous in his arguments for it. Learning that Hannibal was already somewhere in Umbria in the central Apennines, he embarked with his 40,000-strong legionnaires along the road that would lead him to the lake.

The Romans were very sensitive to omens, both good and bad. Well-known are the portents on the 14th of March, 44 BC, when the ground was being littered with the bodies of dead crows and ravens falling at the feet of prominent Romans in Caesar's camp, along with soothsayers wailing; "Beware the Ides of March!." Less well-known are the portents mitigating against a hasty departure for Lake Trasimene by Flaminius. As he leaped upon his horse, the mount stumbled and the Consul was pitched head over heels. As if that were not a sufficient deterrent, then the standard bearer could not pull up the eagle standard, no matter his effort. It was a bad day to march off to war. Flaminius should have stayed home in bed.

Hannibal's intelligence was sufficiently good that he was quite aware of Flaminius' lust for confrontation. In order to provoke the Consul even more, he laid waste the whole area between the nearby city of Cortona and the lake.

The northeast shore of Lake Trasimene is the ideal place for an ambush. Approaching from Rome to the southwest, Flaminius' army initially encountered a broad plain that narrowed tightly as they marched east along the north shore of the lake. Toward the eastern end of the north shore, the passage between the hills that suddenly rise up and the lakeshore becomes very narrow, no more than 75-100 yards in width. The hills today are covered by olive groves, little changed from that day in 217 BC

A little further along, the passage opens once more into a plain bounded on the opposite side by hills. Hannibal made camp in the plain, right out in the open, plainly visible to the Roman army moving toward it along the shore. He sent part of his force around behind the hills and stationed his cavalry at the mouth of the pass, concealed by the hillocks and their olive groves. It proved a brilliant placement. Flaminius' long marching column appeared along the lake road at sunset in mid-April. The consul did not bother sending advance scouts ahead of his main force. He could see the fires of Hannibal's camp in the distance. Confident that he would destroy the Carthaginian force the next day, Flaminius made camp just before he reached the narrowest part of the passage.

One critically important element studied in depth by Hannibal, but not at all by his foe who, after all, had just arrived on the scene, was the consistent early morning fog that invariably settled in the valley next to the lakeshore at precisely this location. It was always a very low-lying fog. Run a few hundred yards up hill through the olive grove and the fog cleared, mired down below.

Early the next morning, Flaminius formed a column and began marching toward the narrow defile, toward Hannibal's camp and directly into the fog.

During the night, Hannibal had re-positioned his troops for optimal strategic surprise, leaving his camp fires burning to distract the Romans. First, his main battle force moved up the hills and hid in the olive groves above the pass and the expected fog. A second, smaller force moved over the hills beyond the defile directly above the Roman camp, but in position so that when Flaminius moved east in the morning, it would be behind him. Hannibal himself remained in his camp with a third, small force. The fourth strategic component of Hannibal's army was the lake itself. The Roman legions were now surrounded.

When Flaminius and his legions were snugly within the narrow passage and rendered sightless by the morning fog, Hannibal gave the order for all three of his forces to attack simultaneously.

The three Carthaginian contingents could see each other quite well since they were above and clear of the fog engulfing the lake shore, and were thus able to coordinate their assaults. The first wave to hit the Romans came from above them and to their left, charging out of the olive groves down the hills into the fog, creating a terrible din that terrified the confused legionnaires, who could hear the enemy but not see him. The shock of this assault decided the battle then and there. The panicked legions (and legions rarely, if ever, panicked) forsook any discipline whatsoever and ran around in disarray, too stunned to offer much resistance.

Meanwhile, Hannibal himself charged the column from his camp while the third force hit Flaminius from his rear. The Roman army was overwhelmed. Thousands of confused legionnaires turned every which way, unable to see the enemy bearing down upon them, but sensing for the first time, quite correctly, that they were surrounded. Confusion turned into horror, and for three hours the Romans were driven into an ever smaller and smaller area. Flaminius valiantly, but in vain, tried to rally them. One Ducarius, a Carthaginian mercenary, managed to break through the protective ranks around Flaminius and kill him, at which point the army's panic became total. Romans by the thousands dropped their arms and ran in the only direction they could, directly into the lake, where they drowned. The rout was complete.

During the morning of the great battle, says Livy, an earthquake devasted much of central Italy, including the Lake Trasimene region. However, the intensity of the conflict was so great that the soldiers at Trasimene did not notice it.

By late morning, at least 16,000 Romans were dead. Another 15,000 were taken prisoner, and now both consuls had seen their armies decimated in only 100 days. Only a few thousand Roman soldiers survived and managed to escape through the fog to nearby Perusia (modern Perugia). However, the next day, one of Hannibal's lieutenants surrounded that hilltop redoubt and the Romans surrendered.

Hannibal lost approximately 1,500 men.

To this day, evidences of the great ambush over 2,200 years ago can still be found on the lake bed and along the shore and the hills and olive groves overlooking tranquil Lake Trasimene. Swimmers constantly bring up bones from the lake bottom. The battle of Lake Trasimene, the greatest ambush in recorded history, is the only time when a complete army lay in ambush. It was a testament to the genius and iron will of Hannibal.

Fourteen hundred years later, Lake Trasimene kicked up its heels for its second and, so far, last brush with glory when St. Francis (see Chapter 4) took up residence on one of the two islands close to the battle site and fasted and meditated there for 30 days.

Hannibal's soldiers were spent after their almost year-long march and campaigning, including two major battles. Both sides repaired to more serene surroundings to lick their wounds and regroup.

When news of the terrible defeat reached Rome a few days after the ambush, a crowd collected in the Forum and the Senate went into closed session for a several-day, nonstop debate about how to cope with the Carthaginian threat. Extreme times called for extreme measures, and one Quintus Fabius Maximus was declared *dictator*, his mission: hold off Hannibal. His delaying tactics later earned his family the surname *Cunctator* (procrastinator), and he has come down to us through history as Fabius the Delayer. However, he did raise a new army and gave Rome, thanks also to Hannibal's next stratagem, time to regroup and catch its breath.

Meanwhile, Hannibal led his troops southeast along the Apennine ridge. He was followed, at a great distance, by Fabius. The two generals played cat-and-mouse back-and-forth across central Italy for 18 months, with no battle to show for it. Hannibal did what he could to provoke his opponent, wasting the land and the villas in his path, but the cautious Fabius could not be goaded into action.

Cannae

As time passed, the Romans became increasingly annoyed with Fabius' delaying tactics and pressured him to make war on the enemy. With the advent of the year 216 BC, two new consuls assumed military command. Rome would soon discover that Fabius had not been such a bad leader after all.

In the late Summer of 216, the time had come. The Roman Senate ordered the army, now 85,000 strong, to march. Eight legions under the two consuls, Lucius Aemilius Paulus and Gaius Terentius Varro, made for Hannibal's camp near the southern village of Cannae in Apulia, approximately 200 miles southeast of Rome. Cannae was a Roman supply depot, a distant outpost a few miles from the Adriatic and 25 miles north of present-day Bari.

According to Livy, it was a miserable place to encamp, a parched, dry region constantly afflicted with clouds of dust. However, the great Carthaginian strategist saw the tremendous tactical advantage this would give him, and decided to form his troops with their backs to the wind so that the dust would blast directly upon the enemy, blinding him.

The two Roman consuls marched together, but made separate camps far away from one another upon arrival at Cannae, due to their differences, which had reached the boiling point during the march across Italy. Bureaucracy was rampant, and as was the custom, the two consuls traded the supreme command daily, which hardly made for a coordinated strategy.

On August 2, it was Varro's turn, and he gave the order for battle without bothering to inform his fellow consul. Paulus, observing Varro's legions crossing the river, had no choice but to form up and hastily follow with his disorganized forces.

The battle lines had the Romans facing south, into the wind and dust, while the 50,000 Carthaginians faced north. Again, it was no contest. Hannibal's encirclement strategy was so bold and innovative that, to this day, it is a subject of mandatory study, dissected in detail at all of the great military academies of the world.

The Romans, blinded by dust and confused leadership, fell into Hannibal's trap as if the outcome had been scripted. As the legions, accustomed to always move forward, did so, Hannibal's center purposely gave way, forming a concavity, a repeat of the Trebia River (and not coincidentally, Marathon [see Chapter 1]). Meanwhile, his flanks closed in from both sides. The Roman army was annihilated.

Casualty figures vary depending upon the historian of record, but the casualty assessments for Rome range from Livy's 48,000 to Polybius' 79,000, against Carthaginian losses of 5,700. In any case, 100 men died every minute during Cannae, and it remained the greatest one day slaughter in history until the First World War Battle of the Somme.

Consul Paulus died along with seven former consuls and 80 serving Senators. Varro, vilified by Rome's panicked citizens, was consigned to the rubbish heap of history's losers. Any way one looks at it, Cannae was the worst military defeat ever suffered by Rome, and left the capital totally exposed to the victors.

It is worth noting that one of the few Romans who survived the slaughter at Cannae was a 19-year old scion of a prominent Roman family named the Scipios.

More Delay

As is so often the case, the victor was slow in following up his advantage, despite the very sound advice of some of his senior commanders. Maharbal, the commander of the cavalry, told Hannibal: " . . . you must realize what has been accomplished in this battle. In five days you will feast victoriously in the Capital. Follow me. I will go ahead with the cavalry and they will learn of your arrival before they know you are coming." Seeing his commander falter, Maharbal said: "You know how to gain a victory, Hannibal, you know not how to use one."

Alas for Hannibal and ultimately for Carthage, he hesitated, feeling that he needed time to develop a plan to take advantage of a victory so huge it was completely unanticipated. As it turned out, the delay saved Rome and gave us the history we now study.

Historians have debated the reasons for, and impact of, this delay for two millennia. It is worth noting that Hannibal lacked sufficient supplies, men, and equipment for a long siege of Rome. He might well have exhausted his strength, as he suspected he would. Instead of a blitz attack on Rome, he opted for a long war of attrition in the Italian countryside. The fact that it proved unsuccessful is less due to Hannibal's generalship than to lack of support from Carthage.

It was not until 211 BC, five years later, that Hannibal made an attempt on Rome itself. In short order he arrived at the gates of the city. Legend has it that he flung a spear over the walls and into the city. It proved a half-hearted attempt, good only for temporarily striking fear into Roman hearts, but for little else. Hannibal soon withdrew and went back to the south.

In any event, like the U.S. industrial juggernaut that eventually overpowered the Axis powers almost 2,200 years later, it was only a matter of time before the superior resources of Rome overpowered the limited strength of her enemy. The Roman tide began to turn against Hannibal shortly after Cannae. In 215 BC, Marcus Claudius Marcellus won the first-ever Roman victory over the Carthaginians (albeit modest in scope and without Hannibal present) at the battle of Nola, which was most important because it broke the psychological thrall the Carthaginian myth of invincibility had held over Rome for so many years.

The Rise of Scipio

Despite Marcellus' first-ever victory over the Carthaginians, the intimidation factor associated with Hannibal remained strong. Roman mothers still admonished their children with warnings of "Hannibal at the gates." The victory at Nola was seen by the sober Roman leadership for what it was, a temporary respite. Wisely, the Roman strategy was reoriented from attempting to defeat Hannibal in the field, where Rome had experienced such dismal results, to keeping reinforcements from reaching him in Italy, the theory being that, without such replenishment, he would eventually fade away.

Nola ended Rome's attempts to join the issue on the battlefield. Rather, she turned her attention to Spain, where her forces were led by two brothers—Gnaeus and Publius—scions of the great, ancient, and much-honored Scipio family. They were pitched against Hannibal's brother Hasdrubal, the Carthaginian general in charge of the Spanish garrisons.

Rome had maintained a token "second front" in Spain since the beginning of the Second Punic War. Now it upped the ante, sending additional legions to Spain. By keeping Hasdrubal occupied, it was hoped that he would be too preoccupied to send help to his brother in Italy.

For several years, the strategy worked, thanks to the generalship of the bothers Scipio. Then, in 212 BC, both Scipios died fighting during defeats of Rome's Spanish armies by Hasdrubal. A window of opportunity was now open for Hasdrubal to help his brother. But thanks to the inadvertently brilliant decision of the Roman Senate, borne of crass nepotism, to appoint the 24-year old son of Publius Scipio to take over in Spain, the window was soon slammed shut.

Publius Cornelius Scipio, one of the greatest military geniuses and wisest leaders of any era, a man whose greatness in the annals of Rome is the equal of any other, was selected proconsul and sent to Spain.

In less than a year, he captured the capital, New Carthage. By then, his gentle treatment of the local population turned them into Roman loyalists and forced Hasdrubal, with a much-weakened army, to follow in his brother's footsteps of seven years before and make for Italy. The decision to follow Hannibal to Italy was not discretionary. Rather, it was a rout followed by a retreat. His decision to depart was taken less to infuse Hannibal with renewed vigor than to escape the Scipian tidal wave that threatened to engulf him if he remained in Spain.

The Relief of Hannibal

Hasdrubal wintered in southern Gaul in 208-207 BC, reinforcing his troop strength with recruits from the local population, most of whom hated Rome and what it symbolized to them, a colonial power. In the spring, he headed up the valleys into and over the Alps. As he crossed the Po River and headed south, his brother, who had wintered in Calabria, headed north for the rendezvous. In Canusium, just a few miles north of Cannae, Hannibal was greeted by the worst news of his life.

For a few months, things had not looked good for Rome. Upon hearing that Hasdrubal had successfully traversed the Alps into Italy, the two consuls left Rome with their respective armies, resigned to fighting a two-front war in order to keep the Carthaginian brothers from joining forces. The crisis was heightened by the disastrous loss of both of the previous year's consuls.

Hasdrubal, however, made a fatal mistake. He wrote a letter to his brother detailing his plans for moving south by hugging the Adriatic coast, and announcing his intention to meet him in Umbria. Thanks to Carthaginian carelessness and superior Roman intelligence work, the letter was intercepted and brought to the commander of one of the two Roman armies in the field, the consul Gaius Claudius Nero, who was near Tarentum keeping a watchful eye on Hannibal. Upon reading it, he hastened to join forces with his co-consul, Marcus Livius.

The now massive Roman army joined battle with the totally overmatched Hasdrubal at the Metaurus River 120 miles northeast of Rome, near the Adriatic. Hasdrubal knew immediately that the situation was untenable and attempted, but failed, to find a ford in the river. Hasdrubal and his entire army perished. What followed was the beginning of the end for Carthage.

The Romans found Hasdrubal's body, severed the head, and rode south with it to Hannibal's encampment, into which it was hurled. Hannibal was in his tent planning for his rendezvous with Hasdrubal when his soldiers brought him his brother's head. As he sat looking at it, he understood that all was lost. He would never again see reinforcements while in Italy. The next day, he reversed course and retreated to Bruttium at the tip of the Italian toe, from which vantage he held off the Romans for another four years.

Scipio "Africanus"

Scipio, meanwhile, continued his Spanish campaign, winning over more and more Spaniards through enlightened governance. Carthage finally woke up to the implications of the Spanish threat, and in 206 BC raised and sent off a massive army to destroy Scipio.

The combatants met at Ilipa in southwestern Spain, approximately 60 miles north of Seville. For the first time during the Second Punic War, the tables were reversed: Rome was outnumbered, but had the superior general.

The first few days of Ilipa consisted of a "feeling-out" process, the two armies probing, but not really clashing. This routine quickly became predictable, with each army marching out to the field in late morning, feinting here and there, and retreating back to camp at dusk. This daily habit lulled the Carthaginians.

One morning, Scipio abruptly broke the routine and attacked before the Carthaginian troops had time for breakfast. The disruption proved the undoing of the Carthaginian force. It was annihilated.

The disaster at Ilipa marked the end of Carthaginian hegemony in Spain, which had lasted only twenty years. It also made the Romans aware that they had found a unique commander in Scipio. Worse for Carthage, the defeat emboldened its allies and subject peoples to flex their muscles and sever their ties to Carthage.

The worst loss was that of Massinissa, king of the Numidians and supplier of much of the Carthaginian cavalry. Henceforth, Massinissa became a loyal ally of Rome, able to wreak havoc on the Carthaginian forces home base in North Africa.

Scipio returned to Rome in 205 BC after mopping up operations in Spain were complete. He was immediately rewarded with a consulship, at 32 one of the youngest consuls ever.

During the events in Spain, Hannibal remained encamped at Bruttium, and the temptation was strong among influential Roman circles to confront him immediately. Scipio, however, wisely resisted the temptation. Instead, he advocated taking the fight to Carthage itself. He was vigorously opposed by the fearful Fabius and his circle, who felt it was dangerous to leave Rome so exposed. Moreover, their judgment was clouded by their envy of the young consul. The old guard won in the Senate and Scipio was denied his army and his strategy. Instead he was sent to Sicily.

The hidebound Roman power structure did not understand what or with whom it was dealing in Scipio. Scipio's immense popularity caused volunteers for an African campaign to flock to his banner by the thousands. In 204 BC, in defiance of the Senate's orders, he sailed for North Africa. While a brilliant and militarily smart move, it would, a hundred years hence, prove a dangerous precedent for the survival of the Roman Republic.

Zama

Arriving in Africa, Scipio met with Massinissa. Soon thereafter, the torment of Carthage began. For two years,

Scipio and Massinissa kept the pressure on the African power. The city became desperate. Hannibal and his army, after almost 16 years of campaigning in Italy, were recalled in 203 BC in a last attempt to save the city and the state.

The stage was set for the final conflict. It took place at Zama, a vast plain approximately 100 miles southwest of Carthage, selected by Scipio because it afforded lots of space in which to employ his newly-acquired Numidian cavalry, which he knew gave him the advantage. The date was October 19, 202 BC.

Hannibal's army numbered 40,000, as did Scipio's. But Scipio's legions were battle-hardened, held together by a few thousand veterans of the epic battles against Hannibal in Italy. Hannibal also had his experienced old guard, but the bulk of his troops were green.

Hannibal realized his disadvantage as soon as he came upon the field of Zama. Always the pragmatist, he immediately asked for a conference with Scipio to discuss peace terms. Always obsessed with husbanding his forces and used to being outnumbered, Hannibal had a remarkable concern for his time—and any other time, for that matter—with the preservation of human life. His regard for the well-being of his men went beyond that of any other classical-era commander.

The two generals met for the first, but not the last, time in the middle of the Zama plain, their vast armies several miles to their rears. The meeting consisted of only Hannibal, Scipio, and their interpreters. It was as stilted and formal as any modern meeting between the American Eighth Army commander and his North Korean counterpart at Panmunjom on the 38th Parallel.

Scipio knew that he held all the cards, and his terms were correspondingly severe. Hannibal found them unacceptable, and the two commanders returned to their armies to prepare for battle. The next day the battle was fought, the balance of power in the ancient world hanging in the balance.

Always enamored with the radically advanced idea of employing an armored cavalry, Hannibal marshaled no fewer than 80 elephants for Zama. He began the battle by charging them into the Roman center.

But Scipio was as clever as his opponent, and was not one to be intimidated by the terrifying sight of fourscore lumbering beasts charging into his center. He ordered his trumpeters to blow with all their might. The elephants were "spooked" and turned around, wreaking havoc among Hannibal's more traditional, but inexperienced, replacement horse cavalry. Massinissa's cavalry charged, right behind and shielded by the elephants. In short order, the Carthaginian cavalry was no more.

Next, the Roman army advanced across the plain. It sliced through the Carthaginian lines until only the old warriors of the Italian campaigns were left. Hannibal's most loyal soldiers fought valiantly, but now Massinissa's Numidian horsemen, having routed the enemy cavalry, attacked Hannibal from the rear. The last veterans of the Trebia River, Lake Trasimene, and Cannae, were decimated. Hannibal was utterly defeated, with the loss of 20,000 killed or wounded and the remaining 20,000 taken prisoner. He and a small coterie of soldiers escaped to the relative safety of Carthage.

Aftermath

Carthage weighed its options, saw none, and had no choice but unconditional surrender. The Second Punic War was over. Rome was supreme in the Mediterranean and in the known world. A peace treaty was signed in 201 BC, and once-mighty Carthage was reduced to a rump state with much-contracted borders, no fleet, and owing an enormous indemnity to Rome.

It could have been much worse (and would be 50 years later), but for the wisdom of Scipio. Like Abraham Lincoln *vis-a-vis* the defeated Confederacy, he argued for an enlightened peace policy. He also made a radical departure from military tradition and refused to demand Hannibal's surrender, for whom his enormous respect bordered on veneration.

On the Carthaginian side, the peace was forced on a reluctant Carthage by none other than Hannibal himself, mindful that anything smacking of resistance would result in the total destruction of the city.

Scipio returned to Rome the greatest hero the republic had ever known. He was awarded the honorific *Africanus* by his grateful nation. This unusual honorific marked the beginning of a stirring tradition that repeats every once in a while when a military leader exceeds the possible and achieves the improbable; Alexander of Tunis and Montgomery of Alamein being two modern examples.

The Roman Senate, however, had a long memory and could not forget that Scipio's victorious African campaign took place in defiance of its edict to remain in Sicily. Consequently, at age 35, his career was essentially over.

Hannibal, in contrast, was made head of government in Carthage and demonstrated that his military leadership qualities translated quite well to civilian life. His leadership made Carthage a prosperous trading nation once more, and he was even able to pay its reparations (10,000 talents of silver–approximately 11-million US dollars today) to Rome much more rapidly than anyone anticipated.

Carthage's rapid recovery did not sit well with the anti-Scipio party in Rome. Spurred by Hannibal's enemies in the Carthaginian Senate, who sent word to their Roman counterparts that Hannibal was plotting to mount an attack on Rome (not true), a Roman delegation went to Carthage in 195 BC, demanding that Hannibal be arrested and turned over to them. Carthage, now militarily weak, had little choice but to comply. Fortunately, Hannibal got wind of the plot against him and escaped, going first to the mother city, Tyre, and then to the Hellenistic Syria of King Antiochus, who permitted him to live in exile in Ephesus, where he spent his early days lobbying unsuccessfully for Antiochus to give him an army with which to avenge himself on Rome.

The Second Encounter

The year 193 BC marked the second and last meeting between the two greatest generals of their era. The Roman Senate became increasingly nervous having Scipio around, fearing that he could become a rallying point for opponents.

They decided to send him far away from Rome. Through a remarkable coincidence, Scipio was made ambassador to the court of Antiochus at Ephesus.

Scipio's first order of business upon arriving in Ephesus was to seek out Hannibal. He had an official purpose in mind, says the Roman historian Livy: to dispel Hannibal's obsessive fear of Rome and thus diminish the likelihood that he might one day re-emerge from exile to command a vengeful army. Scipio did not need to be concerned. Hannibal rightly feared Rome, and spent the last decade of his life hiding from his Roman enemies.

Scipio, sensing that Hannibal would no longer be a threat to Roman hegemony, relaxed and their talk soon turned to another obsession of Hannibal's. Scipio asked him whom he considered the greatest general in history. Unhesitatingly, the Carthaginian answered Alexander the Great, King of Macedon some 130 years before. When Scipio asked for evidence in support of this assertion, Hannibal argued that Alexander had routed countless armies with a small force of his own and that he extended his power into remote lands.

Scipio, intrigued by the game, asked whom Hannibal considered the next greatest general. Hannibal replied that Pyrrhus had taught the art of measuring camps and was singularly adept at selecting a suitable battleground and deploying troops.

Scipio was not done yet, and continued down the same conversational road, asking who was ranked third in Hannibal's estimation. Hannibal named himself.

Scipio smiled and said: "What would you say if you had beaten me?"

"Then," replied Hannibal, "I should have put myself before Alexander and before Pyrrhus and before all others."

That is all we know about the great encounter.

Coda

Scipio's ambassadorship to Ephesus lasted only a short time. He returned to Rome a few days after arriving, having failed in all his endeavors *vis-a-vis* Antiochus.

In 191 BC, after suffering a series of devastating defeats at the hands of the Romans under Scipio Africanus' brother, Lucius Cornelius Scipio (including one at Thermopylae, the narrow pass controlling access to Central Greece where the Spartan King Leonidas and his tiny force held off the mighty Persian army of Xerxes long enough for the Greek defenses to form, making possible the victories of Salamis and Plataea in 480 BC), Antiochus was confronted by the victors with a demand that he give Hannibal up to them. He refused and Hannibal escaped to Bithynia, where he became both advisor to the king as well as commander of the fleet and proved himself a more than able admiral, winning a significant victory over Pergamum. Pergamum, however, was an ally of Rome, and the Romans were outraged that their nemesis was at it again. Hannibal's ancient enemy, Flaminius, was sent to Bithynia in 183 BC to demand Hannibal's surrender to Rome once more.

Again, Hannibal escaped just in time. Only this time he did not sneak away. Old and embittered, realizing that Rome would track him down no matter where he ran, he cheated his mortal enemy out of victory by taking the poison he had always carried with him since leaving Spain 35 years before. He died as the Roman soldiers sent to arrest him arrived at his doorstep.

Scipio's life followed a parallel path. His last public act was serving under his brother Lucius at the Battle of Magnesia in 190 BC, marking the final defeat of Antiochus. Upon his return to Rome, he and Lucius (accorded the honorific "Asiaticus" for his victories in the East) were accused by his old enemies (led by Marcus Porcius Cato) of embezzling some of the indemnity money paid to Rome by Antiochus. Incensed by the accusation, Scipio tore up the account books rather than submit to an investigation, an act taken by his enemies to mean he was guilty. In 185 BC, the conqueror of Carthage was prosecuted and hauled into court on October 19, the anniversary of the Battle of Zama, which prompted a cheering crowd to force an acquittal.

Nevertheless, the Cato faction prevailed, and the Scipios were done as a power bloc in Rome. Thereafter, Scipio Africanus disappears from public view for the remaining two years of his life. He died a natural death in 183 BC, the same year as his great adversary, Hannibal Barca.

****

Two men. Two meetings. One in war between the leaders of the two greatest military powers on the planet. One after the stars of both generals had waned. Hannibal and Scipio were two of the greatest commanders in history. Their transitions into civilian life proved disastrous for both of them. Hannibal had to escape from Carthage and spent the rest of his embittered life in exile. Scipio was run over by the anti-Carthage faction led by Cato and suffered the ultimate indignity of having to stand trial for petty thievery.

Old age did not treat these lions of youth kindly. When death came, they both may have welcomed it. Unlike so many generals, there were no funeral orations for Scipio Africanus or Hannibal Barca. They died quietly, their passing unmarked by a world that had passed them by.

Their meeting at Ephesus is a remarkably modern-sounding event, the kind of get-together we might associate with two great Cold War rivals rather than two generals who lived in far more uncharitable times.

Perhaps too, their careers remind us of something important for our own times: it is the extremely rare general who becomes a successful governor.

Empress Theodora (mosaic)

You do not have to be male in order to qualify for a great encounter. Women have had them, too, and future historians will surely have many such with which to regale their readers.

This particular one took place almost 700 years after Hannibal and Scipio met in nearby Ephesus. The encounter involved one of the most amazing, forceful, powerful, and astute women in history. And a not-so-simple priest.

Chapter 3 - Byzantium

Theodora and the Patriarchs
Tame the Lioness

*For a king, death is better than dethronement
and exile.*

Empress Theodora

Everyone fantasizes about experiencing an epiphany that, in
the blink of an eye, will be a life-changing inflection point
when they finally get a grip on things and go on to happiness
or greatness: Moses and the burning bush on Mount Horeb;
Lana Turner in her too-tight sweater discovered by Hollywood
while sitting at a malt shop counter; Joe Montana's touchdown
pass to Dwight Clark in the end zone as time ran out in the
Super Bowl; evangelicals who suddenly "find" God and are re-
born.

Epiphanies are rare. True, virtually every athlete, movie star
and professional politician proclaims a major life-reversal
after some revelatory experience prompted by a misstep, and
generally involving the (or a) deity. But those, to the extent
they are legitimate, are difficult to write about, since it is not
easy to get the story from the deity's point of view.

In the sixth century AD in the Middle East, there was such
an epiphany, one that caused a diminishing, unprepossessing,
insignificant life to turn itself around. The experience not only
changed the affected person's life, but also the rest of the
world. A millennium-and-a-half later, we still feel the effect.

The Eastern Empire

Westerners know very little about Byzantium. This knowledge gap is made even more incomprehensible when we note that:

a) America will achieve the longevity of Byzantium in the year 2899.
b) Our system of laws was invented and refined by the Byzantines.
c) The great questions of the dominant religion of the West, Christianity, were first argued and resolved by Byzantine churchmen and scholars.
d) Byzantine art and architecture achieved the pinnacle of sublime representation and "set the table" for the Renaissance.
e) The Byzantine Empire was the world's most powerful state for 500 years.
f) Constantinople, the capital of Byzantium, was the greatest city in the world and the most strategically important place on the planet for a thousand years.

So how is it possible for us to know so little about this accomplished mega-state? I don't have an answer. Suffice it to say Byzantium has been shamefully and wrongfully neglected in American education. We don't know what we've missed.

If Americans have heard anything at all about Byzantium, it usually takes the form of a dim awareness that someone named Justinian was one of its emperors. The more knowledgeable among us may also have heard that Justinian had something to do with developing a legal code. And that is where our knowledge ends.

The Imperial City

Constantinople, called Istanbul after 1453 by its Ottoman conquerors, owes its fame and fortune to its location on the most strategic choke point in the world, the narrow series of three channels—the Bosporus, Sea of Marmara, and Dardanelles (from north to south)—that separate the Black Sea and Russia from the Mediterranean and also Asia from Europe. The city itself is precisely positioned on a peninsula bounded on the south by the Sea of Marmara, on the east by the Bosporus, and on the north by the narrow portion of the Bosporus known as the Golden Horn.

Although the Ottoman Horde exploded out of the steppes of Central Asia and overran the Asian portion of the Byzantine Empire, the city itself is oriented to the European side, and for most of its history was the most important capital in Europe. It was often the prize at the end of military adventures. More blood has been spilled contesting Constantinople than perhaps over any other city on Earth, including Berlin and Moscow.

By the beginning of the sixth century AD, Constantinople had progressed to the point where it was called "The New Rome." It was a magnet for ambitious intellectuals, politicians, generals, power-brokers, entrepreneurs, everyone who was anyone in the Roman Empire; a haven for exiles and refugees from the Visigoths who were the new rulers of Old Rome. It was rapidly becoming the commercial, intellectual, cultural, artistic, and political epicenter of the known Universe.

The rulers of the New Rome were shrewd enough to give the 500,000 people who resided within the city's precincts bread and circuses, the latter in the form of entertainments that took place in the great Hippodrome. After the day's races and sports were done, the citizens of Constantinople went home sated, while the support staff and their families who provided the tiring diversions stayed because they actually lived in the Hippodrome.

The Bear Keeper's Daughter

One of these residents was Acacius, the bear-keeper to one of the two major political factions that predominated at the time, the "Greens." Acacius was responsible for the care and feeding of the bears that were employed in bear fights, bear-baiting, and other popular activities involving his beasts. His job, however, was considered the lowest form of employment there was, and he and his wife and family were considered the lowest of the low-born.

Around the year 500, Acacius' wife gave birth to a daughter, the middle child of this dirt-poor family (she had two sisters, Comito and Anastasia). Her father named her Theodora, and she was destined to become the most famous and accomplished woman in the history of her country. Given her origins, this would have been considered the most absurd of predictions to any observer of her birth. Yet it happened. Here is how.

The Hippodrome was a rough and violent place in which to grow up, harsh and brutish in the extreme. Picture 125th Street and Amsterdam Avenue in Harlem in the 1960s, South Central Los Angeles, the *favelas* that surround Sao Paolo or Rio, or central Kolkata where Mother Theresa plied her saintly trade among the hopeless and forgotten, and you will have some idea of what the life into which Theodora was born was like.

Conditions were terrible for the family. Then they got worse upon Acacius' death when Theodora was only four or five years old. Her mother wisely found another man almost immediately, a good thing in the unforgiving world of the Hippodrome. A crafty woman, she attempted to get her new consort appointed to the same position left vacant by her dead husband, but was hooted out of the arena by the Green crowd to whom she made her appeal. Undaunted, she turned to the Blue faction and won her new husband its appointment as bear keeper.

The rejection by the Greens was a humiliation her daughter never forgot. For the rest of her life, Theodora was the sworn and bitter enemy of the Greens, a fact of no consequence at all for the first half of her life when she was a nobody. But once she became the most powerful woman in the world, the Greens suffered mightily for their rejection and derision so many years before.

The rest of Theodora's early childhood is a mystery. There are no written records to give us insight.

Actress and Prostitute

She next surfaces when she is about eleven or twelve, as dresser to her older sister, Comito, who became an actress which, along with prostitution, was one of the lowliest professions in the Byzantine world. Comito was a modest success, and so Theodora sustained this gainful employment for several years. Until, that is, she became so lovely and alluring, and so quick of mind, that she could pick up scripted dialogue instantly and effortlessly. She was persuaded to launch her own acting career.

By age fifteen or sixteen, this ravishing beauty had left her older sister far behind. She was an immediate sensation, thanks in part to an act that combined her physical charms with an uninhibited indecency that found a natural market in this hedonistic fleshpot.

The mosaics and painted images of her as an older woman that survive depict a small woman with an oval face and enormous black eyes, with a perfect complexion and figure. As a nubile teenager, she must have been spectacular. Her bawdy, burlesque routines of Greek myths like Leda and the Swan caused men of all ages to flock to the Hippodrome to see her. I won't go into the details of her Leda act, which is sufficiently outrageous that it would be XXX-rated today. You can read about it yourself in the historian Procopius' *Secret History*. It will shock and titillate even the most veteran aficionado of peep shows or Internet porn sites.

It is said that tens of thousands of Byzantines came to see her perform. But the stage was not her only arena. She became the ancient equivalent of a highly paid and much-in-demand call girl. According to Procopius, there was nothing she would not do, and her creative imagination came up with many ideas for giving pleasure that might escape even us jaded moderns. She was, to top it all off, insatiable, a nymphomaniac capable of satisfying ten men in one night, according to Procopius.

I should note that Procopius was, in his mind, the mortal enemy of Emperor Justinian and Empress Theodora. That may have slanted his writing.

Into Africa

In 520, at the peak of her dubious, low-born career, she suddenly disappears from Constantinople with her current lover, Hecebolus, the most influential man she had been involved with up to this point in her life. Hecebolus had received an appointment as governor of Pentapolis province, later known as Cyrenaica (now part of Libya) in North Africa. Theodora left the stage and her other, more questionable money-making pursuits to accompany him to his new assignment.

Unfortunately, she and Hecebolus did not get along, and the governor threw her out of his house. Theodora was penniless, far away from home, and knew no one. How she survived is not known, although one of the more scurrilous contemporary accounts asserts that she reverted to her former ways and employed her considerable charms to pecuniary advantage.

However she managed, she somehow made her way 500 miles east to Alexandria, second only to Constantinople in terms of glitter, prestige and influence in the Empire.

The Encounter

In the sixth century, the approach to Alexandria by sea, the way Theodora would have most likely traveled, was spectacular. Its great natural harbor was marked by a 400-foot high, all-marble lighthouse on the island of Pharos at the harbor's entrance. The lighthouse was, by then, 800 years old, still in good condition, and deemed one of the Eight Wonders of the World. The architecture she would have seen upon arrival was the most splendid in the world after Rome and Constantinople, and the city's grid system of streets and its storied history must have caused even as calculating and hardened a heart as Theodora's to race with excitement.

Alexandria had been, for centuries, the center of learning in the Empire, home to giants of science, mathematics and geography such as Ptolemy, Euclid, and Eratosthenes. The contributions to the measurement and mapping of the Earth of just these three alone were relied upon by discoverers and explorers for over 1,500 years, and heavily influenced visionaries like Prince Henry the Navigator and Christopher Columbus.

Alexandria was also one of the great commercial hubs of the planet, an international market through which passed the corn that kept the peace in the Byzantine Empire (cornbread was distributed free to the inhabitants of Constantinople), as well as olive oil, fruit, ivory and gold from deep in the heart of Africa, spices from India, silk from China, and precious gems from Ceylon.

The wealthiest city in the world, it was also one of the most corrupt. Like so many metropolises where licentiousness and depravity are rampant, Alexandria was also an eminent religious center, overflowing with theologians, Patriarchs of the Orthodox Church, ascetic and charismatic monks (one, Antony of the Desert, reveled in the sanctity of not having washed for 40 years, which not only made him legendary, but also quite easy to detect at a distance), and a pantheon of saints in its history, unparalleled anywhere else. The monastic movement, in fact, was born in the deserts of Egypt, a stone's throw from the city.

The Christian Church in Alexandria was founded by St. Mark in the year 43. Mark died a martyr in the city in 63, and the power of the Church took off from that point. Strabo describes Alexandria as a universal melting pot, full of Greeks, Italians, Jews, Indians, Persians, and Syrians. Until the founding of Constantinople in the fourth century, it was the second city of Christendom, after Rome. It was so important a religious center that, very early on, the Bishop of Alexandria was the first one given the title Pope.

The city also spawned some of the more fractious heresies to afflict early Christendom. Monasticism, perhaps the most important contribution of Alexandria to the faith, began here in the third century. Initially, it was looked upon by the Church fathers with great suspicion. Origen, the great cathecist of the early Church, was an Alexandrian who was so controversial he was excommunicated. Arius, the proponent of what became Arianism, which was to vex the Church for centuries, was an Alexandrian. Monophysite Christianity, another of the great heresies and a powerful influence on Theodora's life and the Byzantine Empire, also originated here.

Until the Second Ecumenical Council in 381, the Patriarch of Alexandria ranked second to the Bishop of Rome. In that year, the Patriarchate of Constantinople was formally accorded second place status by the Church, but this was not recognized by either Rome or Alexandria for more than 100 years.

When the Monophysites emerged into the open in the middle of the fifth century, Alexandria became embroiled in controversy, and Orthodox and Monophysite Patriarchs vied for power, alternating in the Patriarchate for many years. The disruptions and disturbances that colored the Alexandrian Church eventually led to its demise.

In fact, when the Council of Chalcedon purported to finally and once-and-for-all settle the doctrinal disputes that were tearing apart the Church, it was the people of Alexandria who were united in their opposition and who rioted in support of a heretical patriarch.

The zenith of Monophysite power in the city occurred during the 60 years between the 480s and the 540s, when the Catholic succession was finally restored to the city by the Emperor Justinian.

When Theodora made her inconspicuous entrance into the city, she waded into tremendous, intertwined political and religious ferment. Since the time of Constantine the Great 200 years before, the fundamental religio-political principle governing the affairs of the Empire was Christian Orthodoxy. Any deviation conjured memories of the chaotic and lawless days before Constantine adopted Christianity as the official religion of the Empire. And that was not to be tolerated.

While this is not the place to go into the technical details of the religious disputes and debates that convulsed the Empire in the sixth century, most of which would seem ridiculously arcane and "nitpicky" to us, they were of central importance to the population of the Empire in general and to the citizens of Alexandria in particular. Theodora, heretofore not exactly a paragon of religiosity, could not avoid them and jumped into the middle of the controversy with both feet.

A brief summation of the debate is necessary at this point in order to understand what all the shouting was about and to appreciate the position of Theodora later in her life when she had enormous influence over its outcome. Oversimplified, the crux of the dispute was this: The peoples of the desert, the eastern provinces of Syria and Palestine, along with the Egyptians, were "fundamentalists," believing in a simple and pure religion and in one transcendent God bereft of any images or likenesses. Their opponents who, for the most part, lived in the more settled parts of the Empire—Italy, Greece, and the precincts around Constantinople—enjoyed the pageantry associated with Christianity, replete with icons and images of all sorts in order to remind the faithful that Jesus was the image of God.

More people have suffered and died in the name of religion than from all other causes, including war and pestilence, combined. This sixth century debate was no exception. Passions were fevered on both sides, and no quarter was permitted by either to the so-called "enemies of the Faith," i.e., anyone who harbored opposing views.

The Greco-Roman (western) peoples of the Empire analyzed Christianity as they did everything else, and in so doing, appeared to strip away the layers of mystery which the more mystical peoples of the East preferred. To top off the unbridgeable chasm between East and West, the espousal of the Trinity by Orthodox Christians was considered blasphemy by the Monophysite East, akin to worshipping three gods instead of the one and only God of the monotheistic tradition that came out of the desert wanderings of Abraham, Isaac and Jacob.

While the Trinitarian argument had largely been settled a hundred years before by a succession of Church councils, the bitter feelings left by the debate were never far from the surface, and arose once more in the context of a dispute over the nature of Jesus Christ. Orthodoxy held the position that Christ was of two natures, divine and human, peacefully coexisting. The Monophysites, in contrast, believed that Christ's humanity had been absorbed into his divine nature during his sojourn on Earth. Monophysite derives from the Greek words *mono* (single) and *phusis* (nature). The Monophysite belief is generally considered the most important of the early Church heresies, producing a vast literature and more death and suffering than any heresy until the late fifteenth century.

This highly technical debate was destined to obsess Theodora for all of the days of her life following her encounter in Alexandria.

Her arrival in the city coincided with a sea change in official religious policy by Constantinople. The previous tolerance of Monophysitism (which from time-to-time was not only tolerated, but even favored by some Emperors), was suddenly reversed by the Emperor Justin. By decree, the Monophysites were given only one choice: embrace Orthodoxy or suffer the torments of Inquisition. Much blood was shed, many monasteries were torched, and hundreds of priests were martyred when they refused to conform.

The worst persecutions fell on the Monophysites in the East, excepting Egypt which, as both the granary of the Empire and the home of the militant Archbishop of Alexandria and his powerful army of monks, received gentler treatment regardless of the extent of heresy to be found there. Consequently, Theodora found herself among thousands of Monophysite refugees from Palestine and Syria, all of whom were welcomed and cared for by the Patriarch Timothy.

Not all of the Monophysite refugees resettled in the great port city. Thousands who were even worse off, having lost everything to the Inquisition, wandered into the immense desert stretching thousands of miles to the south and west of the city, where they, in essence, created the concept of the solitary life in search of God. Their saintly enterprise was an inspiration to many in the Empire and of the most intense interest to the people of Alexandria, the gateway to the desert, Theodora among them.

The Meeting

The question naturally arises how a 21-year old actress and prostitute from an insignificant background, with a dubious history to say the least, even got to meet Patriarch Timothy. There is no recorded answer to that question. Meet, however, they did, and the encounter changed Theodora's life. Looking back years later, she invariably referred to Timothy as her spiritual father.

All that we know about Timothy, the militant Monophysite, is the following—mindful that history is written by the victors and the Monophysites were big losers. He had only recently become Patriarch. He was politically sophisticated and publicly played the role of compromiser, seeking a middle ground between his fundamentalist followers and the purveyors of Orthodoxy.

We can only speculate that Theodora was impressed by this selfless individual who took in the wretched of the Earth (of whom she herself was one) and treated them with dignity and human kindness. Theodora's experience with men had not been a positive one, and it must have struck her profoundly that here was a man who was different, one who demanded nothing in return for his compassion and good works. Theodora's reaction to this living manifestation of undemanding spiritual love was not very different from a hundred stories we have all heard or read about in the intervening centuries. She went through a sudden and deep-seated religious conversion . . . and was "born again."

Timothy must have been equally impressed by the young woman, for he took the unprecedented step of recommending her to one of the great theologians of the time in order to advance her education. Timothy introduced her to his counterpart and fellow believer Severus, the exiled Monophysite Patriarch of Antioch, who had fled to Alexandria when the Monophysites came under attack in 518.

Severus had studied law and rhetoric in Alexandria as a young man and then had spent years living as a monk in the Palestinian desert (like Antony of the Desert, he also renounced baths). The leading Monophysite intellectual of the era, he went to Constantinople in 509 to answer heresy charges, and was so compelling a proponent of his beliefs that he became a confidant of the Emperor Anastasius, a Monophysite sympathizer, who nominated him Patriarch of Antioch in 512 (he was ousted from his post upon the accession of the orthodox Emperor Justin in 518).

Severus was the most productive of all the Monophysite writers, and generated a massive body of work (his 3,700+ letters were later collected in twenty-three books) that was likely absorbed by Theodora. His polemics against the Council of Chalcedon make for difficult reading. Serendipitously for his eager pupil, he also wrote diatribes against the abuses of the Hippodrome in Constantinople, where he denounced cruelty to animals, especially the horses used in chariot races. This must have sat well with the bear-keeper's daughter.

At his feet, Theodora learned enough about religious doctrine to put some intellectual depth behind her new-found Monophysite beliefs. She also learned how to debate from this most formidable of debaters.

For a woman of this era, any kind of formal education was out of the question, so Theodora's experience was totally unique. We do not know how she managed to defy both rigid custom and overwhelming odds, but she did. Obviously, she must have affected Timothy (and by extension, Severus) equally as much as he affected her. Her studies completed, this prodigiously bright, articulate and confident woman was now ready to tackle the world.

Back to the "New Rome"

Following her conversion, Theodora returned home to Constantinople via Antioch. She took simple quarters and made her living spinning wool, a dramatic change of life. She did not know that an extraordinary fate awaited her. For all of that, the story might have gotten lost at this point, were it not for the fact that she was destined, in short order, to be elevated to the position of the most powerful and influential woman in the world.

Soon after her return, Theodora met a man named Petrus Sabbatius—soon to be called Justinian—the nephew and adopted son of the improbable Emperor Justin, who himself had begun life as an illiterate Thracian peasant from the even-then unhappy region we now call Serbia. It was lust at first sight and the two quickly became an inseparable couple. Petrus was intoxicated with her. As far as we know, this was Theodora's only relapse into the life she had known before her conversion. It proved to be an excellent regression.

Constantinople in the Sixth Century

In order to understand Theodora's impact on her time and on history, we need some background. What happened in Constantinople in the early years of the sixth century was a serendipitous confluence of people and events that gave rise to a great period of prosperity, power, and (relative) enlightenment. It was to become the apogee of the Eastern Roman Empire.

Let's digress briefly and examine why there even was a Constantinople and how it came to be the world's greatest and most powerful city.

When Constantine proclaimed himself Roman Emperor in 307, he was only one of seven self-proclaimed emperors simultaneously vying for power in Rome. Strangely for one who was ultimately drawn east, his power base was in the extreme north and west of the Empire: Gaul and Britannia. It took him 17 years to eliminate his competitors and consolidate his power. Thanks to a celestial phenomenon on the eve of an important battle (the Battle of the Milvian Bridge) that he took to be the sign of the cross, Constantine became a Christian and elevated Christianity to official and preferred status in the Empire.

The Empire pacified, Constantine looked for a new capital, Rome having lost her credibility and luster over the centuries. He selected Byzantium, an ancient Greek city strategically situated at the point where Europe meets Asia. He renamed it after himself and moved the capital there in 330.

The city he chose was then almost a thousand years old, and its location on the divide between Europe and Asia where the Black Sea and the Mediterranean meet gave it the most strategic and enviable location on the planet. By the time two centuries passed, the new capital had experienced phenomenal growth. Its 500,000-plus population made it far and away the largest city in the world.

Most of this teeming multitude was crammed into tightly interconnected, wooden structures situated on a small peninsula jutting into the Bosporus Straits, with the waterway known as the Golden Horn to the north. Crowding caused the city its two greatest vexations: the ever-present danger of fire and the equally-omnipresent problem of citizen unrest.

Peace and relative prosperity prevailed for much of the fourth century. But as time went on, the eastern and western halves of the Empire grew apart, and as the century waned, there emerged from time-to-time two rival Emperors, one Greek and one Latin.

The end of the century brought these differences into sharp focus. The Eastern Empire became wealthier and stronger than the West. Rome's vulnerability was not lost on the aggressive Germanic and Slavic tribes salivating on its borderlands. Moreover, the western surges of the Hunnish tribes of the steppe lands put increasing pressure on these tribes and forced them to look south to the temptations and fleshpots of warm, sunny Rome.

At first, the Goths attempted to negotiate a peaceful solution that would have had them settling south of the

Danube. When negotiations failed, they resorted to force. First against Constantinople, then when that failed, against the more vulnerable Rome.

Constantinople was saved by Emperor Theodosius (378-395). When he died after a strong reign, he was succeeded by two young sons. Arcadius was given the purple in Constantinople. His younger brother was sent to rule over Rome. The division of the Empire now became permanent, as did the contrasts between the two realms. The East was quite able to protect itself, but was less and less interested in protecting a weakened Rome.

When the Visigoth king Alaric and his hordes moved on the Empire in the early fifth century, Constantinople's deft diplomacy turned him from eying it as a prize, toward Rome. On August 24, 410, he captured Rome (the first time anyone had done that in 800 years!) and left it ravaged. The sack of Rome shook the world. St. Augustine was stimulated to write his *City of God* by the event. Constantinople withdrew even more deeply into itself.

Things went from bad to worse in the West, as a raft of new invaders, encouraged by Alaric's success and Rome's obvious weakness, took advantage. Rome had no choice but to accede to the invaders' demands that they be granted land in Gaul and Italy upon which to settle. A standard practice was to give a barbarian chief one-third of a Roman estate in return for military service—the earliest manifestation of feudalism. This marked the beginning of the end of Rome as the world knew it, its demise preordained by this disastrous, short-sighted policy.

By the middle of the fifth century, the barbarians were already in *de facto* control of the Western Empire. Barbarian "Masters of Soldiers" controlled the succession to the Imperial throne. In 476, Odovacar had had enough of this charade and deposed the child-ruler Romulus Augustus, taking the throne himself. He in turn was replaced by Theodoric the Ostrogoth. The break with the Eastern Empire was virtually complete.

Schism

While there was always going to be tension between Rome and Constantinople, the East's attention now shifted from geopolitics to religion. Divisions in the Church, whether doctrinal or organizational, were part of its evolution since its earliest days. With the increasing strength of the Church, the stakes for the winners and losers became higher, and these divisions became more pronounced.

The first major issue to divide believers was over the nature of the Trinity. Arius, an Alexandrian priest, espoused the position that the Father was dominant over the Son, and condemned as heretics the majoritarian view that they were of the same nature. This doctrinal debate divided virtually every Christian community in the world, and drove Emperor Constantine crazy. When blood began to be spilled over the issue, he convened a council of bishops at Nicaea in 325 to resolve the matter, and put considerable pressure on them to declare Arianism a heresy. They did, and thousands of Arians were exiled to the far reaches of the Empire. In time, the heresy died out.

Outside the Empire, it was a different story. Arianism took hold among the barbarian tribes and became the prevailing doctrine of faith in the West. Church divisions died down for a while and soon became a non-issue in the West, which had a more immediate problem—survival—with which to contend. In the East, however, the next great threat to the Church was Monophysitism.

On July 9, 518, the 87-year old Monophysite Emperor of the East, Anastasius, died during an epic storm. He had ruled for 27 years, and ruled well, surprising everyone. His undistinguished early career had given no hint that he would make a good and strong emperor.

Religious turmoil had, however, marked his reign. Six years before his death, a Monophysite revision of the liturgy in Constantinople's great Cathedral of the Holy Wisdom—the *Hagia Sophia*—caused a riot in the city. Imperial troops brutally suppressed the uprising, provoking a revolt against the government. Anastasius himself was compelled to go to the Hippodrome, where he offered to abdicate. His appearance and bearing overwhelmed the opposition, and the city quieted. It was a brave and risky move, a close call.

Outside the city, a general named Vitalian saw his opportunity, and with the support of the mainstream Orthodox Church and probably of Rome as well, marched against the Emperor. His rebellion was also a close thing, but ultimately failed. Vitalian, however, escaped and bided his time while the Emperor aged in Constantinople.

The Succession of Justin

Orderly political succession is something we Americans take for granted, thanks to our long, remarkable, and rather unique history of peaceful and uneventful transfers of power. Then 2000 and 2016 presidential elections certainly underscored this amazing achievement. Consequently, we don't appreciate the fact that, historically, peaceful successions are an extreme anomaly.

Succession for most nations of the world and for most of history has rarely been easy or seamless. Rather, it has been a monumental problem, usually the stimulant for political murder and sometimes mass destruction. Indeed, without the long history of succession problems over which to obsess, what would Shakespeare have dramatized to such effect?

The Eastern Empire was no exception. When Anastasius died, the succession had not been planned for at all. While his immediate predecessors had taken some pains in this regard—nominating co-emperors or designating a successor when the end was near—Anastasius had done nothing of the sort. His wife was dead and his illegitimate son had vanished without a trace years before. It was clear that the "right of conquest" would govern this succession.

There were four contenders: Hypatius, nephew of Anastasius and Master of Soldiers in the East (Antioch). Acceptable from a religious standpoint, he was unacceptable otherwise, having been militarily humiliated by Vitalian some years before. Vitalian, also an imperial contender, was at least ten days march away to the north and would not hear about the Emperor's death for at least a week. Too late for him to assert his claim.

Two of the contenders, however, were in Constantinople. Celer, the Master of Offices (i.e., civil service chief), was the first to learn about the Emperor's death. He had a few troops under his command (the *Scholae*), but they were more ceremonial than real. Justin, Count of the *Excubitors*, a palace regiment, although already 68 years old, had real soldiers loyal to and ready to fight for him.

The morning after Anastasius died, Celer summoned the court and patriarchs to the palace to choose a successor. Meanwhile, the people, as was the custom, gathered in the Hippodrome and argued the succession themselves. Palace representatives came to the Hippodrome at intervals to put forward the names of candidates, all of whom were rejected by the mob. Skirmishes broke out between the Scholae and Excubitors as they moved back and forth between the palace and the Hippodrome. Justin decided to go to the Hippodrome to attempt to restore order. It was a brilliant tactical move.

When he appeared there, his troops called out his name as emperor. He very publicly and humbly declined, and, order restored, repaired to the palace. Soon chaos reigned once again in the Hippodrome and the mob moved on the palace. The Senate was in session and heard the crowd trying to beat down the doors to their chamber. Terrified, they offered Justin the throne if he could restore order. He refused once again. The mob almost upon them, they begged Justin to accept. He did. The Excubitors elevated him upon a shield, a long-time Roman practice originally adopted from the Germans, and paraded him before the mob. An officer placed a golden chain on his head. He was carried to the Hippodrome where the Patriarch John placed the crown on his head to acclamation. The power play, shrewdly planned and executed, was complete.

Like his predecessor, Justin had an undistinguished career before becoming Emperor. He was of peasant origin, a

Romanized Thracian and Latin speaker, hailing from a village in what is now the Nis region of Kosovo. But he was an exceptionally intelligent peasant.

He had arrived in the capital as a young man. By the time he ascended to the throne, he had lived in Constantinople for almost 50 years. He was married to a former concubine, Lupicina, who took the more exalted name of Euphemia when she became Empress. The couple was childless, but the desire to pass something on to the next generation was strong in Justin. When the time was right and he was able to afford it, he brought four of his young nephews from Kosovo to Constantinople, essentially adopting them as his sons and giving them all of the advantages he himself had never enjoyed.

They were all talented boys. Three of them rose quite high in the ranks of the Byzantine military and had successful careers by any measure. The fourth was the most talented of all. In the absence of historical proof, speculation is widespread that this young man was the mastermind behind his uncle's deft *coup d'etat*.

The Rise of Petrus Sabbatius

The fourth nephew, Petrus Sabbatius, came from the tiny village of Tauresium, close to where his uncle was born. It is likely he came to live with his uncle in about 490, when he was only eight years old.

His uncle enrolled him in the finest schools, where he excelled. Other than his arrival and elite education, virtually nothing is known about Petrus' early childhood. However, his educational influences must have been quite strong, since he remained a gifted and eminent scholar all his life.

Like his cousins, he began his career in the military, in one of the palace guard units. By the time Justin became emperor, Petrus was an officer of the Scholae regiment. But barracks life was not his forte. Justin's advent to power provided the young man a once-in-a-lifetime opportunity. Being far more comfortable in the rarified air of court life than his uncle, and being worldly wise and knowledgeable, he soon became Justin's right-hand man and key advisor. He was appointed Count of the Domestics, a vital position at the epicenter of power despite its unprepossessing title. It gave him daily, official access to the emperor, to complement his unofficial role. During the nine years of Justin's rule, Petrus pulled the strings of power. At about the time of his uncle's accession, Petrus added the name Justinianus to his given name, which might have meant that he had been formally adopted by Justin. It is logical to think that Justin wanted as his successor someone from his own family, and he did not have to look far to find the most talented man in the Empire.

Justin's Reign

Two overriding issues obsessed the Empire: the old bugaboo of religious schism was the major one, followed closely in importance by deteriorating relations with the Goths ruling Rome and the West.

Justin was a "mainstream" Orthodox believer, a follower of the doctrine laid down by the Council of Chalcedon in 451, which had attempted, unsuccessfully, to unite the Church behind the predominant views expressed at Nicaea 125 years before. Despite Chalcedon, Monophysitism was stubborn and would not go away. It was particularly strong in Egypt—where Theodora had become a fervent adherent—and in Syria as well.

Despite intermittent attempts at a compromise pushed by the palace, the Monophysites, like all zealots, were not satisfied with half a loaf. Various imperial attempts at conciliation only encouraged their zealotry and made the situation even worse, provoking a horrified reaction in the West.

The Pope in Rome in 484 went so far as to excommunicate the Orthodox Patriarch of Constantinople for having influenced the Emperor toward conciliation with the Monophysites. The decree, however, did not stop with the Emperor. It also encompassed the whole of Orthodoxy! This was to prove one of the bigger mistakes of the Church of Rome, as it locked the political schism between East and West in stone and isolated the Roman Church from any possibility of succor from the East in the face of the barbarian threat in the West. The political division of East and West was now complete.

Religious unrest meant that the new regime thus faced a grave crisis from its first day. The Emperor found himself between the Scylla of the excommunication decree, which threatened to undermine his political authority, and the Charybdis of Monophysitism. There was also the added twist that Egypt—the hotbed of Monophysitism—was the breadbasket of the Empire, the granary that was the source of free bread for the citizens of the capital. Without free bread, there was no telling how long the quick-tempered Constantinopolitans would tolerate any government. This meant that Egypt's heresy had to be tolerated, which would outrage the majority of the Imperial theocracy.

Justin turned to his astute nephew for advice on how to handle the problem. The advice was quickly forthcoming and unambiguous. First, the Patriarch of Constantinople was forced to repudiate his Monophysite beliefs and publicly proclaim his adherence to the pronouncements of Chalcedon. Second, Monophysite bishops were expelled and Orthodox exiles recalled. Only Egypt was ignored, for obvious reasons, and it soon became the haven for persecuted Monophysites. Third, a reconciliation with the Pope was sought—and achieved.

The brilliance and simplicity of Justinian's solution was much admired by his uncle. Henceforth, he would rely even more heavily on his indispensable nephew.

Marriage

By the time Justinian met Theodora, he was starved for intellectual companionship equal to his own. She must have impressed him enormously. They soon became lovers, and Justinian was so smitten with his new mistress that he immediately and very publicly moved her into his Palace of *Hormisdas* on the Marmara shore.

Soon the lowly bear keeper's daughter was swimming in riches unimaginable and loving every minute of her good fortune. Her influence over her lover was enormous, so much so that she soon persuaded Justinian to intervene with his uncle to halt the Monophysite persecutions.

But an illicit relationship was not enough for Justinian. He was determined to marry Theodora, despite the formidable obstacles to such a match, the most formidable being the Empress Euphemia, who herself began life as the slave-girl Lupicina. Like many persons raised to high rank from society's lower rungs, the Empress was adamant in her opposition to anyone seeking to follow her route up the ladder, especially a former Hippodrome tart who may have reminded her too much of herself.

Euphemia's opposition would have ended the matter but for the fact that she died suddenly, unexpectedly, and most opportunely for Justinian and Theodora in 523. Rumors have persisted for the past 1,500 years that her death was not wholly prompted by God's sudden desire to have his daughter with him; however, no hard evidence has emerged.

After a decent interval, Theodora and Justinian were married in the *Hagia Sophia*, the original of which burned to the ground in 404, was rebuilt, and is now the great mosque of Istanbul. Theodora's triumph was almost complete.

Three years intervened before she reached the pinnacle of power. During that time, Theodora impressed her husband more and more each day with her formidable intellect. By the time Emperor Justin died, Justinian deemed her his key advisor and the person upon whom he relied for both the most cogent counsel and the most unvarnished assessments.

Marriage caused Theodora to undergo a remarkable transformation, one traceable directly back to the ideas and values she absorbed from Timothy. The former whore and lewd performer became the most devout, loyal, and faithful wife imaginable.

Theodora in Power

She also quickly became the most powerful force in the Empire, and it was said about her by her enemies that she held the Emperor under a spell. To an extent, that was quite true. Most of Justinian's many achievements during the relatively brief time Theodora reigned by his side (she died at age 47 of cancer and was survived by her husband for almost two decades) owed either their origin or their eventual shape to her influence. On more than one occasion, her bravery and resolve saved the Empire and the throne when her husband and his closest official advisors were inclined to run away.

One of Theodora's chroniclers called her "surpassing in intelligence all men who ever lived." While obviously hyperbolic, she was arguably more intelligent than any man of her time. She proved that time-and-time again with her uncanny ability to stymie plots and intrigues against her husband as well as emerging as the foremost military strategist of the Empire. She was also a champion of gender equality, chiefly for the right of women to own property and to inherit from their husbands, a remarkable position for any woman in the sixth century to take. She successfully lobbied for criminal laws against rape and human trafficking. By the time she died, the position of women in the Byzantine Empire reached unprecedented heights never before achieved in the entire world and unattainable for more than a thousand years elsewhere.

Her finest hour occurred during the *Nika* Revolt of 532. It is not stretching the truth to say that she saved her husband's throne, perhaps his life, and possibly the Empire.

Like so many modern political crises, this one originated with a funding problem; more precisely, a critical lack of funds. Emperor Anastasius had left his successor Justin with full coffers and a large reserve, whereupon the much less sophisticated Justin proceeded to dissipate most of the Imperial treasury. Justinian was equally profligate, spending huge sums on building and rebuilding superfluous churches.

The Byzantine Empire, however, was rich, and replenishing the treasury was a realistic enterprise. There were taxes aplenty to be collected, and Justinian set about collecting them. The tax system, however, had fallen prey to numerous government inefficiencies, thanks to a half-century of abundance that made the tax collectors fat and happy. It was time to render them lean and mean again, and also to make sure that every taxpayer paid his fair share.

To achieve this, Justinian chose one of the most interesting characters of the era, John of Cappadocia, as Praetorian Prefect, i.e., chief tax collector. John, a dour, gruff, and volatile man, did not exactly endear himself to the taxpayers. He set about his mission with religious fervor. In short order, he succeeded in whipping the tax system into shape, and revenues began to rise. So did public anger at his high-handed methods, among them the imprisonment of tax scofflaws and the imposition of new fees for any and every imperial service.

John's stellar results impressed the Emperor, and he conferred additional powers on him, chief among them being to find creative ways to balance the budget. John was no less an attack-dog enthusiast when it came to cutting spending. He immediately slashed the wonderful Byzantine postal system to the bone, so that the only surviving communications conduit was between Constantinople and the Persian frontier.

This had the unintended consequence of making it more difficult to provision the capital, which in turn meant that the quality of the free bread deteriorated. It is worth noting that bread policy changes have probably prompted the fall of more governments throughout history than any other single factor.

At the same time, disgruntled citizens gravitated to the city from all over the Empire, either because they sought a better standard of living there than back home where John's tax collectors wreaked havoc with local economies, or because they sought to petition the Emperor for redress of their grievances. The pot began to boil over.

In January 532, during an unseasonably wet and cold winter, the Greens, suppressed for several years, gathered in the Hippodrome and began to mutter against the authorities, especially the hated John of Cappadocia. Emboldened by their numbers, they soon began to agitate against the Emperor himself. At first, the Blues defended Justinian and a number of skirmishes and street fights broke out between the two factions, spilling over into the city streets. There were some arrests and several of the rabble-rousers were sentenced to be hanged.

A huge crowd gathered on the traditional hangman's hill on the opposite shore of the Golden Horn on January 10th, execution day. The nervous hangman, not used to a large audience, botched the job and two men, one a Green and one a Blue, fell off the scaffold, still alive. Whereupon the crowd gathered them up and carried them by boat across the Golden Horn to a church sanctuary. The police surrounded the church, escalating the confrontation. The mob, in turn, demanded an acquittal. The stalemate lasted three days.

On January 13, the annual chariot races began in the Hippodrome. This time both the Greens and the Blues were present in large numbers, and facing resistance from the authorities, joined together to demand that the two condemned men be freed. As one, the two factions suddenly burst out of the Hippodrome shouting "Nika, Nika," the traditional slogan used to urge charioteers to victory. The throng rapidly made for the City Prefect, killed all the policemen who had the misfortune to get in their way, and freed all the prisoners from their cells. Once the prison was vacated, they burned it to the ground.

The fire renewed the mob's violent energy, and now they surged toward the palace, setting fire to the main gate. The fire spread and consumed the *Hagia Sophia*. Outside the palace, the huge crowd demanded the dismissal of John and all his tax collectors.

Within the palace walls, Justinian feared for his life and immediately gave in to the crowd's demands. But as so often happens in these situations, the protestors realized they had power, liked it, and wanted more. They laid siege to the palace.

Justinian and his closest advisors panicked. They did not know what to do. After two days, the crowd, further emboldened, proclaimed a new Emperor, one Probus, a nephew of Anastasius. When he did not immediately respond to the mandate, the crowd burned his house, too.

On January 16, Justinian decided upon a desperate measure. He went to the Hippodrome through the secret tunnel connecting it to the palace, and suddenly appeared in the imperial box. There he publicly accepted blame for everything and promised the revolutionaries total amnesty. Events, however, had gone much too far. Not only was the crowd dangerously contemptuous, disrespectful, and hostile, but also the situation had inspired a group of nobles to attempt a *coup d'etat*. The old general Hypatius was even crowned Emperor in the Forum. Meanwhile, Justinian hastily retreated to the palace.

Back in the palace, the discussion now took the form of whether to attempt to capture Hypatius or attempt to flee via galley to Thrace. Belisarius, one of the great generals of history, took a small unit of soldiers and went back through the tunnel to the imperial box in the Hippodrome, but he never got there. To his shock, his small force was barred by some of the palace guard. When he reported this development to Justinian, the Emperor ordered an immediate flight to the harbor and the waiting galley. All appeared lost.

Suddenly, Theodora rose to her feet and held up a hand for silence. She had been present for days during the debate over what to do, and had remained silent until this moment. According to Procopius, this is what she said:

> "Whether or not a woman should give an example of courage to men is neither here nor there. At a moment of desperate danger, one must do what one can. I think flight, even if it brings us to safety, is not in our interest. Every man born to see the light of day must die. But that one who has been emperor should become an exile, I cannot bear. May I never be without the purple I wear, not live to see the day when men do not call me 'your Majesty.' If you wish safety, my Lord, that is an easy matter. We are rich and there is the sea, and yonder our ships.

But consider whether if you reach safety you may not desire to exchange that safety for death. As for me, I like the old saying, that the purple is the noblest shroud."

Imperiously, Theodora sat down. There was a long silence. When the discussion resumed, the tone of the debate changed dramatically, from whether to flee to how to put down the rebellion. A plan was hatched.

Pro-Justinian agitators were sent into the streets. They cried out "Long live Justinian," and soon the two permanent factions resumed their ancient rivalry. Fighting broke out between the Blues and the Greens. As it escalated, Belisarius and another general, Mundus, fell upon the rear of the crowd. Their troops were merciless, cutting down everyone in sight. Meanwhile, Belasarius' great rival, the eunuch Narses, slaughtered every rebel who streamed out of the palace grounds.

Having cleared the streets, the imperial troops made for the Hippodrome. Within hours, thirty thousand people were dead, and Hypatius was captured and brought to the palace. The terror-stricken, would-be emperor fell to his knees before Justinian and begged for his life. Justinian was about to show mercy when Theodora stopped him. The next day Hypatius was put to death and his body thrown into the sea. The *Nika* Revolt was over.

Thereafter, for the remaining sixteen years of her life, Theodora became Justinian's closest and most respected advisor. John of Cappadocia was immediately restored to power and resumed his vigorous tax collecting ways.

Death

For the rest of her life, Theodora ruled alongside her husband as Empress. As the year 547 wound down, Theodora began to feel fatigued and soon her throat began to pain her. The doctors were unanimous in their opinion that the Empress was under a death warrant.

Her decline was rapid. On June 28, 548, she died of throat cancer, leaving her husband grief-stricken and virtually unable to function. Justinian was 66, old for the time, but he had many more years—seventeen—of governing ahead of him. He did not remarry. During the remainder of his reign, he often interrupted his official duties to journey to the nearby Church of the Holy Apostles and light candles before his wife's tomb.

Despite the scurrilous polemics directed her way by the disgruntled and frustrated office-seeker Procopius, who wrote the only contemporary biography of Theodora, she comes down to us through history as a remarkable personality: a woman at a time when women were little more than pack-mules and property, who elevated herself from origins so mean that her rise to power is quite improbable. Moreover, without the influence of the Monophysite Timothy, her rise would have been impossible.

There is a spectacular mosaic of Theodora in the Church of San Vitale in Ravenna, Italy, for a brief time the capital of the late Western Roman Empire. It was a contemporary portrait, completed in 547, a year before her death. While in the stiff, iconographic style of Byzantium, it nevertheless is a revealing image of the Empress. Her strength seems to exude from the painting, which she totally dominates, and not only because she occupies the center of the portrait. She overpowers the scene, much as she overwhelmed the life of Constantinople in her time.

The Orthodox Church made Theodora a saint.

St. Francis of Assisi
(As depicted in the Sacred Grotto, Mt. Subiaco, Italy)

Now we move from the center of Eastern
Orthodoxy to the center of Western Orthodoxy,
and a 700-year quantum leap into the future.
From the intrigue of the (aptly-named)
Byzantine court, we shall proceed to the sublime
mysteries of the Church of Rome and into the
inner confines of the Vatican and the curia in
order to dissect one of the most remarkable
religious coincidences of any era.

Chapter 4 - Rome

The Pope Invests Two Saints

It is better to be a hammer than an anvil.
St. Dominic

It is in pardoning that we are pardoned.
St. Francis of Assisi

With apologies to Sergio Leone, Clint Eastwood and the "Spaghetti Western" genre, gradations among good, bad, and ugly are usually very difficult to make. We carry every one of these ambiguous and often overlapping potentialities inside us all the time, and know better than anyone else outside our personal turf which one will prevail at any given time.

The late Twelfth and early Thirteenth centuries were a simpler time, at least retrospectively. When we examine the remarkable lives of the protagonists of this chapter, it is not very difficult for us, imposing our twenty-first century values, to categorize each of them. History does not easily countenance gray areas. For observers closer in time to these great events, however, pigeonholing these men was not quite as easy.

San Francesco

It was a hot summer day in 1198, the most important day that the small, insignificant town one-third of the way up

Mount Subiaco was to experience in many years. Gian Bernardone was in his late teens. He and his friends watched in fascination as Conrad of Urslingen, a German knight, rode with his retinue down the mountain into the valley, away from the little town of Assisi, for the last time, saying his farewells to the lands he had ruled for two decades. Several days later, he knelt in abject submission before the Papal legates and handed over his fiefdom to the new Pope, the soon to be legendary Innocent III.

When the dust from Conrad's retreating horses finally settled, a blood-red banner was hoisted over the ancient hill town which had been founded almost 2,000 years before as an Etruscan hill fortress. The banner contained only one word: "Liberty." Within minutes the sack began, and included stones from the fortress, which were used to build a wall around the town, a project that took remarkably little time. While there is no hard evidence, it is highly likely that Gian Bernardone was one of the young men who sacked Assisi in the name of freedom.

The powerful impression made by these events was to stay with young Bernardone throughout his life and influenced not only him, but generations to come.

Young Gian, a rowdy and bawdy teenager who led a gang of partying ne'er-do-wells as they wreaked mayhem in Assisi, suddenly transformed himself in his early twenties into the legendary Francis of Assisi, probably the most deservedly sainted Catholic in the two-thousand year history of the Church. In his brief time on Earth (44 years), half of which he spent fighting, carousing and debauching, he devised a legacy that has since influenced millions to lead an ethical existence and positively affected the lives of tens of millions beyond his own order and even beyond his own faith.

Santo Domingo

Several hundred miles across the Tyrhennian Sea to the west of the Italian peninsula, another young man, about ten years Gian Bernardone's senior, was at approximately the same time elected sub-prior of his Augustinian chapter at the Cathedral of *Osma*, his home parish, about a hundred miles north of Madrid.

Domingo Guzman had destiny written all over him. When his mother was pregnant with him, she had a dream in which her womb bore a dog who broke away from her and ran through the world setting fire to it with a torch he carried in his mouth. Deeply disturbed by this dream, she went to the Benedictine abbey of *San Domingo de Silos* twenty miles away and prayed for an interpretation. The sanitized answer was that her son would set the world on fire with his preaching. There could have been another answer, more ominous, but equally plausible, as it turned out. When the baby was born, she named him Domingo after the abbey.

Unlike his rowdy young Assisi contemporary, the inordinately pious Domingo Guzman spent his youth doing good works for the poor and praying. Both of his older brothers were studying for the priesthood, so the same path was a natural for him. He went to the University of Palencia at age fourteen, and after a decade of study, was ordained a priest.

The Pope

There is a saying among papal historians that goes something like this: there was no saint among the twelfth century popes. The pope to whom that saying was the most applicable was Innocent III. He was a lawyer by training, which may have had something to do with his lack of saintliness. He came to the highest office of the Church having been, from the age of 24, a close advisor to three popes.

At his coronation, he proclaimed something quite innovative and quite shocking to the secular authority:

> "The Lord entrusted to Peter the government not only of the whole Church, but of the whole world."

Upon assuming the papal ring, he attempted to live those words to the fullest and assume the secular crown, too. He presided over the papacy during the culmination of its period of transition from a purely religious authority to a combined religious and secular power. Obsessed with territorial aggrandizement and with being perceived as supreme lawgiver, he was intoxicated with power. No pope before or since (with the possible exception of Julius II at the beginning of the sixteenth century) has been so involved with worldly affairs. And no pontiff left a more lasting imprint on his Church and his flock than this remarkable, determined man.

Resurgence of the Papacy

Innocent succeeded to the papacy after it had been occupied for almost twenty years by a series of five tired, old men chosen for their feebleness, narrowness of mind, and malleability by a curia reacting against the political involvement of the great Pope Alexander III, who died in 1181. At best, they were placeholders, put in the papacy until the church leaders could sort out what Alexander had wrought.

This interregnum had its salutary effect. In the 1180's, tensions between the papacy and the Holy Roman Empire eased considerably. The secular and the clerical appeared to come once more into balance, a *modus vivendi* satisfactory to almost all. But both science and history teach us that equilibrium generally does not last. And in this case, it went out of balance very quickly, as soon as one side or the other produced a strong personality to lead it.

In 1191, Pope Celestine crowned Henry VI Holy Roman Emperor in Rome. Henry took his title seriously, and conquered Sicily in 1194, then moved to consolidate his holdings in central Italy, impossible to do without threatening the temporal lands of the pope. Celestine was not a strong man and avoided conflict at all costs, negotiating incessantly, delaying and filibustering to the point of exhaustion, his strategy being to avoid giving up any of his lands.

The two chieftains—Emperor and Pope—died within months of each other at the end of 1197 and the beginning of 1198, respectively, and the historical stage was set. The militant wing of the College of Cardinals had had enough of imperial encroachment and, in one of those sudden fits of pique that afflicts the curia approximately once every two or three-hundred years, rejected Celestine's chosen successor and instead turned to the youngest of all the cardinals, 37-year old Lothari of Segni. On January 8, he was unanimously elected *Vicarius Christi*—Vicar of Christ, a new title.

Lothari came from the Roman nobility and had been made a cardinal eight years before by his uncle, Pope Clement III. He was not very religious, but had made his reputation as a brilliant law student in Bologna and as a pragmatic and highly effective lawyer. This most worldly, down-to-earth autocrat, power politician, and papal patriot, took the unlikely name of Innocent III.

A portrait of the pope painted during the early years of his reign shows a man who has seen it all before. There is nothing innocent about Innocent's gaze. There is only a quiet assurance, a shrewdness of eye and mouth, a look that says something about not-suffering-fools-gladly. It is not a picture of a man someone would want to cross.

Innocent III has come down to us through history as the archetype of the medieval pope, seeking and attaining both theocratic and temporal power, and exercising it relentlessly to advance the interests of the Church. He played the feudal land game to the hilt, gaining overlordship of Hungary, Aragon, and Sicily in addition to the Papal States. This was a remarkable achievement for the time, worthy of the greatest kings and emperors.

He was the first pope to successfully assert the right to supreme power over all affairs of the Church, from exclusive authority to canonize to the right to dispose of benefices. Unlike some of his predecessors and successors who asserted similar rights, he wielded the power to back up his claims and enforce them, even against secular princes who would dispute him.

More interested in the accumulation of power and territory than in its wise implementation, his government in the territories he either conquered or finagled was a disaster. Like many a conqueror and politician since, once he won the chase, he lost interest in the hard work of administration.

His goal was to permit the papacy to respond positively to the age-old question so aptly put by Josef Stalin 750 years later when told the church would disapprove of his moves against it in Eastern Europe: "How many divisions does the Pope have?" To a great extent, Innocent belied this put-down, not only rendering Rome dominant in churchly matters worldwide – a tremendous achievement in itself – but also making the papal states dominant in Italian political affairs as well.

He also claimed the right to interfere in secular affairs "where sin might be committed," a rather broad mandate subject to interpretation. This is the setting of this chapter's great encounter.

And a Resurgence of Heresy

Every action incites an equal reaction; so Newton told us in his Third Law. Innocent's corollary went further: every action against Church doctrine must incite a far greater reaction.

The centralization of papal authority over the Church in every aspect of its insinuation into its followers' lives caused a great deal of resentment in the bishoprics and provinces distant from Rome. Suddenly, the local experimentation that is the lifeblood of innovation of any institution was stifled by papal decrees from Rome, a distant and alien place.

The reaction provoked by Rome's rise to supreme ecclesiastic power in the last years of the twelfth century has never abated and has vexed every pontiff since. To put this in a contemporary perspective, consider if, overnight, local control of public schools were decreed out of existence and replaced by centralized control of every facet of educational affairs by Washington, DC. No more school boards elected or appointed by the affected citizens or their local representatives. No more

Parent-Teacher Associations. No more citizen advisory committees. At a minimum, there would be a great furor in the land.

Something like this happened to the Catholic Church 750 years ago. The election of bishops, for example, up to then a matter for local clergy and worshippers, was taken away by Rome. Active lay participation, always vast and ubiquitous in local church affairs, was reduced to insignificance.

The reaction was quick in coming. It began with a back-to-basics movement, led by individual preachers who pursued the original ideal of Christian poverty. Preaching itself was something new – and very dangerous from the perspective of the traditional clergy and curia, since the formal mass concentrated exclusively on the liturgy and the sacraments and the suppression of questioning thought.

In no time, heresies were sprouting up everywhere. Their growth and rapid expansion were remarkable. These were protest movements against the secularization of the Church and the loss of local control and rights.

From the Church's earliest days, there had always been heresies. Any divinely-inspired organization interested in survival and expansion has no choice but to consider virtually any difference of opinion, no matter how insignificant to outsiders, as an assault on its very existence. The Church had always coped with such divergences by letting the stresses build up to the point where a council of official clergy was convened in order to mediate the dispute. The important term is "mediate," and this mode of dispute resolution was spectacularly successful through the centuries.

The differences this time were threefold:

- First, whereas before there was generally one orthodox and one opposing viewpoint, the thirteenth century spawned a multitude of dissident ideas and doctrines, magnifying the threat and making the suppression of heresy extremely difficult to manage.
- Second, the doctrinal controversies of the past were largely argued among the elite, the senior

clergy. Now they involved local priests and
members of the flock as well.

- Third, and perhaps most important, the nature
  of the debate changed drastically. No longer
  were the great questions ones of philosophy or
  interpretation of the divine vs. human nature of
  Christ (see Chapter 3), conducted within the
  broader acknowledgement of the authority of
  the Church. Now they questioned the very
  organization and existence of the Church itself.

The South of France was the hotbed of this radicalism and
the epicenter of Church criticism. The "Poor Men of Lyons,"
the Albigensians, and the Waldensians each advocated a purist
religion based on the lives of Jesus and the Apostles. Their
representatives moved among the cities and towns of the
region preaching poverty, morality, and movement away from
Rome, generating tremendous excitement and garnering
enormous support and enthusiasm from the common folk.

The natural reaction of the Roman curia was repression.
But repressive measures had little effect and only firmed the
resolve of the heretics. Not fully comprehending the broad-
based social forces behind the religious revolts, the Church
first attacked the symptoms, not the disease. The most
enduring legacy of Innocent III may be that he eventually
recognized the Church's error and had both the intelligence
and fortitude to reverse course. He shrewdly decided to co-opt
the social forces tearing at the fabric of the Church in order to
popularize its religious message. By doing this, he gave a new
character to the Church and brought it back to respectability in
the eyes of most of its constituents. The importance of this
revolution from the top cannot be overemphasized. In essence,
it saved the Church.

Innocent's accomplishments did not stop with making the
Church a secular power to be reckoned with politically and
militarily, nor with his many ecclesiastic reforms. He also
radically altered the mass itself, rendering the conversion of
the bread and the wine into the body and blood of Christ

through priestly utterance the centerpiece of the ritual. Transubstantiation was added to the mass.

It was said about this remarkable politician and lawgiver when he died at age 55, in the prime of his life and at the pinnacle of his power, that he was:

"less than God, but more than man."

Few remembered that Lothari himself had coined the phrase to describe himself at his coronation eighteen years before.

The Transformation

The means by which the Pope accomplished his revolution were brilliant: He recognized and gave formal authority to the two greatest mendicant orders – the Dominicans and the Franciscans. The formal investiture of the Dominicans, a much more mainstream group than the Franciscans, and one with whom the Pope was quite familiar and very comfortable, came in 1206. While formal recognition of the Franciscan order had to wait until the Fourth Lateran Council in 1215, *de facto* authorization to proceed came from the Pope himself to Francis of Assisi much earlier. The year that this took place was also 1206. The day that Francis was given the go-ahead by the pope was the *same day* in which Dominic Guzman and his Dominican order were given their formal marching orders. Both of these remarkable men—St. Dominic and St. Francis— came to Rome at the same time to receive the Pope's sanction. They met each other that day for the first and only time, kneeling before Innocent III. Following the papal blessing for their endeavors, they talked with each other for several hours before going their separate ways.

The *quid pro quo* for the Pope's marching orders was a pledge of absolute obedience to the dictates of Rome. Both men had little problem with this requirement, eager as they were to gain endorsement of their orders. They and their successors and eventual imitators were quite comfortable with the notion of being instruments of papal policy. They became agents of reform, but of *controlled* reform under the thumb and watchful eye of Rome.

The two orders achieved enormous popularity very quickly. By mid-century, they were fixtures throughout European universities and essentially guided the intellectual life of the Church and Empire. They also amassed considerable wealth, which, for the Franciscans, became a source of great tension, splitting them into two camps, the Conventuals and the Spirituals, or *Fraticelli*, who adhered strictly to Francis' vow of apostolic poverty.

Inquisition

The Dominicans experienced no such problems. They expanded rapidly throughout Southern Europe and, true to the origins of their founder, became the most influential institution in Catholic Spain, reaching their apogee in the late fifteenth century through their zealous efforts on behalf of the Inquisition, where St. Dominic had gotten his start.

The small city of Albi in Languedoc in the south of France was the center of radical revolt against Church dogma. In Albi in the late twelfth century, an extremist sect known as the Cathars lived lives in keeping with their purist perception of the life and teachings of Jesus—hence the term "catharsis." Taking the name of their epicenter, they have come down to us through history as the Albigensians.

Much more radical than the Waldensians, who desired to remain within the Church, the Albigensians preached rejection of both priests and the priesthood. They electrified the people with their ideas, and the movement spread rapidly through the land and even seeped across the Pyrenees into heavily conservative, Catholic Spain.

Rome was deeply troubled by the wildfire spread of the Albigensian heresy, and not only because of its assault on the existing bureaucracy and organization of the Church. The Albigensians went far beyond clerical opposition. Perhaps their greatest heresy was political: denunciation of capital punishment and secular government.

Something had to be done about this "spiritual pestilence," as it was labeled by the curia. At first Innocent, the lawyer and protector of order, tried to reason with the heretics. Initially, he sent representatives to talk to them in hopes of achieving an understanding. Cistercians, dressed all in white robes, rode into the middle of the revolution and tried logic. It didn't work. Some of them did not come back, having been either converted to the rebel cause or killed. It was time for more drastic measures.

Innocent then made a delegation that would have enormous consequences for the history of the world over at least the next half-millennium. He fixed upon two Spanish priests, Bishop Diego of Osmar and his sub-prior and disciple, a young man of prodigious intellect and religious fervor, Dominic Guzman.

The two Iberians rode bravely forth into the froth of Languedoc, arguing the merits of the Church's case. It was both a spiritual and an intellectual contest. Only it did not work. The situation deteriorated rapidly, accompanied by renewed violence against Churchmen and Church property.

Meanwhile the heresy spread rapidly. Innocent was deeply disturbed and worried. Within a few months, Albigensianism had moved along the Danube as far as Passau on the German-Austrian-Czech frontier, through the *Ostmark* (Austria) and into Illyria (the Balkans), deeper into Spain, and most alarmingly, into the Po Valley of Italy and south down the peninsula. The time for reason and peaceful negotiation was over.

The pope did what popes had always done when the Church was threatened: he summoned the secular kings and nobles of Europe to a crusade against the heretics.

> "Arise, Christian soldiers! The blood of the righteous cries to you to protect the Church against its enemies . . ."

A crusading army, one hundred thousand strong, soon gathered in northern France. As spring 1209 turned into summer, they marched south. In July, they laid siege to the town of *Beziers*.

Motivated by *Masada*-like fervor, the Albigensians inside the town walls refused at first to surrender. However, starvation tends to change minds rapidly. Upon surrendering, Church records show, 20,000 inhabitants were massacred. When the crusaders finished their handiwork, Beziers had gone the way of Carthage at the hands of Scipio Africanus and Cato.

In calling for a crusade, Innocent was following precedent, although he took it to a new level. Unlike its predecessors, this crusade was not directed against the Infidel in faraway, exotic lands. No Church leader had previously contemplated a crusade against Europeans or Christians (albeit lapsed Christians), so the war against the Albigensians was a first. And since it was carried out primarily by troops from northern France, the religious war soon turned into a secular civil war of conquest, with northern warlords vying for supremacy in the south, while quarreling with each other over the spoils.

One pre-eminent figure deeply involved in the Albigensian affair refused to take part in the crusade, being opposed to violence and having invested a goodly number of years and a great deal of energy in the possibility of achieving a *modus vivendi* with the heretics: Dominic Guzman.

Eventually it became apparent that the crusade was going the route of its more well-known counterparts in the Near East. It was fundamentally a failure. More creative measures were needed. Thus was born the most terrible (and shameful) instrument in all of Church history: the Inquisition. Yet another ecclesiastical "reform" attributable to the Great Reformer, Innocent III.

The idea derived from the pope's earlier demands for stringent diocesan control over each parish throughout the realm of the Holy Roman Church. First came severe restrictions on the right to preach. Anyone who preached without either the pope's or the local bishop's consent was summarily excommunicated. Moreover, twice a year, it was required that the bishop or his archdeacon conduct a personal inspection of each parish. Reliable parishioners were recruited as spies, placed under oath, investigated, and tasked with informing the Church authorities about suspected heretics, secret meetings, and unauthorized preaching. The accused were examined by the bishop and punished if they refused to recant or if they later relapsed.

Thus, all of the ingredients were in place when the Fourth Lateran Council met in 1215. A decree was issued creating an Episcopal Court of Inquisition. Interestingly, the "legislative history" of the decree, gleaned from the Council debate, indicates an intent to establish an orderly legal procedure for this examination, replete with witnesses in open court offering testimony under oath, the right of the accused to examine documentary evidence, and even hints of a right to confront witnesses.

Somehow, all of these rights got lost in implementation in the Languedoc. Denunciation was almost always the trigger. Political authorities agreed under oath to expel heretics from their domains. The property of heretics was confiscated. Topping it off was Innocent's order of capital punishment for all found guilty of heresy.

It took almost three centuries for the Inquisition to reach its terrible, cold-blooded zenith. But the seeds were sown in Rome and took root in Languedoc, under the tutelage of the new Order of Preachers, the first Order in Church history for priests. The Order took to its role with eagerness and zealotry and performed its function most ably, hardly stopping for breath for the next 400 years. The Dominicans, whose founder Domingo Guzman was a barefoot, 45-year old, obscure priest who had spent his whole adult life in Albigensian territory pleading for nonviolence and understanding on both sides of the terrible debate, became the most violent and dogmatic Order in the Church, a brutal collection of holy thugs.

The Seeds of Sainthood

Let us return now to the principals of this chapter and their historic encounter.

One balmy day, the pope was strolling in his garden when one of his cardinals brought a small, rather forgettable-looking young man to see him. He had a jet black beard and eyebrows to match, and he was introduced as Francis from the hill town of Assisi. He had the audacity to request permission to found an order and submit its harsh, monastic rule for the Pope's approval. Francis explained that he and his brothers wanted to live the life and poverty of Christ, including His sufferings. Francis' most radical rule, in Innocent's eyes, was the requirement that anyone who wanted to join the order had to sell all his worldly possessions and give the proceeds to the poor. This went so far as to include the applicant's shoes!

Francis and his followers had actually been living like this for some years already. After he found God, Gian Bernardone had taken the name Francesco and moved with his acolytes, who flocked to his side from all over Umbria and soon from throughout the Italian peninsula, to the monastery high up Mount Subiaco above Assisi, in order to live a life of poverty, quiet contemplation, and good works.

Young men came to him in droves, attracted by his simple, yet powerful message of faith and love. They found in the simple life high up near the clouds exactly what they were seeking.

The Franciscan monastery has changed little in 800 years. The strongest impression one senses upon entering the grounds is of peace, an almost palpable tranquility. An aura of non-denominational spirituality infuses the place, affecting even cynical religious skeptics. This feeling is underscored further upon visiting St. Francis' humble cell—cave rather—in which he slept on a rock floor barely big enough for a small child. He found comfort in the uncomfortable home he made for himself, and became one with nature and with his God. The modern visitor finds this uncomplicated and virtuous existence, bereft of any materiality, very attractive and exhilarating, and hates to leave.

Innocent was shocked by Francis' plea, but also intellectually intrigued. He questioned Francis on practical grounds. What would happen in winter, he asked, with no adequate clothing or footwear to protect the brothers? "When there glows within us the longing for a heavenly home," replied Francis, "we do not feel the cold outside." "What would the brothers actually do?" queried this most pragmatic of pontiffs. Francis said he would send them forth to every country and continent, two-by-two, to promote peace . . . with penitence, the forgiveness of sins. Innocent felt the voices of the early Church reaching out to him over twelve centuries . . . and hesitated.

Initially, the Pope rejected Francis' audacious petition outright.

Nevertheless, he was intrigued and impressed, and his momentous conversation with young Francis stimulated his brain cells to overtime. Despite the slap-in-the-face implications pervading their exchange—to wit, that there was another path, the path to the human heart, to love and to peace, in contrast to the path to power and world domination honed to near-perfection by Innocent himself—the practical pope saw an opportunity here: If their worldwide preaching increased the numbers of the faithful, who would benefit? Why, the traditional, power-seeking Church and its leadership, of course.

Consequently, Francis was recalled to Rome. The pope gave him his preliminary consent. He put the order on probation, as it were. The Franciscans would be allowed to preach and receive the tonsure (the bald spot on top of the head that symbolized admission to clerical status). Formal authorization would have to wait to see how Franciscan practices worked out.

The Council

That took another five years. At the Fourth Lateran Council in 1215, Innocent presented the Franciscan petition to the assembly, with the 34-year old Francis sitting among the church luminaries in his tattered brown robe a startling contrast to the richly garbed princes of the Church. Sitting nearby was another contrasting figure, also barefoot and simply attired. Domingo Guzman was in Rome for the same reason as Francis: to secure formal recognition for his Dominican Order of Preachers. Unlike the layman Francis, Domingo was a priest. Their differences went beyond simple status, however. Domingo was formed by his experiences among the Albigensians. His order would be focused totally on campaigns against heretics. Admission into the Dominicans would be limited to priests like himself.

Strangely, the Lateran Council embraced the unconventional, Francis, and rejected the conventional Domingo. It was an unusual call for such a conservative body, and one that has befuddled historians to this day. Here were priests who wanted to stamp out heresy, largely mainstream types with a very establishment idea, one that the Dominicans represented and fully supported. Yet they turned it down.

On the other side was an idealistic dreamer, a layman, perhaps a dangerous radical who wanted to go forth among men and preach love and peace and poverty, not exactly themes that moved the thirteenth century curia, and which would seem to be very much contrary to their interests. Yet they approved the petition.

Innocent was deeply troubled by the Council's vote against the Dominicans. He mulled the matter over for a few days, then took an extraordinary decision. He granted Domingo permission, with some modification of his rule, to set up his order in defiance of the Council. Domingo went back to the French province of Languedoc to carry on the fight with new weapons.

The contrasting decisions of the Council can, I think, be explained rather easily. True, if one examines only the intellectual arguments for and against sanctioning each order, it seems that the decisions should have been reversed. If the Council were to have acted purely in its own (i.e., the Church's) best interests as these were perceived in 1215, then the Dominicans should have won easy approval and the Franciscans should have been just as easily denied.

The answer, it seems, lies elsewhere, not in the sphere of logic and intellect, but rather in the sphere of the personalities of the two applicants.

By all accounts, Francis was an angelic, innocent-appearing soul, one who spoke simply, openly and non-threateningly to all. He appeared frail and small. It would have been very easy to underestimate him. The raging fires that burned within him were well-concealed. He was charismatic to like-minded folk (of which there were few in attendance at the Council), but not charismatic-looking—an easy person to underestimate. The prevailing attitude among the cardinals and bishops must have been: what possible harm can such a simple little fellow do?

Domingo Guzman, on the other hand, was a smoldering Spaniard who looked the part. He was stockier than Francis, much more of an intellectual, and therefore easier for the assembled Church dignitaries to understand. Domingo, it seemed to them, could have been one of their number if only he had been born to their advantages. They knew him well from his work among the heretics and his participation in the Albigensian Crusade. And to know him was to fear him. He was physically brave, having proven that on many occasions in France, and he was a prodigious and passionate debater, having had to argue the position of the mainstream Church often while being railed against by angry mobs. The Council was afraid of him and of his potential.

Hindsight would conclude that the Council's two decisions were correct. For the wrong reasons, they were absolutely right to approve the Franciscan petition. The Franciscan example compelled millions to become part of the flock and thereby, as Innocent alone had the foresight to realize, vastly expanded the power and influence of the Church. The Franciscans were, perhaps, the finest public relations vehicle ever devised by the mind of man.

The Council was also correct in fearing the dangers inherent in Domingo Guzman and his more mainstream monastic approach. The Dominicans rose to supreme power, particularly in Spain where they essentially captured the government and *de facto* held it for almost 300 years, holding kings and queens like Ferdinand and Isabella in thrall. Of course, their presumption, arrogance, and ill-advised decisions eventually decimated Spanish power forever, and made a mockery of the fundamental teachings of the Church, becoming perhaps one of the worst public relations vehicles ever devised by the mind of man. They also became immensely powerful in curial circles, spawning four popes, numerous cardinals, and thousands of archbishops and bishops.

The year 1215 was not the most propitious moment for either Domingo Guzman or Francis of Assisi to come forward and petition the pope for confirmation of their new orders and concepts. Yet the pope, if not the Lateran Council, was sufficiently intrigued by their innovative approach to religion, and his influence prompted the Council to summon both founders to appear before it and argue their cases.

The threat that both orders of friars represented to the established routine was, quite simply, freedom of speech, that most uncontrollable human urge, one that once unleashed could prove more dangerous than any attacking army. What could possibly be deemed more destabilizing to a Church hierarchy that had become preoccupied in recent years with rampant heresies that required the most stringent intervention to eradicate?

Domingo, as we have seen, was considered the more extreme of the two petitioners, and not only because of his steely-eyed countenance and hot Spanish blood. In an age when only bishops had the right to preach, he had the audacity to boldly call his creation the "Order of Preachers!" This was a slap in the curia's face.

Encounter

The few histories that chronicle the Council tell us that Francis and Domingo met there in the winter of 1215-16, and that although they were complete opposites, they got along famously. According to a Dominican chronicler, Domingo saw Francis in a vision before he actually met him. The vision was quite vivid, consisting of the Virgin Mary presenting both himself and Francis to Christ, announcing them as the two men who would accomplish the conversion of the world. Francis appeared so clearly to Domingo in his vision that, when he first accidentally encountered him on the streets of

Rome, he recognized him immediately.

One of Francis' biographers says that Cardinal Ugolino, the pope's cousin, brought the two founders together in Rome, and suggested that they should join forces, combining Domingo's managerial abilities with Francis' charismatic magnetism. While they respected and admired each other for their respective abilities and achievements, they both apparently realized that, in their particular case, the whole would not be greater than the sum of the parts. It should be noted that ensuing history demonstrates the wisdom of the separation. As the years rolled by, the Dominicans and Franciscans became bitter enemies and did much to subvert each other.

The legend of the meeting of the saints may well be embellished, but it is a great story nonetheless. The two men, both barefoot, were ordered to cool their heels in the papal gardens where, deep in thought and prayer, they both wandered among the blossoms and topiary, suddenly coming upon each other.

Domingo, as noted, recognized Francis from his vision, and it was he who took the initiative. They exchanged small talk and discovered their common purpose. To two such holy men, it must have seemed an encounter decreed by heaven. They found they had much in common, these polar opposites, and got along well. We do not know with any more precision what they talked about.

Once called upon to go and meet the pope individually, their confidence levels were sky-high, and each one argued his case with extraordinary eloquence and forcefulness.

The pope was impressed, and both orders were invested by the pope that same afternoon.

Had history scheduled this encounter only a half-year later, we might not be reading and writing about it almost 800 years hence. Innocent III died suddenly on July 16, 1216, struck down by a fever at Perugia, nine miles across the valley from Assisi. It is said that the last thing of this Earth that the Pope saw before he died was Assisi, clinging precariously to the side of the mountain so close in distance, but so distant in philosophy, to where he lay dying.

Francis of Assisi journeyed from his hill town to pray beside the Pope's body before burial.

*Portrait of a man said to be
Christopher Columbus*

The next encounter is about power of a different sort. To some extent, several of the same issues were involved as were pertinent to the Vienna summit (the subject of the last encounter in this book) 500 years later. A lot of "might-have-beens," had things gone differently, and had the Great Discoverer not been the forceful personality that he surely had to be.

The setting is the mouth of the Tagus River near Lisbon, Portugal. The encounter took place in the aftermath of one of the greatest events in the history of the planet: the discovery of the New World.

Chapter 5 - Lisbon

The Discoverers and the King

Following the light of the sun, we left the Old World.
Christopher Columbus

Destiny created two encounters between Christopher Columbus and Bartolomew Dias, two of the greatest explorers of all time, and two related ones between Columbus and King Joao II of Portugal, one of the most powerful and influential monarchs of the era. Each of these four, very brief meetings was momentous, dripping with implications for the fate of the world.

Missed Opportunity

In late December, 1488, the Westerlies and Northerlies swirling together off the extreme southwestern coast of Europe chilled the air and kept the population indoors. At the court of King Joao II of Portugal in Lisbon, the destinies of Iberia, Africa, India, and the Americas were being determined.

It had been two years since the king's initial introduction to a most unusual Genoese sailor and mapmaker, one who had become a Portuguese citizen and married into the local nobility after his merchant ship foundered in battle off the coast 13 years before. Significantly, the ship went down just off the jutting spar of Cape St. Vincent, the *Sacrum*

Promontorium of the Romans, the "Sacred Headland" that demarcates continental Europe's farthest penetration into the Atlantic and the place selected a half-century before by the *Infante Dom Henriques*, better known to us as Prince Henry the Navigator, for his famous school at *Sagres*.

At that first encounter, Christopher Columbus presented King Joao with a scheme for crossing the Atlantic Ocean, replete with supporting documents including the reports of Marco Polo and a famous letter from the Italian mapmaker, Toscanelli, claiming that India lay just over the horizon to the West. While the King had a track record of interest in a Western endeavor to find a route to the riches of the East, Columbus botched his opportunity, as reported by Juan de Barros, a historian who wrote of the encounter 50 years later:

> "The king, as he observed this Christovao Colom
> to be a big talker and boastful in setting forth his
> accomplishments, and more puffed up with
> fancy and imagination about his island Cypango
> [Japan] than certain of the things he told about,
> gave him small credit."

Contemporary accounts imply, to the contrary, that the king was intrigued by Columbus, even amused and entertained by his passion for his project and his equal ambition to "bootstrap" his family up the social ladder. The future Discoverer asked for virtually everything that he ultimately received from the Sovereigns of Castile and Aragon, Ferdinand and Isabella:

- Three caravels for a period of one year, outfitted and manned;
- Appointment as caballero with the title of Don for the Discoverer and his heirs (in other words, advancement of the family into the nobility);
- The title "Great Admiral of the Ocean," attended by the same rights granted the Admirals of Castile;

- A grant of viceroy and governor of all islands and mainlands discovered during the voyage;
- Ten percent of all revenues and precious metals derived from the newly discovered lands; and
- One-eighth of the proceeds of all trade with the newly discovered lands.

That was *chutzpah*. The price was too high for King Joao, according to Columbus' son Fernando. To get rid of him diplomatically, the king turned Columbus over to his scientific council which ultimately rejected his grand plan after much delay.

The king's interest in Columbus' scheme *sans* Columbus was manifested by his secret chartering of a voyage of discovery that left the Azores, sailing west, a year later (1489) and of which very little is known after that other than the fact that the ships were never heard from again.

Undaunted, the obsessed Italian relocated to Spain to pitch his project to the Sovereigns. He got nowhere, chiefly because King Ferdinand and Queen Isabella were totally preoccupied by their campaign against the last bastion of Moorish power on the Iberian peninsula, the stronghold of Granada. Frustrated, Columbus wrote a letter to King Joao, requesting a safe conduct to visit Lisbon and petition the king once more. The safe conduct was required because Columbus had left Portugal owing considerable sums to creditors. The king granted the request, intrigued once again by the audacity of the man and concerned that Portugal's almost 70-year effort to reach the Indies by circumnavigating Africa had foundered somewhere on the continent's South Atlantic coast.

More than a year earlier, buoyed by the exploits of Portuguese explorers who, in the quarter century since The Navigator's death had pushed the national effort past the Bight of Benin and beyond the Equator and the immense mouth of the Congo River to latitude 22 degrees South, the king sent one of the greatest of all Portuguese sailors out on the most ambitious voyage yet. Bartolomew Dias took two caravels and a storage ship, determined to go where no man had gone before: around the southern tip of Africa and into the Indian Ocean all the way to India.

Now in the waning months of 1488, after almost a year-and-a-half with no word from Dias, King Joao and his court could only conclude the worst: Dias and his crew must have failed and perished in the effort. Given the circumstances, the idea of a revival of Columbus' bold idea to go east by sailing west carried renewed weight.

Columbus hurried to Lisbon and the court, carrying his charts and ancient treatises, marshalling his arguments. This time he was sure he would succeed.

Meanwhile, half a world away, Bartolomew Dias passed latitude 22 degrees South and kept on going, much to the trepidation of his sailors who were certain they were teetering at the edge of the abyss. In late January, 1488, Dias had been blown rapidly south by a great gale, so much so that the Southern Cross appeared high in the night sky, a sight never before seen by Europeans. When the gale blew itself out, Dias tacked northeast and made landfall on a new, unexplored coast. He did not know it, but the landfall was already 200 miles east of what he would call, when he discovered its spectacular setting and magnificent harbor on his return trip, the *Cabo de Boa Esperanca*, the Cape of Good Hope, the southernmost tip of the African continent.

Dias kept sailing east-northeast, certain now that he had doubled the continental tip. With the aid of dead reckoning (other than Columbus, Dias was the greatest ever at this sailing technique), he believed he would soon land in India (an accurate assessment). However, near what is today the Great Fish River, approximately halfway between Port Elizabeth and East London, South Africa, Dias' men balked and refused to go further. He was forced to turn back.

In late December 1488, the king was at his court in Lisbon, ready to receive Christopher Columbus and hear his argument once more. Columbus was ready, pacing anxiously in the antechamber to the throne room. Literally just minutes before the scheduled meeting, a great shout went up in the courtyard facing the Tagus River. Runners suddenly appeared with the news that two caravels had entered the Tagus, breached the

Lisbon Bar, and were about to anchor below the palace. The meeting with Columbus was postponed until the king could satisfy his curiosity about the mysterious ships. Within the hour, Bartolomew Dias climbed up from the docks and appeared before the king. In an annotation to his personal copy of Pierre d'Ailly's influential work, *Imago Mundi*, Columbus wrote about the encounter:

> "Dias plotted out his voyage league by league on
> a chart before the king . . . I myself was present
> at the occasion."

Africa having been doubled, the sea lanes to India were open (although it would be another ten years before Vasco da Gama reached the Subcontinent). There was no longer, in the king's mind, any need to spend money attempting a Western route. The grand design of Henry the Navigator was on the verge of being realized. The meeting between King Joao and Columbus was canceled. Bartolomew Dias, not Christopher Columbus, was the hero of the day, the sensation of Portugal and of all Europe.

Back to Spain

Christopher Columbus was a forgotten man, consigned once again to a hurtful anonymity. Despite a rare reunion with his brother Bartolomeo, who happened to be Dias' cartographer on the epic voyage around the Cape, it must have been the darkest day of Columbus' life. Devastated, he left Portugal again and went back to Spain. Days later, Bartolomeo Columbus went to England to try to interest King Henry VII in his brother's plan. Unfortunately, he was captured by pirates who confiscated his money and landed in England, destitute with only the now shabby clothes on his back. This did not enable him to make a favorable impression when he arrived at court. King Henry rejected his pitch, whereupon he crossed the Channel and tried, unsuccessfully, to interest French King Charles VIII in his brother's great enterprise.

Christopher Columbus, of course, did not give up. We all know the outcome of Columbus' prodigious persistence in the face of a lifetime of failure and frustration. After the defeat of Muhammad XII (a.k.a. Boabdil) and his Moorish forces at Granada in early 1492, Ferdinand and Isabella were able to turn their attention to Columbus' plan. Stimulated in large part by concern over an impending Portuguese monopoly of trade with the East, they approved the scheme.

Columbus set out on the greatest voyage of discovery in history in the summer of 1492. Thirty-three days after leaving *El Hierro,* the westernmost Canary Island, sailing almost due west largely by dead reckoning, maintaining two logbooks—one for the crew that hid how far they had gone from home, and a secret one for posterity that was close to accurate—he made landfall on one of the outer islands of the Bahamas (no one is quite sure which one was his "San Salvador"), went on to explore Cuba and Hispaniola (where he believed he was in Japan), lost his flagship *Santa Maria* on the treacherous rocks of *Cap Haitien* on its northern coast, and sailed for home aboard the *Nina.* He brought two Arawak Indians with him as proof of his success.

After reaching the Azores, he made for Cape St. Vincent and *Palos de la Frontera,* his embarkation point, but was blown off course by a tremendous hurricane that separated him from the *Pinta* and landed him in the clutches of the chief competitors of his Castilian sponsors, the Portuguese.

Detour to Portugal

As dawn broke on March 4, 1493, Columbus, who earned his sea legs sailing up and down the Portuguese coast, recognized the Rock of *Sintra* dead ahead of the *Nina,* and realized with a sick feeling in the pit of his stomach exactly where he was. The rock marks the entrance to the Tagus River and is only a few miles from Lisbon. Despite his queasiness, he had no choice but to round *Cabo Raso* and enter the Tagus estuary. The *Nina* was simply too beaten up by the crossing and the hurricane to risk making Spain. She desperately needed repairs. The Admiral of the Ocean Sea had to make landfall.

The reasons why Columbus was anxious about this encounter with the Portuguese had nothing to do with his epic discovery. He sensed, quite correctly, that they would not be particularly interested in a Western route to the Indies, having exerted themselves so long, so heroically, and at such enormous expense in blood and treasure to develop an Eastern route around Africa. In the few years following their discovery, they had made rapid progress in developing trade monopolies with Eastern potentates that gave them both *de facto* and *de jure* control of the lucrative spice trade. Columbus knew that, despite the convenience of a much shorter Western route to Asia, which he mistakenly believed he had found, breaking the Portuguese monopoly would be difficult if not impossible. His argument for a Western route had nothing to do with the spice trade. Rather, his interests ran to gold and God.

Columbus had another, very personal, reason for fearing the Portuguese reaction to his surprise reappearance in their land. To understand it, we have to know a little about fifteenth century Portugal, the centrality of seafaring and exploration to its national identity and survival, and the role that maps and charts played in its economic life.

As the fifteenth century opened, Portugal found itself in a tenuous position. The gradual coming together of its Iberian cohabitants into what would soon become a unified Spain—a development 700 years in the making—was a serious threat to Portuguese independence. At the same time, Spanish dominance of the Straits of Gibraltar, the gateway to the Mediterranean, threatened Portugal's trade with the East through the Mediterranean. Finally, the steady march of the Ottoman Turks toward their ultimate victory over the Eastern Roman Empire in 1453 was gradually cutting off Western Europe's access to the all-important land routes through Asia Minor that had connected it to the spice-producing regions of Asia for hundreds of years. Portugal was desperate and had to do something.

Fortunately, Portugal was blessed with a prince of the royal family who understood the geopolitical and economic issues better than anyone else. His name was Henriques, and we know him as Prince Henry the Navigator. This remarkable man was the half-English grandson of John of Gaunt, the Duke of Lancaster, father of King Henry IV and grandfather of the great Henry V of Agincourt fame. Through force of personality and a dogged persistence that should be the envy of all modern politicians, he established a sailing school at Cape Saint Vincent, the promontory that marks the southeasternmost extension of the European continent, and set forth on a long-term mission to find an alternate route to the Indies that would avoid both Spanish hegemony, Gibraltar, and the Turks. Henry's thesis was that one could sail around Africa and reach the East Indies by sea. It was a tremendously bold and futuristic theory for its time, and met with enormous skepticism among the powers-that-were in Portugal. Nevertheless, Henry was a persuasive advocate and, being a scion of the royal family, was given the resources to embark on his great adventure.

For the next 40 years, he sent expedition after expedition further and further down the West African coastline, each year's fleet required to advance farther from home and deeper into the unknown.

Henry himself never left *Sagres*, the town where he founded his sailing school. Rather, he exercised his incredible managerial abilities to develop the greatest repository of sailing and geographical information the world has ever seen, before or since. It included the most extensive set of maps and charts on the planet, documents that soon become among the most valuable intellectual property in Portuguese hands, so valuable, in fact, that they generated the world's first security classification system, giving rise to such modern notions as "Top Secret," "Secret," "Confidential," "Eyes Only," and "Need to Know." These maps and charts were the lifeblood of the Portuguese economy and its international trade for two hundred years. Nothing was more protected.

In the 1470s, Christopher Columbus' brother Bartolomeo emigrated to Portugal from Italy and became a successful map and chart maker. After several years, he was trusted enough to receive a security clearance and access to some of the most sensitive charts and maps in the possession of Prince Henry's school. While never proven, it has been widely assumed by historians that he illegally shared some of these highly classified documents with his brother, the Discoverer. This is what was uppermost in Columbus's anxious mind as he involuntarily blundered into Portuguese waters on his return home from the greatest exploration in history.

At sunrise, the *Nina* passed the quiet fishing village of *Cascais* and went over the bar of Lisbon. A crowd of people began to gather on shore, gaping at the strange sight. At 9:00 a.m., the ship dropped anchor off *Restello* (now *Belem*), four miles from the capital. The anchorage today is occupied by a landfall upon which sits the convent of *Jeronymos*, where lies the body of Vasco da Gama, as well as the remains of the man who gave his exploits to history in verse, the great national poet of Portugal, Luis de Camoes.

Columbus had picked the worst possible place to anchor. Moored right next to his tiny *Nao* ship (the Nao design dates back to about 1200 AD and owes its design to the fusion between Mediterranean and Northern European-style ships, creating a wide and deep vessel ideal for carrying bulk cargo), separated by only a short stretch of water, was a huge and heavily armed Portuguese Man-of-War, the greatest fighting ship ever built up to that time. The contrast between the two ships could not have been greater. The minuscule *Nina* was like a dinghy, dwarfed by the huge and mighty Man-of-War.

But worse was to come: The master of the powerful naval vessel was none other than Bartolomew Dias, the same Dias who had, by his serendipitous arrival 51 months before, destroyed the chances of Columbus' proposal to King Joao.

Columbus must have thought that the gods had yet another cruel twist of fate in store for him in the person of the master of the Man-of-War when he spied him making his way across the open water in a launch. And the way the conversation began, Columbus' worst fears were immediately confirmed.

Dias boarded the *Nina* for his second and last encounter with Columbus. He immediately and imperiously ordered the Spanish captain to return with him to the Man-of-War and give an account of himself. Columbus refused, replying that he sailed under the orders of the sovereigns of Spain, and that he was answerable only to them. Moreover, that as *Admiral of the Ocean Sea*, he outranked everyone the Portuguese had on hand. He said he would only be removed from his ship by *force majeure*.

Dias was taken aback by Columbus' audacity. In addition, he could see by the conspicuous presence of the two Arawaks on board that Columbus had, in fact, succeeded in his westward trek. His tone changed immediately, from that of an arresting officer to that of an admirer. If the Admiral would not come, would he send his second-in-command? No, replied Columbus, my men are as bound to our service to Spain as I am. Dias again backed off, and asked only to see Columbus's papers, meanwhile peppering the Admiral with questions about his voyage. Then he politely took his leave.

Later that day, Dias visited the *Nina* again and offered Columbus all of his men and any material Columbus might need to make repairs and be on his way. Quite an attitudinal shift!

Columbus, however, was not out of the woods yet. Word rapidly reached King Joao, ensconced in a monastery 22 miles from Lisbon. He summoned Columbus to him.

King Joao's court historian, Ruy de la Pina, recorded the meeting. The king was torn between two extremes: showing courtesy to Columbus—he ordered the refitting of the *Nina* at his own expense—while at the same time making plain his annoyance that Columbus had succeeded in his great endeavor on behalf of the King's archrivals, Ferdinand and Isabella. According to Ruy, he blamed himself for his wrongheaded prior dismissal of Columbus. He also questioned whether Columbus was not in fact in the jurisdiction of the Lord of Guinea (i.e., the King of Portugal) when he made his Discovery.

Though for the most part cordial, Columbus correctly suspected that he was in an extremely difficult and dangerous situation. Before mounting his horse for the journey to the convent housing the king, he sent a letter off to the sovereigns announcing his discovery. But King Joao did not know this, and Columbus feared the king wanted his head in order to suppress all news of the great accomplishment. Ruy tells us that the king's advisors recommended that the Discoverer be killed. Columbus became even more certain of the kingly intent when the latter recommended to him that he travel overland to Spain, advice which, if followed would almost certainly have resulted in his demise, whether by royal command or at the hands of the many bandits that controlled the difficult route. He graciously declined, citing the need to get back to his ship, and left as quickly as possible.

Following a brief detour to pay his respects to the queen at a nearby convent, he was off to the *Nina*. He sailed the very next morning. Blessed with a powerful northerly wind, he soon rounded the ominous black promontory of Cape St. Vincent and made landfall in *Palos*.

The Navigator's Influence

A powerful, ghostly presence overlay all of these encounters: the overriding influence of Prince Henry The Navigator, whose single-minded obsession with exploring beyond the farthest reaches of the known Earth, sending brave sailors where no one had ever gone before and where those who went were certain that they would be sucked into the firmament if they ventured too far from home, was largely responsible for the similar single-mindedness of all three men whose story is told in this chapter.

Bartolomew Dias and Christopher Columbus learned about sailing and about the sea and what could possibly be found beyond the horizon from the students of Prince Henry himself at Sagres. King Joao II's career and policy were also the direct result of Prince Henry's pushing the edge of the envelope. It was left to him to complete the work of The Navigator, sending Dias farther south than previous explorers had ever gone, setting the stage for Vasco da Gama to sail as far east as European man had ever gone, and, indirectly, impelling Christopher Columbus as far west as any European had ever traveled.

Ludwig van Beethoven

From two of the greatest explorers in the world, we move to the greatest duo in another field: music. In eighteenth century Habsburg Vienna, in a fleeting few minutes electric with potential and possibility, the two greatest musical geniuses of their—and perhaps any other—era, looked each other in the eye . . . and neither blinked.

Chapter 6 – Vienna I

Mozart Auditions Beethoven

The music is not in the notes, but in the silence between.

Wolfgang Amadeus Mozart

Tones sound, and roar and storm about me until I have set them down in notes.

Ludwig van Beethoven

Let me suggest that you listen to Mozart's and Beethoven's music while reading this chapter. I did that the entire time I was researching and writing it, and it made a difference, inspirationally at least. Every time I listened to the same piece, it said something different to me. As my understanding of the two geniuses and their music grew, I heard their personalities in their work and I was profoundly affected.

A "Clash" of Giants

The musical equivalent of irresistible force meeting immovable object was just a fleeting moment in the lives of Mozart and Beethoven. But it was one that resounded with "what if" possibilities that render it riveting to this day.

When you are asked to name the greatest composers of all time, who is it that comes to mind? Naturally, anytime anyone is asked to compile a "Top Ten" list, there is room for argument. People love to argue incessantly over such matters. Without the possibility of such debate, the number of movie and television critics, sports writers and college raters appearing online and in daily newspapers and magazines would plummet. Witness the college football polls. Or arguments over whether *Casablanca* is a superior movie to *Citizen Kane* or *Gone With The Wind* (it is).

There are few arenas of human endeavor not subject to dispute about which is Number One. The 1927 Yankees or the 1970s Big Red Machine? The Steelers of the 1970s or the Forty-Niners of the 1980s? Michelangelo or Leonardo? Washington, Jefferson, or Lincoln?

Musical composition, however, may be an exception. Two names appear by consensus on everyone's list, from rank, musical illiterate to avid concertgoer to sophisticated connoisseur: Joannes Chrisostomus Wolfgangus Theophilus Mozart (1756-1791)—the "Amadeus" moniker became popular only after his death—and Ludwig van Beethoven (1770-1827). Certainly the history of music lends itself to argument about some other candidates: Bach, Handel, Haydn, Mendelssohn, Liszt, Schubert, Wagner, Chopin, Tchaikovsky. Nevertheless, there is a remarkable consensus that Wolfgang Mozart of Salzburg and Vienna and Ludwig van Beethoven of Bonn and Vienna bestride the music scene like two colossi. No others come close.

I can confirm this as I write these words while listening to selections from both composers: First, Mozart's monumental *Requiem* followed by Beethoven's achingly beautiful *Sonata Number 14 in C Sharp minor ("Moonlight")* and *Sonata Number 8 in C minor ("Pathetique")*. If there are more sublime sounds in the world, I haven't heard them.

We all know the story of Wolfgang Mozart, the most prodigious of child prodigies and *wunderkinds* the world—not just the world of music—has ever seen. He was born in 1756 in Salzburg, a not-quite-real fairyland of gingerbread houses in the middle of spectacular Alpine scenery and bucolic cows wearing sonorous bells and tended to this day by actual shepherds. An accomplished pianist at age three, a composer and gifted musical polymath at four (he could already play the harpsichord, organ, and violin), a terrific public performer at six who lacked any formal education, and suddenly dead at the much-too-young age of 35, he left us with a prodigious body of work that transports us to musical heights unrealized before or since. His musical obsession marks every day of his life like no other composer, with one exception—Beethoven. Mozart could concentrate like no one else since Michelangelo sculpted, excluding everything else from his sensory life.

His total absence of formal education was "supplemented" by a very unorthodox musical training. He never studied music in any conventional way. He learned by listening and playing.

Beethoven, while something of a prodigy in his own right, was of more human proportions in his early talent. He was not born a composer like Mozart. He took a more conventional route to musical glory. He had to *learn* composition, the way virtually every composer has and does. Mozart was one of those extremely rare geniuses who never had to learn anything. It was already inside him.

The Structure of the Music

Musical composition is a complex mathematical undertaking. It reaches its apogee of complexity and performance notoriety in the symphony which, naturally enough, gave rise (in much the same way as the chicken-and-egg debate) to the symphony orchestra. The latter, like the symphony, is a complex organism, one that evolved logically over several hundred years from random collections of instruments to the balance we see (and more importantly, hear) today.

To have an idea of how complicated an endeavor it is to write a symphony, much less a good one, it is instructive to have some understanding of how a symphony orchestra is constructed.

The number *four* is tremendously significant:

1. The symphony orchestra is based upon the *four*-part harmony that impacts on all music;

2. It has four sections: strings, woodwinds, brass, and percussion;
3. Each section has enough instruments to play at least four parts simultaneously; and
4. The symphony, the most important and elaborate work played by an orchestra of the same name, most commonly has four movements.

The orchestral balance is achieved by overloading the string section, which dominates not only symphony orchestras in terms of number of instruments, but dominates much of the musical world, period. Witness how much music has been written for just strings alone. Out of 80-100 total instruments in a symphony orchestra, over half are likely to be strings.

The seating arrangement is also important, since different instruments produce sounds at varying decibel levels. After several centuries of experimentation, the arbiters of such things determined that the most balanced arrangement was for the strings to be in front, arrayed around the conductor, violins to the left, cellos to the right. The louder, shriller instruments are positioned farther away from the audience so that the sound that reaches the listener is close to equilibrium.

The woodwinds consist of 2-3 flutes, perhaps a piccolo, several oboes, maybe an English horn, two bassoons, a contra-bassoon, and a bass clarinet (optional).

The brass section has at least two trumpets and two trombones, four French horns (although they are usually seated apart), and a tuba for deep bass sounds.

The percussion section offers the widest latitude for experimentation, since there are so many percussive possibilities, i.e., a bewildering variety of drums, triangles, xylophones, glockenspiels, marimbas, vibraharps, chimes, carillons, bells, castanets, rattles, cymbals, barrels, kegs, tubs, gongs, celestas, and more. Kettle drums are considered vital, since they actually can be tuned. Often, a large bass drum and a small snare drum are also mandatory features of the percussion section since they provide rhythm, but beyond these, the possibilities are virtually infinite.

Contemplate for a moment that you are charged with writing music that should last for half an hour or more for a symphony orchestra. Help!

A symphony is to serious music what a literary novel is to serious literature. Mozart and Beethoven wrote 50 symphonies between them. Despite dying so very young, Mozart was responsible for 41 of them.

Symphonies have certain rules that composers customarily follow, rules that govern each of the movements, a theme and contrasting "countertheme," generally in related keys. The themes are usually introduced in the opening movement, like the protagonist and antagonist in a novel. Sometimes there is a "bridge" melody that supposedly binds them together. As the symphony develops, the themes hop around, break up, turn inside out, move in and out of different keys, are played by different instruments, and go through a gauntlet of variations designed to create something of a "plot." The plot ultimately resolves itself via a return to the original melodies ("recapitulation").

In summary, the symphony is the most complex of all musical compositions and calls upon all of the creative and technical genius of the composer for its realization and, of course, its success.

Mozart could dash off whole symphonies without a mistake, without a rewrite, without any proofreading or editing. Anyone who has ever had to write even so modest an expostulation as a high school paper can appreciate how remarkable this statement really is. More unbelievable, he could do it in weeks. And even more remarkable (the limited superlatives available to the author do not do Mozart justice!), many of them are fantastic, considered by expert and listener alike to be the zenith of musical accomplishment.

Beethoven, in contrast, took apart the classical symphony and, in putting it back together, made it into something greater than it had ever been. However, squeezing the notes out of his turbulent brain and committing them in final form to paper was agony for him. His willpower had to have been enormous.

Every author of any merit brings a point-of-view to his work, and I am no exception. However, the one I advance in this chapter is quite different, at least in intensity, from the rest of this book. While I have strong opinions about both Hitler and Napoleon, my assessment of their "meeting" on the second floor (described later in this book) of an obscure building in a tiny village tucked away in a bend of a second-tier river in Central Europe is, well, neutral. And while I think Francis of Assisi was a great, great man whose influence for good still deeply moves mankind 800-plus years later, whereas his counterpart Dominic Guzman spawned one of the great scourges that ever afflicted mankind, I save my strongest-held opinion for the one, brief meeting between these two towering figures of the musical world.

That opinion is this: their meeting could have been a disaster had its original intent been realized. Only the intervention of a tragic fate prevented an even more tragic encounter that would have deprived the world and posterity of the extraordinary music of Ludwig van Beethoven.

The original drafts of the music created by these two geniuses are worth examining for another reason, too. Mozart's creations are full of clear, powerful, confident notes that leap off the page and into the ears of listeners everywhere, with nary a correction to be found anywhere. They were perfect as they emerged from his celestial gift and immediately committed to paper. For Mozart, the creative process was a walk in the woods. His compositional methodology was to lay out each part (instrument) on the floor, then combine them in his head. No one else in the history of music before or since could do that.

For Beethoven, however, composition was a nightmare, not only because his manuscripts look like an excursion across a Jackson Pollock canvas, but also because of what they tell us about the *process*. In addition to scribbles and cross-outs everywhere, fits-and-starts, they are full of hesitations, uncertainties, losses of confidence, and abrupt deviations into other realms. Where Mozart could dash off innumerable musical pieces effortlessly with an incredible lightness of being, Beethoven's music had to be squeezed out like a caterpillar struggling to emerge from a cocoon. Mozart did not have to become a beautiful butterfly. He was born one.

It should be noted that, for virtually all composers with the exception of a Mozart (or a Franz Schubert), composition was—and is—extremely hard work. Beethoven was no exception. Indeed, being deaf for a good portion of his creative life, he was at a singular disadvantage.

Every composer begins with a musical idea. It plays around in his head and, at a certain point, he plunks it out on the piano and commits it to notes on paper. For Mozart, it was a short, facile step between the musical idea and the full-blown final product, be it *lied*, sonata, concerto, or symphony. Beethoven, on the other hand, sweated bullets in order to nurture the musical idea into a complete musical piece. Where Mozart could not write fast enough to keep up with his mental musical explosions, Beethoven's inspiration was far less spontaneous and required diligent effort and many dead ends and blind alleys before it bore fruit. But, ah, what fruit it bore!

Mozart's musical ideas are sublime, delightful, full of symmetrical spirit and uplift. They are, in their own way, as close to perfection as human endeavor is likely to get. Beethoven's musical ideas, in contrast, are much deeper, heftier, more profound, and perhaps more achingly beautiful. They take your breath away in a way that Mozart's do not, with the possible exception of his very serious works like *Don Giovanni* and the unfinished *Requiem*. Mozart's work is the voice of genius; Beethoven's the voice of God.

Had logic prevailed and fate not intervened, it is likely that the young Beethoven would have become Mozart's student. A few lessons from that artistic Andromeda and Beethoven might well have chosen another career. Who can endure perfection thrown up in one's face day in and day out?

Consider playing basketball one-on-one with LeBron James. Or debating Winston Churchill. Of course, these examples fail to make the point. The gap between the compositional ease of Mozart and the epic struggles of Beethoven is huge, much bigger than anything described above. Any human being would have become deeply discouraged when confronted with an otherworldly talent like Mozart's.

If daily exposure to Mozart's effortless musical talent would not have discouraged him, the two composers' sharply contrasting personalities probably would have caused the relationship to collapse. Mozart was a happy-go-lucky, good-time Charlie, a *bon vivant* whose pursuits outside of music were so mundane and earthy as to defy credulity. He compartmentalized his life like no genius before or since. Creative splendor coexisted within him with crude enjoyment, bathroom humor, and buffoonish behavior.

Beethoven, in contrast, was at the other extreme when it came to a sense of humor or the ability to truly enjoy oneself. He elevated seriousness to a higher plane. Had he fallen into Mozart's orbit, subjected there to both genius that transcended the rational and boorishness that sunk to depths that most good young men from Bonn did not know existed, he likely would have slunk home discouraged or disgusted or both, perhaps beyond repair. Easily embittered, he may have re-enveloped himself in his cocoon and, at best, become an anonymous, undistinguished member of the musical staff of the Elector of Cologne. After all, how do you follow in footsteps so big they take up galactic space?

Mozart was the king of the tonal architects, the ultimate master of the classical design, the emperor of Form. He was the evolutionary idealization of what had begun a hundred years earlier with Johann Sebastian Bach, was continued by Georg Friedrich Handel, and came closest to Mozartian perfection in the person of Franz Josef Haydn who, himself, wrote 125 symphonies, almost three times the output of Mozart (Haydn, it should be noted, was granted 77 years by the Book of Life, more than twice as many as Mozart).

First Movement: Early Life

The comparisons and contrasts between the two composers are best exemplified by the two extremes of life. Their origins and early years' influences on the one hand demonstrate their similarities. At the other extreme, their deaths and funerals represent the clearest contrast.

They were almost contemporaries. They came from the same part of the world: Central Europe. They were exposed to similar influences. Both, for example, were born into *very* musical families. Leopold Mozart, Wolfgang's father, was a professional musician in the service of the Archbishop of Salzburg. Johann van Beethoven, the father of Ludwig, was a professional singer in the service of the Archbishop (and Elector) of Cologne. Moreover, his grandfather, the first Ludwig, was *Kapellmeister*—musical director—to the Archbishop and became Beethoven's role model and guiding spirit.

Leopold was a shameless and mercenary promoter of his son's talent. Never did a parent, not even a modern Hollywood stage mother, exploit a child like Leopold did his son. The boy was a sensation, possessing not only the uncanny ability to compose on demand in almost any style requested; he could also write-to-order, adapting his compositions through variations to the idiosyncrasies of any group before which he was playing. As a child, his existence was little different from that of an organ grinder's trained monkey.

Leopold's aim was to secure a patron for his son. He moved frantically from town to town across Europe seeking a deep-pocketed Daddy Warbucks. It never happened. The child (and later, the adolescent) was almost too facile at the piano and with his compositions. Not to mention too young to serve in the serious role of *Kapellmeister* or court composer. His audiences were dazzled, heaped praise on the boy, and then sent him on his way.

In addition to whatever musical genes he passed along, the father also passed on his extreme anxiety for patronage to his son, whose life was marked—and marred—by an eternal, unsuccessful quest for precisely such patronage. It was never to be. The best he ever did was as a teenager, serving for a time as concertmaster to the Archbishop of Salzburg's orchestra, for the decidedly unprincely wage of the equivalent of $75 per year.

When Leopold Mozart rendered his famous description of his wondrous son, "the miracle which God let be born in Salzburg," one has to wonder how he meant it. Today, he might even be accused of child abuse.

Johann van Beethoven, like Leopold Mozart, was very much aware of his son's huge talent. And also, like Mozart-*père*, of the fame and fortune that could be the family's if he played his cards right and nurtured that talent to its logical conclusion. Beyond that, and most interestingly, Johann was acutely cognizant of how Leopold Mozart exploited his family prodigy, pushing his son up the musical and court ladders, and of the economic and attendant consequences of having fathered a musical genius. Beethoven-*père* was also more than a little jealous of the early display of young Mozart's abilities, so much so that he lied about his own son's age, passing him off as two years younger than he actually was, and doing it so often and routinely that, in later years, Ludwig had a problem determining for himself how old he was! All thanks to the prodigal talent of the young Mozart.

Yet Johann van Beethoven was not sufficiently disciplined to do the same as Leopold Mozart to and for his offspring. He was also, in contrast to Leopold, a harsh taskmaster, daily beating and flogging his son if he played a wrong note on the clavier or if a practice session was not up to his demands. Ludwig's childhood was a prolonged misery, a dark period that had a powerful influence on his adulthood.

A disorganized alcoholic, Johann deteriorated gradually until, when his son was seventeen, the torch of responsibility for the family essentially passed from the older to the younger generation.

Second Movement: Commonalities and Contrasts

The linkages between these two musical geniuses go much deeper than their origins and forebears. Both men were Bach obsessives. Mozart used to attend Sunday salons in Vienna where he would join other musicians to play the best of Bach.

Beethoven performed Bach in Vienna in his early years, creating quite a stir. "Not *Bach* (brook)," it was said, "but *Meer* (ocean) should be his name."

Haydn too, was a mentor to both Germanic giants. Beethoven even studied composition under Haydn. It was from Haydn as precursor that Mozart and shortly thereafter Beethoven created and refined the form we call the classical symphony. Alas, unlike Haydn, who waltzed through a life of princely patrons, economic certainty, and easy success, Mozart and Beethoven had to suffer cruel financial and physical fates. Mozart died much too young after a mysterious final illness that gave us the incomparable *Requiem* in return for the snatching away of one of the great talents of history. Beethoven, the ultimate gratifier of the auditory sensibilities, was condemned to the ultimate irony: early and total deafness. The audiences could hear and exult in his celestial chords. He could not.

Mozart and Beethoven had much more in common than that, however. Each was deeply devoted to his mother, and suffered intensely when his mother died unexpectedly when each boy was only a teenager, not yet able to go about on his own in a hostile world.

Like all human beings, there was also much to contrast between these towering personalities. Mozart was all fun and games, a simple, immature, devil-may-care, and uncouth fellow aside from his divine gift. His musical virtuosity aside, he was the most common of common men, a fact that drove his musical peers to despair. How, they wondered, could so much sublime talent repose in such an otherwise coarse character? It did not seem fair. The role of Antonio Salieri in the great film, *Amadeus*, brings this out. This dichotomy even became the premise for the most appealing myth that Salieri, a minor composer and court favorite, actually poisoned Mozart, causing his death. A myth, I should add, that has made more than one author, playwright, and movie maker rich.

Ludwig van Beethoven, on the other hand, could never be accused of frivolity. He was as serious and humorless an individual as Mozart was facile and fun. Beethoven was all *sturm und drang*. He smoldered. Just look at his portraits.

Third Movement: The Meeting

The central European community of musical giants was a small one. It would be natural to conclude that Olympian figures like Mozart and Beethoven crossed paths many times during their overlapping adult years. After all, they were only 14 years apart in age. But that was not the case. In fact, Mozart and Beethoven met only once, for an hour or so, on a slow spring afternoon in Vienna.

Beethoven was already known as the "young genius" in March, 1787, when he left Bonn on the 20th of the month for Vienna. After a leisurely journey, he arrived in Munich on April 1st, stayed a few days, then set off again for his destination. In those days and for more than a century thereafter, if you were going to make it big in the world of music, you had to go to Vienna, the musical capital of the world.

Beethoven arrived at *Domgasse No. 5* with an extremely modest entrée, namely a letter of recommendation from the Elector-Archbishop in Bonn to Emperor Joseph II. Hardly the guarantee of a brilliant career. In contrast, Mozart first made his way to Vienna directly to the Imperial Court of the Empress Maria Theresa 25 years before, at the age of six. He was a sensation, an enormous success, and charmed the court not only with his music, but with his spirit and audacity (two qualities that were with him until the end), promising his contemporary, the ill-fated six-year old Marie Antoinette, daughter of the Empress, that someday he would marry her!

Beethoven was to stay in the Habsburg capital this first visit less than two weeks. Five years later, Vienna became his permanent home. He remained there almost 40 years and produced all of his great masterpieces there, stimulated by the political and musical history of his adopted city.

Mozart, during this spring marked by the arrival of the young Beethoven, was working on *Don Giovanni*, his great tragic opera. Beethoven, according to his biographer, Otto

Jahn, was taken to Mozart one afternoon to audition to become the latter's composition student.

Mozart had a reputation as a strict musical taskmaster. At Mozart's request, Beethoven played something for him. Mozart assumed it was a showpiece, prepared especially for this occasion. Hence, he was very cool in his praise. Beethoven, sensing Mozart's reserve and the reasons for it, begged the maestro to give him a theme for improvisation. Extremely excited by being in the presence of Mozart, whom he greatly admired, Beethoven played brilliantly. Mozart noticed well enough, and was duly impressed. Silently, he stole from the room and went to an adjoining one to tell some friends: "Keep your eyes on him; some day this youth will make a noise and give the world something to talk about!"

Beethoven, ripe for discipleship, wanted desperately to become Mozart's pupil. But that was not to be. The very afternoon he sat at Mozart's clavier dazzling the assemblage, a messenger arrived with a letter for him from Bonn, informing him that his mother had suddenly fallen gravely ill. He hurriedly excused himself and left Vienna that very day, at the same time leaving posterity to wonder what might have been.

We have no record that Beethoven ever mentioned anything about his brief encounter with Mozart. There was, however, some residuary influence: musical scholars consider Beethoven's early Bonn works to have been heavily modeled on Mozart. Mozart's *Violin Sonata in G Major* (Kochel 379), for example, is considered the model for Beethoven's *E-flat Major Piano Quartet*. Beethoven's early melodies, too, are based on the *suspension*, a style characteristic of Mozart and the eighteenth century. Gradually, as he matured, Beethoven eliminated the suspension, but never shed himself completely of the influence of Wolfgang Mozart.

We can only speculate about what, if anything, the world lost because Beethoven *did not* become Mozart's piano composition pupil. Perhaps the uncommonly serious younger man would have been offended by the playful, carefree lifestyle and manner of his mentor. Perhaps Beethoven would have been so overwhelmed by the stupendous scope of Mozart's "gift," by how easy composition was for the teacher, that he would have become disappointed and begun to doubt his own abilities. No one before or since Wolfgang Amadeus Mozart could sit down and create whole sonatas overnight, whole operas in just weeks. Mozart could, and did. Many times. His output during his short life was prodigious, over 600 compositions all told, many of them among the greatest pieces of music the world has ever heard, accomplished in only one draft.

Beethoven, in contrast, struggled mightily over his music. It must have been hell for him to extract the proper combination of notes from his deaf ears and fevered brain. Mozart's compositions signify divinely inspired genius; Beethoven's, the doubts, turmoil, and overwhelming stress of the creative process.

All of which leads to the conclusion that both he—and we— are much the richer for what never came to pass between the two maestros. While poignant that Beethoven was about to lose his mother, the sad fate that intervened that afternoon probably made for some of the greatest music ever. By being abruptly called back to his mother's deathbed in Bonn, the world benefited. The otherworldly talent of Ludwig van Beethoven was permitted to be unleashed for posterity to enjoy, unconstrained by the prodigious, intimidating talent of his almost mentor.

The young Beethoven did not return to Vienna for another five years. When he did, Mozart had been dead for almost a year, in a way opening opportunities for younger composers and pianists for the first time in over a decade. Beethoven was one of the first to avail himself of them. It might seem reasonable to conclude that he returned to the capital prompted by the disappearance from the musical scene of the otherworldly talent of Mozart. He now would have the field open for himself. In fact, war prompted Beethoven to relocate to Vienna in 1792. The French revolutionary armies had invaded the Rhineland, threatening Bonn and Cologne.

Beethoven's intention on arriving in Vienna was to study with Joseph Haydn, then considered the greatest living composer. Presciently, Beethoven's friend and patron, Count

Waldstein, wrote to him: "Mozart's genius mourns and weeps over the death of his disciple. It found refuge, but no release with the inexhaustible Haydn; through him, now, it seeks to unite with another. By means of assiduous labor you will receive the spirit of Mozart from the hands of Haydn."

Beethoven studied piano with Haydn and vocal composition with Antonio Salieri (whose obsessive envy of Mozart was the theme of the film, *Amadeus*). He quickly developed a reputation as a virtuoso pianist especially good at improvisation. In stark contrast to Mozart, Beethoven easily accumulated numerous patrons among the Viennese aristocracy and did not want for either lodging or money.

He debuted in March, 1795, performing his first Piano Concerto in C Major (there is some dispute among scholars if that was, in fact, his first piece for public consumption). He followed that with the publication of three piano trios, which were an immediate critical and financial success. Upon debuting his Symphony No. 1 in C Major in 1800, he established himself as one of Europe's greatest and most widely recognized composers.

As the new century moved on, Beethoven experienced one success after another. At the same time, Europe was fixated on the person of Napoleon Bonaparte, who was rapidly rising to the height of his power and mastery of Europe. Beethoven had very mixed feelings about Napoleon. He both admired and loathed him while also identifying with him—they were roughly the same age.

In 1804, Beethoven debuted his Symphony No. 3, the "*Eroica,*"originally written in Napoleon's honor, a dedication that was abruptly withdrawn when Beethoven heard that Napoleon had declared himself emperor. This is a tremendously powerful work that broke new ground in classical music. It was the first "heroic" symphony and served as the platform for much of the great music that followed during the remainder of the nineteenth century. It was so original and unique that the musicians rehearsing it had great difficulty figuring out how to play it. Consistent with the agony and anguish that Beethoven brought to all of his compositions, it took him more than two years to write it. The original score is circled, highlighted, and otherwise marked up to the point where few original notes survived revision.

Simultaneous with these great compositions, Beethoven was forced to come to grips with something beyond horrible for a musician and composer: hearing loss. He tried to conceal his malady for years, but it became increasingly apparent to his friends and patrons that he was going deaf.

Deafness profoundly affected him. He lived in misery, cutting himself off from society. He became deeply depressed at a time when there were no therapies available for melancholia. People viewed him as a misanthrope. He was miserable and lonely on top of being painfully shy, ill-tempered, and paranoid. He was constantly at odds with his family (brothers), pupils, patrons, publishers, and everyone else who crossed his path.

It is beyond belief that, despite his tragic circumstance, Beethoven could continue to compose and churn out great works at an incredible pace. From 1803-1812, he produced 72 songs, seven piano sonatas, six symphonies, six string sonatas, five string quartets, five sets of piano variations, four overtures, four trios, four solo concerti, two sextets, and an opera. They included some of the greatest music ever created, including: the resounding *Fifth Symphony*, the unearthly *Moonlight Sonata*, the *Kreutzer Violin Sonata*, and *Fidelio*, his only opera. This would be an incredible lifetime work product for any composer with all his senses intact. The originality of these pieces is breathtaking; their complexity incomprehensible. Like Mozart, Beethoven heard the music in his head before committing it to paper.

Beethoven never married. He suffered the added tragedy of being hopelessly in love with a married woman, Antonie Brentano, to whom he wrote a heart-rending love letter that he never sent.

He ached for children and, in 1815 upon his brother's death, launched a seven-year legal battle with his sister-in-law for custody of his nephew, Karl van Beethoven, in which he ultimately prevailed.

Ludwig van Beethoven is widely considered the greatest composer of all time, although you would get an argument from Mozart admirers. Strikingly, for his first three years in Vienna, Beethoven was deemed a virtuoso pianist, not at all a composer of any note. He earned a modest living performing for various aristocrats and occasionally in public.

Everything changed for him, however, when in 1798 he first became aware that he was losing his hearing. By 1801, his was completely deaf. There is much speculation concerning why Beethoven lost his hearing and at such an early age (he was not yet 30). It ranges from syphilis, lead poisoning, or typhus to his habit of immersing his head in cold water to stay awake.

The onset of deafness made him turn more toward composing and away from performing. For a second time, his personal misfortune became the world's great good fortune.

Beethoven is the major transitional figure connecting the Classical and Romantic eras of Western music. Beethoven's body of musical compositions stands with Shakespeare's plays at the apex of human accomplishment.

That Beethoven composed his most beautiful and extraordinary music while deaf is an almost superhuman feat of creative genius, perhaps only paralleled in the history of artistic achievement by John Milton writing Paradise Lost while blind. Summing up his life and imminent death during his last days, Beethoven, who was never as eloquent with words as he was with music, borrowed a tag line that concluded many Latin plays at the time. *"Plaudite, amici, comoedia finita est,"* he said. "Applaud friends, the comedy is over."

Fourth Movement: Finis

Perhaps the biggest difference between the two musical titans was the way in which they died and were honored at their deaths. Mozart, as is well-chronicled, died quietly, surrounded only by family and a few friends, ignored by the society at large whom he strived so desperately all his life to impress. He was convinced that he was being systematically poisoned, but gave no indication by whom. He first expressed this to his wife, Constanze, in June 1791 while walking in the

Prater, Vienna's large amusement park which in later years provided one of the city's iconic symbols, a giant Ferris Wheel, the *Riesenrad* (known to most Americans because of the Orson Welles movie, *The Third Man*). He told her that someone (unnamed) was giving him *aqua toffana*, a "popular" poison known for killing its victims slowly—it takes several months to work. It had been invented in 1659 by a Neapolitan mother and daughter who sold it to wives intent on dispatching their husbands. Aqua toffana easily escaped medical detection in that era.

While this was gnawing at Mozart, he was also tremendously busy. In addition to working on two operas, *The Magic Flute* and *La Clemenza di Tito*, he had been commissioned to write a *Requiem* for an Austrian count in honor of his wife's recent death. For the first time in several years, he was earning good money and did not have to plead for handouts from rich patrons and admirers.

As stated above, the myth that Antonio Salieri was the poisoner, implied in *Amadeus,* is just that: a myth. Late in life, when Salieri was confined to a mental institution, he claimed that he had poisoned Mozart, then quickly retracted that claim. The only actual event in that part of the *Amadeus* that is true is that Mozart was composing the *Requiem* when he died. Contrary to the film version, he did not view his composition as some kind of ominous portent and was not dictating it to Salieri while he was dying. At his death, the great work was only half-finished (it was completed later by his pupil, Franz Süssmayr).

Mozart's death came quickly. For most of the second half of 1791, Mozart was full of life. At the end of August, he traveled with Constanze and the young Süssmayr, rumored to be Constanze's lover and possible father of her last child, to Prague for the first performance of *La Clemenza di Tito*, which the audience greeted with acclaim. Mozart and his companions returned to Vienna in mid-September.

The Magic Flute was first performed at the end of September. In an early October performance, Mozart himself played the role of *Papageno*. Constanze went off to *Baden,* a nearby spa, and in letters to her Mozart expressed no intimation of poor health. Quite the contrary. The letters describe his daily comings and goings and, as was his wont, were full of jocular gossip.

Weeks before his passing, he still appeared to be in good health, mentally as well as physically. Constanze returned home in November. In mid-month, Mozart conducted his new cantata for the Masons, of which he was a member, to celebrate the opening of a new lodge. It is a joyful piece that belies any depression or ominous foreboding.

Things were definitely looking up. In fact, a group of Hungarian nobles announced that they intended to send him an annual payment, fabulous news for someone constantly living way beyond his means.

Returning home from the Masonic performance, Mozart felt ill and took to bed. Two weeks later, at 12:55 AM on December 5, 1791, he died. He was only 35 years old. The doctors were unable to do anything for him. The cause of death remains a mystery.

His funeral was poorly attended (even his wife, Constanze, was not present). The hearse was followed through the misty winter's day (the winter storm scene in *Amadeus* is a fiction) by only a handful of mourners. They included his patron, Baron Van Swieten, his disciple Süssmayr, and Salieri. He was laid to rest in the Cemetery of St. Mark, either in a common grave, a pauper's grave, a mass grave, or a potter's field. The historical sources are all over the map regarding this. All we know for certain is that Mozart's grave was—and is—unmarked. We also know that the mourners only accompanied the funeral cortège to the cemetery gates, so only the grave-diggers who lowered the coffin into the ground knew where he was buried. The mourners instead repaired to a *gasthaus* to get warm and toast their colleague. When the greatest artistic genius since Michelangelo Buonarotti passed away, no one outside of perhaps Salieri truly understood what the world had lost.

Ludwig van Beethoven died 36 years later. March 26, 1827. The greatest composer of the nineteenth century lay in a rough bed on the second floor of the *Schwarzspanierhaus*, the "House of the Black Spaniard," only a few miles from where

Mozart had lived and died. Beethoven's last act on Earth was prompted, fittingly by a thunderclap, at which he opened his eyes, and much in character shook a clenched fist heavenward, then passed on. He was 56 years old. God had granted him a life span of two decades more than Mozart. For the most part, they were two decades of holy hell for Beethoven. Had they not been so tragic for him, the question can legitimately be asked if his legacy would have been the same? Did it take the inhuman suffering that this ironically most auditory of men had to endure to produce some of the most inspired sounds— ones he could not hear—to assault and delight the human ear?

Despite his infirmity and personal misery, Beethoven continued to compose great music as he neared the end of his life. The *Missa Solemnis* and *Ninth Symphony* (his last) were composed in 1824.

In contrast to Mozart, an autopsy was performed on Beethoven. It concluded that the cause of death was cirrhosis of the liver and strongly inferred that his deafness was the result of arterial disease. Now, almost 200 years later, scientists who analyzed a skull fragment detected inordinately high lead levels, leading to speculation that the actual cause of death might have been lead poisoning.

Also unlike Mozart, Beethoven died a very public death. The funeral, which took place three days later on a lovely, warm day, was a mass event. Even Vienna's schools and theaters were closed. In contrast to the pathetic handful of mourners at Mozart's funeral, approximately 15-20,000 people came to the *Schwarzspanierhaus* to pay their last respects. A ceremonial carriage pulled by four horses carried the coffin through the streets of Vienna while a band played the funeral march from his *Opus 26 Piano Sonata*. Following the ceremony, the cortège, consisting of the carriage carrying the coffin and no fewer than 200 following carriages, made its way to the suburb of *Wahring* where the great man was laid to rest in the parish church cemetery. The Austrian national poet, Franz Grillparzer, delivered a stirring eulogy.

Beethoven, the embittered misanthrope who lived a reclusive life amidst the tragedy of his hearing loss, yet continued to create music like no one else, was massively feted at his death by the society he hated and despised. Mozart, the devil-may-care, lighthearted *bon vivant* who loved society and always wanted to be in the center of it, and whose life resembled a party more than anything else, died totally ignored by that same society he so savored, and only attained the adulation he craved after it was too late for him to revel in it.

Coda

Mozart paid a terrible price for his seminal talent. Two terrible prices, in fact; one being relative anonymity during his life, the second being his tragically premature death. Perhaps he suspected that his passionate flame would flicker only fleetingly, and that there was much to be done in the short time allotted him. And so, from age four on, he worked furiously to get it all accomplished. For which we, the beneficiaries, must give thanks.

Beethoven was blessed to live what for the time was a normal life span. However, he was condemned to a living hell. Both during his active years and since, he has been consistently considered one of the greatest of all composers, if not the greatest.

However, public attitudes about composers can change dramatically over time. Mozart did not realize more than fleeting fame during his life. However, shortly after his death, he was deemed the greatest composer of all time and performances of his operas and compositions were in high demand. However, by the late nineteenth century, he was relegated by a musical public steeped in ponderous Wagnerian romanticism to "lightweight" status not worthy of a serious music lover's attention, a minor composer of largely frivolous pieces. By the middle of the next century, however, he had regained his place at the top of the musical podium.

Both men were complex, poignant characters. The one a merry prankster, never quite growing up, constantly unable to manage his finances, always suffering from slights by the aristocracy he so desperately wanted to admire and honor him, any maturity evident only in the sublime grandeur of his creative works. The other, a perennial old man, misanthropic and grumpy, his brow always furrowed, tormented by a cruel fate that robbed him of the sense that was, perhaps, better developed in him—and certainly more sensitive—than in any other human being. His Sisyphean torture was to hear things in his head that he could never hear for real. In both cases, their sufferings were all for our benefit.

Henry Morton Stanley

The next encounter relocates us from perhaps the most civilized place on the planet to perhaps the least civilized—one of the last great undiscovered plots of land on the globe at the three-quarter mark of the nineteenth century, the Congo. There, we will meet two immensely brave adventurers and visionaries, one an Italian in the service of France, the other an Anglo-American in the service of Belgium. Their meeting was a clarion call to colonialism, a lust for power that flickered briefly, then expired with a whimper, but left a lasting bad taste that is reluctant to fade away.

Chapter 7 – The Congo

Stanley and De Brazza
Scramble for Africa

Dr. Livingstone, I presume?

Henry Morton Stanley

Popular history demands that any chronicle of nineteenth-century African encounters concern itself first and foremost with the legendary meeting of two great African explorers, David Livingstone and Henry Morton Stanley at *Ujiji* in 1871. They had much in common, these two Englishmen who were not truly English (Livingstone was a Scot, Stanley a Welshman who became an American):

- They were the only two of the many Victorian lions of African exploration who came from humble beginnings.
- They were extremely uneasy in "polite" society.
- They had few close friendships.

In the four months they spent together, they grew intensely close to each other, with Livingstone the mentor and Stanley the disciple.

While certainly fascinating, Stanley's highly publicized "finding" of Livingstone was not the momentous historical event Victorian society and historians would have us believe.

First, Livingstone was not "lost." At least he did not consider himself lost. Second, Stanley's finding of Livingstone did nothing to change the world. True, it brought Stanley great fame, but he would have become famous regardless, thanks to his later explorations. It is impossible to know whether Stanley was spurred to explore and attempt to tame the Congo River because Livingstone had failed, or if he would have done it anyway, under any circumstances.

The encounter that is the subject of this chapter occurred several years later, at what became known as Stanley Pool, a giant lake in the middle of the Congo River. It was more confrontation than encounter, one between two tremendously obsessive, ambitious, and charismatic men (Livingstone was an obsessive, but neither ambitious nor charismatic) who shared much in common and were also very different, and who epitomized the great colonialists who captured the public imagination for a brief duration of less than a hundred years. Henry Morton Stanley was one party to the encounter. The other was the enigmatic Pierre Sauvergnon de Brazza.

Europe Rediscovers Africa

By the late nineteenth century, when what is popularly known as the "scramble for Africa" took off, African exploration by white Europeans was already over 400 years old. The fascination with "Darkest Africa," the impenetrability of the "Dark Continent," the mysteries that might be hidden below the immense Saharan barrier in the north, covering a land area larger than the continental United States, captured the imaginations of generations of Europeans. The wonders to be found in the recesses of the rain forests, the strange creatures lurking there—some ominous and terrifying, others just odd-looking and behaving—and the great quests associated with this most sinister and mysterious of continents—for gold, for slaves, for the secrets of the Mountains of the Moon, for the revelations hidden in the bones of our ancestors, for explorers who themselves disappeared and were never heard from again, and above all, for the sources of the Niger, the Nile, the Zambesi, and the Congo, the great rivers that were the highways to the interior— riveted their interest much like the real-time televised events of the modern era enthrall us today.

"Civilization's" interest in Africa goes far back into the mists of history. Classical civilization was equally intrigued, and even reputable scholars like Herodotus wove fantastic tales about remarkable African animals and men who could perform incredible feats of speed, strength, and endurance. The *literati* who were the market for Herodotus' histories and his contemporaries' second-hand reports about Africa were just as hungry for this sensational material as their Victorian Era counterparts 2,500 years later.

Roman traders routinely traveled down the Red Sea along the coast of the Horn of Africa for a thousand years, and Rome regularly recruited soldiers for its famed Third Legion exclusively from Africa. Yet, in all of its long tenure as the dominant power in the western world, Rome only touched tangentially on Africa. Its frontier garrison settlements on the continent were concentrated on a narrow strip of coastal plain between the Pillars of Hercules (the promontories that flank the Straits of Gibraltar) and Carthage in the east. The primary purpose of these African footholds was to provide the Roman circuses with their entertainers—slaves from the tribes of the Sahara and beyond, and lions, leopards, and other wild beasts to tear the slaves apart. This carnage reached such extremes that, over the centuries, North Africa was denuded of wildlife and numerous species were rendered extinct.

Carthage, still to this day the greatest-ever African nation- state, threatened the predominance and very existence of Rome for 118 years, thus reinforcing the ominous message received by generations of Europeans concerning things African. The cry "Hannibal at the gates" struck terror into the hearts of Romans in the late third century BC and had a lingering effect that endured many centuries beyond the grinding of Carthage to dust by the Roman *revanchists* who followed in the footsteps of Scipio Africanus.

Hence, by the time the first European explorers set foot in sub-Saharan Africa, the continent had a reputation. A dreaded one.

What happened during the four-century period of intense exploration beginning in the fifteenth century did nothing to calm the lurid imagination of Europeans concerning Africa. New and even more sinister horrors were systematically revealed. The harshness of the landscape, the debilitating nature of the climate, the decimating diseases—dysentery, malaria, and a host of exotic illnesses yet unnamed—and the fearsome look of many of the painted inhabitants strange to European eyes, all contributed to fixing firmly in the European psyche the early images of Africa as a malevolent, menacing place.

The impenetrability of Africa became dogma. No place was more impenetrable than the great Congo River, the rumored thoroughfare into the deepest, darkest, most mysterious recesses of the continent where who knew what new wonders—and riches—might await.

The immense mouth of the Congo was first seen and mapped by Europeans—

Portuguese sailors on missions launched by Prince Henry the Navigator, who for a generation sent his brave sailors and hardy *caravels* and *naos* ever farther south into *Terra Incognita*—in the late fifteenth century. The next 400 years of upriver exploration managed to chart only 130 miles of the Congo's 2,718-mile course. In other words, more than 95 percent of the river remained to be explored and exploited, for whatever it might be worth.

Three centuries after first arriving on the West African coast, the Europeans were still basically on the beach, intimidated by hostile natives, plunging cataracts, impenetrable rain forests, and stark terror at the thought of what might lurk therein. The Portuguese explorations had, by the mid-sixteenth century, evolved into a thriving slave trade with Arab slave masters acting as intermediaries who plunged into the African interior in search of human chattel. The Lisbon slave market handled more than 10,000 slaves per year.

When Africa's profitability became evident, the other seafaring nations of Europe were poised to compete for a share of the wealth. English, Dutch, French, and German trading companies were established and financed in order to exploit West African trade. They sent ships, struck treaties with local chiefs, built fortresses, and began trading.

It is noteworthy that the Amazon, which was discovered in 1500, or about 25 years later than the Congo, was fairly accurately charted for its full course more than 300 years before the Congo or the Nile. Such was the forbidding power of the African myth.

The great African rivers were not at all like the friendly, open waterways to which Europeans and Americans were accustomed. No traversable Mississippis, Ohios, Missouris, Rhines, or Danubes here. In contrast, the African rivers were downright dangerous, full of treacherous rapids, falls, and whirlpools, some hidden from view until it was too late. More than one famous African explorer lost his life thanks to the pitfalls of an African river. Mungo Park, for example, the well-traveled geographer of the Niger, was swept to his death over Bussa Falls.

Risks to life and limb were not limited to water. Wild animals were everywhere in the water and onshore, and not yet experienced and sophisticated enough to be intimidated by rifles and bullets. The world's most venomous reptiles and insects, as well as poisonous plants, proliferated and found creative ways to lay African explorers low. Diseases against which there were no defenses were also everywhere and took an enormous toll.

David Livingstone's life, for example, was almost ended by a hungry lion who did not understand the power of firearms. Livingstone survived, but one of his arms became virtually useless thereafter. Livingstone, by the way, had an absolute phobia of snakes, definitely not a good way to be when exploring the African rain forest. Whenever he encountered one, he was rendered speechless and immobile, rooted in total terror, unable to function. While this was undoubtedly the best defense, it made African exploration a problematic career choice for him.

Why did they do it, these explorers? Like their oceangoing counterparts of earlier centuries, hell-bent on discovery in the New World, these diverse individuals went to Africa and risked life and limb for a variety of good and bad reasons: to spread the Word among the heathen (most were stunningly unsuccessful at this—witness Livingstone the missionary who, it is said, made one convert in 30-plus years of effort); for self-glorification; to hunt big game, for the sport of it all, like Samuel Baker; because they were smitten with the place; for lucre; for national glory and territory; for science, like Heinrich Barth, the chronicler of Saharan anthropology and languages; to soldier; to start new lives, like the Boers in South Africa; and to escape from dysfunctional lives and criminal sanctions in their homelands.

The explorers who did not die in Africa usually returned home broken men, felled by illness and exhaustion. They were lionized by the Royal Geographic Society and its continental European counterparts, and the public, fueled by books written by the explorers and by breathless newspaper accounts, became insatiable for more. For the explorers, the suffering was worth it, paid for in public acclaim today reserved for movie stars and sports figures.

The public was electrified by news of one momentous discovery and quest after another:

- The search for the source of the Nile and the adventures to that end of the enigmatic Richard Burton and his rival, the intrepid John Hanning Speke.
- The announcement by David Livingstone of the discovery of the spectacular Victoria Falls on the Zambesi.
- The grandeur of the Great Rift Valley of East Africa, which ran for a distance that dwarfed the 700-mile stretch of Britain from John O'Groat's to Land's End.
- The exotic natives who dressed oddly, wore bizarre and often oversized jewelry, and were

often outsized (Tutsi) or undersized (Pygmy) to an extreme, and their alien habits, such as drinking the blood of their cattle and wearing plates in their lips.

For the British and other Europeans, the frenzied explorations of Africa became their national pastime before sports such as soccer cricket captured the public's imagination.

Thus was the scene set for one of the most momentous and far-reaching meetings of the nineteenth century. It was between two men who courted and laughed at danger many of the days of their lives, two improbable adventurers in search of glory for their patrons. Both were expatriates, often ridiculed by "serious" scientists, and accustomed to overcoming impossible odds and obstacles in their quests for personal and national glory.

John Rowland, a.k.a. Henry Morton Stanley: Rejection in Wales

No one would have ever predicted greatness for the young boy who would become Henry Morton Stanley. Small in stature, he was a giant of the Victorian era who strode across the planet as if it were only there to serve his whims. It was said of him that he had a "Napoleonic Complex" that Napoleon would have envied.

The late nineteenth century was a propitious time for uniquely determined individuals like Stanley to make their mark. It was, perhaps, the first time in history when dreams, combined with an incredibly strong will, could really be made to come true, when optimism could overcome harsh reality and being born to a low station, and when an innocent, uncynical public could still become excited about amazing feats of discovery and adventure. Henry M. Stanley was a man for this time.

He was born "John Rowlands, Bastard" (according to the church register) on January 28, 1841, the illegitimate child of 19-year old Elizabeth "Betsy" Parry, a housemaid in Denbigh, Wales. His name came from the man alleged to be his natural father, but there is reason to doubt that claim by John Rowlands, Sr., who was the town drunk. One of the rumors afoot in Denbigh at the time (there were many more later, when Stanley became famous) was that Rowlands had sold the right to assert his paternity for drinking money from the true father, a wealthy—and married—local solicitor named Vaughan Horne.

The little boy was both unwanted and unloved. Not a single one of his natural or purported parents or other relatives took the slightest interest in him. He had a childhood that would have made Charles Dickens cringe. Coupled with the further misfortune of having been born into the bleakest of Dickensian circumstances, his personality and his life's course were molded to an incredible extent.

His mother ran off to London immediately after his birth, leaving the infant with his itinerant butcher grandfather, Moses Parry, and two of her brothers, all of whom considered baby John a burden. Moses died when the boy was four, and he then passed to the care of his two uncles, who immediately boarded him with an elderly couple, the Prices, for half-a-crown (35 cents) per week. Soon the Prices asked for more money and when it was not forthcoming, divested themselves of the young boy by consigning him to the St. Asaph Union Workhouse on the pretext of taking him to visit his aunt. In his autobiography, Stanley recalled that he had never felt so utterly desolate before or after.

The workhouse was the ultimate manifestation of the already brutal concept of the Victorian orphanage, really a penitentiary in which the impoverished young and old were imprisoned, out of sight and out of mind of "polite" society. In essence, they were prison inmates. At St. Asaph's, John Rowlands became Oliver Twist to the overseer James Francis' Fagan. He toiled in the workhouse until he was 15 years old ... at first crying himself to sleep every night after being frequently beaten during the toilsome day, then gradually accepting the cruel fate to which he had been consigned, after which he never shed a tear again in his life.

He worked constantly, a regimen broken up only by sleep, a monotonous diet of bread, rice, gruel, and potatoes, but a surprisingly decent education. Beaten incessantly by his overseers, he was fortunate to survive. Others among the thirty or so boys in the workhouse did not. The only boy who could remotely be called a friend of John's was beaten to death at age eleven by a purported schoolmaster because he had not done his lessons.

John, on the other hand, did his lessons extremely well. Workhouse colleagues remembered him being particularly adept at geography, mathematics, and penmanship. His very legible diary, written years later in Africa, is a testament to his remarkably neat handwriting.

At age twelve, John for the first time learned that he had a mother who was alive. She actually was admitted to the workhouse for a few weeks, along with a son and daughter, John's half-sister Emma (Betsy, in total, bore four illegitimate children by four different fathers). After a few weeks, she left, taking the little boy with her, but leaving Emma. During her stay, although Francis had pointed her out to John as his mother, there was no contact whatsoever between mother and son. They exchanged no words, only a glance which Stanley later described as "so chilling that the valves of my heart closed . . ."

His mother's disinterest and hostility hardened the oft-rejected young boy even more. Although his sister also became a permanent inmate, the two siblings also had no contact at all with one another.

At the age of fifteen, John abruptly left St. Asaph's under somewhat mysterious circumstances. He claimed that he ran away after a major confrontation with—and thrashing administered by him to—Francis, while the workhouse records say that he went to his uncle in Holywell.

His first stop was the village of Lys, where he went looking for his paternal grandfather and namesake. That encounter also resulted in a cruel rejection. He next sought out his two maternal uncles in Denbigh, received the expected hostile reception from them and, tired and hungry, made for Brynford where his cousin was the master of the local Anglican school.

His cousin, Moses Owen, became the first and only relative to show him any decency and gave him a position as pupil-teacher, payment being in room, board, and clothing. However, the decent treatment was short-lived. Soon, Moses drove his bastard cousin out.

From there he went to his Aunt Mary in Fynnon Bueno where he was given lodging and food in return for help on her farm. That also did not last long, and Rowlands was shipped off to Aunt Mary's brother Tom Morris in Liverpool who took him into his large family and overcrowded home with something resembling good cheer, despite the fact that Morris was steeped in poverty.

After weeks of an unsuccessful job search, John found employment at a haberdashery, but the workload was so intense that he fell ill and had to be replaced. At the same time, the Morris family suddenly turned against him and he suffered rejection once more. Ordered out of the house, he found a job making deliveries to the docks for a butcher, a position which was to change his life. One day while making a delivery to the United States-registered ship *Windermere*, out of New Orleans, the ship's captain offered him a job as a cabin boy. He made up his mind instantly, and in three days was off to America.

For the rest of his life, Rowlands/Stanley was driven by his early, brutal memories of being abandoned. Instead of feeling compelled to prove himself to his unusually irresponsible family, he went far beyond them, feeling he had to prove himself to the entire world.

Turnaround

Author's Note: The account that follows of Stanley's life in the United States and reversal of fortune must be viewed with some skepticism. I have taken most of it from the explorer's own autobiography. However, there are other sources that vigorously dispute the heroic version that Stanley leaves us and claim that much of what he said was a complete fabrication, an invention of his own construction and a reinvention of himself. Regardless, the true facts are less important than the point that, whatever the truth, he underwent a stunning reversal of fortune, brought about largely by dint of his own determination and against incredible odds, and in relatively short order transformed himself from unknown pariah to world hero. The account that follows necessarily compresses Stanley's amazing journey of self-identification.

John Rowlands was a terrible sailor, and after only a few days at sea was demoted from cabin boy to deck hand. The seven-week voyage kept him constantly seasick and abused by his colleagues, probably sexually as well as physically, given the guiding principles of shipboard life in the mid-nineteenth century ("rum, sodomy and the lash," according to twice First Lord of the Admiralty Winston Churchill's assessment of the Royal Navy).

Once arrived in New Orleans, Rowlands immediately jumped ship. Walking the streets, he experienced the most important encounter of his life. Spotting a man on a warehouse porch, he asked him if he needed a boy for work. The man was a cotton broker named Henry Hope Stanley. Impressed by the boy's bold approach, he hired him to do a few tasks. Impressed also by John's voracious reading habits, he warmed to him and took him to live in his home. Shortly thereafter, he declared that he wanted to be responsible for John's future and assumed the role of surrogate father. John was both astounded and delighted with his good fortune and with having found another human being who actually liked him. He immediately changed his name to that of his benefactor (it is unclear where the middle name—Morton—that he chose for himself originated).

Both Stanleys allegedly spent the next two years traveling together up and down the Mississippi on business. When the senior Stanley's brother took sick in Havana, Henry Hope left for Cuba, never to return. Young Stanley wound up in a backwater, Cypress Bend, Arkansas, where he found employment in a general store. It was a miserable existence, but Stanley derived two valuable experiences from it that would serve him very well later in life. He was exposed to the local variety of malarial mosquito, which probably helped him resist the more virulent *anopheles* that afflicted the African rain forest. And he spent his extensive idle time sharpening up his shooting skills, which became legendary during his Congo explorations.

The year was 1861, and war was imminent in America. Pushed by a young lady on whom he had a crush, Stanley volunteered for the Dixie Greys and was soon Private Henry Morton Stanley of the Sixth Arkansas Volunteers.

On April 4, 1862, Henry Morton Stanley experienced another baptism, this one of fire, at Shiloh on the Tennessee River. In short order, he was captured, became a prisoner of war, and was incarcerated near Chicago. Advised that he could be freed if he joined the Union Army, he donned the blue uniform of the Illinois Light Artillery and marched toward Virginia. On the way, he came down with dysentery and was hospitalized at Harpers Ferry. Shortly thereafter, he received a medical discharge.

Friendless and penniless, he walked from the hospital nine miles to Hagerstown, Maryland where a family took pity on him and nursed him back to health. Once on his feet, he made for Baltimore and took ship to England. There, he made one last attempt at securing his mother's love. When that failed, he sailed back to New York as a deck hand once again. In very short order, he served aboard merchant ships, took a job as clerk to a judge, and enlisted in the Union Navy in 1864 as the Civil War was winding down. He did not last long in the sea service, and abruptly jumped ship and deserted in Portsmouth, New Hampshire in early 1865.

Stanley next went to St. Louis, where he persuaded the editors of the *Missouri Democrat* to make him a free-lance reporter covering the Far West. This job did not last long either, and soon Stanley was back in New York looking for adventure. He soon found it in an abortive round-the-world tour fraught with ill-conceived adventures that collapsed in Turkey. Stanley next went to Wales, actually spent a few days with his mother and at St. Asaph's as an honored alumnus, and then sailed back to New York. He went back to St. Louis and a reporting job with the *Democrat* covering the state legislature in Jefferson City.

For the first time in his life, Stanley received professional recognition, and was soon promoted to special correspondent covering General Winfield Scott Hancock's campaigns against the Plains Indians. Seeking to supplement his income, he also sold his dispatches to Eastern newspapers, including the future sponsor of his Livingstone quest, the *New York Herald*. Also for the first time, he was able to save money.

After covering the Indian wars, the *Democrat* sent him back to the plains to cover the deliberations of the Indian Peace Commission, headed by General William Tecumseh Sherman. The Commission soon forced the Indians to sign a one-sided treaty and Stanley returned to St. Louis. In later years, he said that his assignments on the Plains were an apprenticeship for his dealings with the indigenous peoples he encountered in Africa.

Feeling confident by virtue of having $3,000 in the bank, Stanley gave up his position with the newspaper in late 1867 and decided to try his luck in the major leagues of journalism, New York. His first try was Horace Greeley's *New York Tribune*, where he was turned down (despite having taken to heart the publisher's exhortation to "Go West, young man").

He next called on James Gordon Bennett, Jr., editor-in-chief of the *New York Herald*, which had published some of his stories of the Indian wars. Stanley proposed that he cover England's punitive expedition to Abyssinia (where King Theodore was holding British hostages) at his own expense, and a deal was struck along those lines, with payment to be by the story for good material.

He made his way via Liverpool and Suez to Eritrea, where General Sir Robert Napier's punitive expeditionary force was primed to tackle Theodore in his mountain redoubt of *Magdala* four hundred miles into the interior. The British effort was rewarded with a huge and total success, the hostages safely retrieved, British losses minimal, and Theodore deposed and dead, his troops routed. Stanley had his story and it was a doozy. Now the problem was to get it to New York.

The British correspondents gave their dispatches to an officer who made for the coast. Stanley, however, wanted desperately to scoop them, so he followed the officer himself. Braving a raging flood, he made the coast in time to catch a steamer to Suez, along with the British officer. However, arriving at Suez, the ship was quarantined for fear of cholera. Stanley then smuggled his dispatches to the telegraph office along with a handsome bribe so that his stories would be sent first. They were, and immediately thereafter, the Mediterranean telegraph cable broke, preventing the British stories from reaching London for weeks. Stanley had his worldwide exclusive. By the time he was luxuriating in a fine Cairo hotel, the word came back that Bennett had appointed him to a permanent position as a foreign correspondent.

Presuming Dr. Livingstone

When I was born three-quarters of a century after the event, the most famous phrase in the English language was still probably:

> "Dr. Livingstone, I presume?"

I remember, as a child, playing with friends in my backyard, pretending to be Stanley in darkest Africa, crashing through impenetrable rose and currant bushes, peonies, and raspberry plants in the quest for my neighbor Livingstone.

The need to "find" David Livingstone first percolated into the public consciousness in late 1868, when that most celebrated Victorian era explorer had not been heard from for more than three years. Rumor had it that Livingstone was on his way out of the African interior to the East African coast, and the *Herald's* foreign correspondent in Africa was directed to secure an interview with him when he emerged. Stanley went down the Red Sea to Aden to await news of Livingstone's reappearance, but the rumors proved to be unfounded.

Stanley spent the next, frenetic year covering conflict after conflict on behalf of his paper, while at the same time contemplating marriage to a Greek woman, then a Welsh beauty, and reconciling with his mother and sister Emma, both of whom he even took on a vacation to Paris. He was a prolific writer and his dispatches from exotic war zones were popular and widely read.

In late 1869, he was abruptly summoned to Paris to meet his publisher, Bennett. The meeting has become the stuff of legend. In it, Bennett purportedly directed Stanley to "find Livingstone" and report on the quest to the *Herald's* readers. Strangely, however, he wanted his young reporter first to detour all over the map of the Middle East, North Africa, and the Subcontinent in search of other interesting stories. Despite the heroic encounter status accorded the hotel meeting by Stanley in his autobiography, it is highly likely that finding Livingstone did not rank very high on Bennett's priority list.

After completing Bennett's tour of the East, Stanley finally was able to embark on the search for Livingstone in early 1871. First he went to Zanzibar to recruit for and provision his expedition. When ready, he and his recruits crossed the straits to *Bagamoyo* on the African coast and headed into the interior in March, 1871.

After an excruciating trek, sickened by fever and risking death at the hands of battling native tribes, Stanley reached the shores of Lake Tanganyika, only a few hours from Ujiji, where his intelligence network told him that an old white man was resting after his own arduous journey from the interior. A stranger made his way to Stanley's camp, asked him who he was, then ran back to Ujiji to report the impending arrival to Livingstone.

Stanley arrived in Ujiji a few days later to the excited exclamations of two long lines of people who formed a corridor. At the other end stood David Livingstone in front of a semicircle of Arab traders. When he came up to him, Stanley tipped his cap and uttered the famous greeting.

Amazingly, these two very different men got along famously. Stanley stayed with Livingstone for four months and became his fast friend and disciple. Their parting was extremely painful for both. They wept as they clasped hands for the last time and went their separate ways.

The Making of a Legend

At 4:00 am on April 30, 1873, Livingstone was discovered kneeling by his bedside as if in prayer. He was dead. The events that followed added mountains to the legend of African exploration surrounding Stanley.

First, Livingstone's loyal servants cut out the great man's heart and buried it in the heart of the continent he so loved. Then they partially mummified the body and carried it to the east coast, from where it was shipped to Southampton. Almost a year later, on April 18, 1874, Dr. Livingstone took his honored place among the giants of British lore in Westminster Abbey after a state funeral that was the envy of monarchs.

Stanley was given the place of honor among the pallbearers, first on the right, fitting since he revered the father figure Livingstone above all other men. Then he completed the Scotsman's work, opening up the African interior like no one before him.

The Great Quest

Seven months after the funeral, Stanley set forth on the great "Anglo-American Expedition for the Discovery of the Nile and Congo Sources." He left Zanzibar with over 200 men, funded by the *Daily Telegraph* and the *New York Herald*. The smartest thing he took with him was the *Lady Alice*, a 40-foot boat that consisted of five severable sections that could be portaged when necessary. Ultimately, the *Lady Alice* sailed almost the entire length of the Congo and fought off more than 30 attacks by hostile tribesmen.

Unlike Livingstone, Stanley was both a terrific manager of expeditions and men, and a formidable enemy to those who "crossed" him, native or European. These traits and his general indomitability served him extremely well and made him by far the most successful of the many African explorers.

And in stark contrast to Livingstone, who often managed to soothe the hostile natives by gentle words, Stanley, in true Wild West fashion, shot first and asked questions later. Moreover, he was hardly averse to forging alliances with the most reprehensible African slavers and marauders if such alliances advanced his cause.

Like his counterpart James T. Kirk of the Starship *Enterprise* four centuries later, Stanley did not think twice before going where no man had gone before. The take-off point was the town of *Nyangwe* on the *Lualaba* River, almost the exact geographic center of Africa.

Nyangwe was where Livingstone had been forced to turn back during his attempt at the Congo. It was the dividing line between what was known of Africa and the great unknown. Until Nyangwe, Stanley had been following others' footsteps. After Nyangwe, he was on his own, treading where no other white man had trod.

The Lualaba was already the stuff of enormous speculation. Livingstone thought it could be the source of the Nile. Other explorers believed it to be the origin of the Niger. And a third contingent opined that it might be the headwaters of the Congo. All anyone knew was that once on the Lualaba beyond Nyangwe, one would be in the deepest recesses of the heart of darkness itself. When Stanley stepped off the riverbank onto the *Lady Alice*, he had no idea if he would emerge at the Nile Delta at Alexandria on the Mediterranean, the outlet of the Niger at the Bight of Benin, at the vast mouth of the Congo, or would perish in whatever the attempt.

On November 19, 1876, the *Lady Alice* embarked and floated down the Lualaba, soon to be swallowed up by *terra incognita*. Within days, illness and hostile natives had slowed progress to three miles a day. Attack after attack by natives armed with poison arrows had to be fended off. Six weeks later, when the calendar turned to 1877, the expedition had advanced only 200 miles and Stanley's Arab ally and land force commander, the redoubtable Tippu Tib, called it quits and left with his army, amounting to almost half of the total force that had left Nyangwe. Stanley was now down to only 48 guns.

At the place where the Lualaba met the *Aruwimi*, Stanley's small force was attacked on both flanks by 44 war canoes and an overwhelming force of over 1,000 men. His by now battle-hardened troops were well-prepared to defend their boat and their lives, employing river tactics that had served them ably before.

The victory both exhausted and elated the small band. Their confidence was high and infectious, and for a few weeks thereafter they made great progress downriver without much in the way of resistance, news of their martial exploits having preceded them.

But the easy going was not to last. The river curved first to the northwest and then due west. Stanley was now certain that the Lualaba was in fact the great Congo. He also knew from the timid upriver explorations from the Congo's mouth that had been chronicled that he was likely to confront cataracts somewhere along its path. These appeared sooner rather than later, bunched into two widely separate groups. They proved exceedingly difficult obstacles, both resembling flights of stairs. The upper group were named Stanley Falls and the lower group Livingstone Falls, and each set required two months to traverse. To do so, Stanley had to hack his way through the densest rainforest in the world, where each step forward required several minutes of vigorous defoliation.

At *Inkisi*, he and his men had to carry their boats and supplies up a 1,500-foot mountain in one day. On other occasions, he decided to shoot the rapids. At times the boats had to be lowered through rapids on hawsers.

The trip downriver was brutal and carried a heavy price. Tragic accidents were commonplace, due in large part to the powerful Congo current. On March 28, 1877, Stanley watched in horror as the current clutched the canoe *Crocodile* and swept it downriver and over the falls, drowning his beloved young African aide Kalulu and seven others. Ten weeks later, his last European companion, Frank Pocock plunged to his death over the *Zinga* cataract with Stanley watching through field glasses. His death came as close as anything could to defeating Stanley and decimating his iron will. His diary entry for that day is difficult reading even 140 years later, full of rambling, incoherent, grief-stricken, sorrowful words, as well as detailed instructions to his own executors in case he should die.

Now he was truly alone, having lost his father-figure Livingstone, his virtual son Kalulu, and his closest companion, confidant, and sharer of sufferings and elations, Pocock. On top of these personal setbacks, Stanley also had to cope with his rapidly dwindling band of dispirited Zanzibaris. Many deserted. Others died. Several went mad. It is hard to imagine that Stanley could go on. But go on he did.

What pushed him forward? It had to be more than his incredible determination. His losses were immense, especially for a human being so unloved in his youth.

I suspect that his motivation to continue was that, on the very same day that Pocock died, Stanley experienced his first hint of success. He ran across a Zinga region native who wore a jacket that had to have been made in Europe. Further investigation revealed that the Zingas also could distinguish between Portuguese, French, and English. He knew that the sea must be within reach.

Stanley forged on, overland to *Boma*, less than 100 miles from the river mouth. A messenger was sent ahead to Boma, carrying these words from Stanley: "You may not know me by name; I therefore add, I am the person that discovered Livingstone in 1871. - H.M.S."

On August 9, 1878, exactly 999 days after leaving Zanzibar, a relief party from Boma found Henry Morton Stanley, who now completed this greatest of all African explorations and took his rightful place on the pedestal formerly reserved exclusively for Livingstone in the public mind.

Consolidating the Gains

Henry Morton Stanley, Welsh-born, a British subject, now an American citizen, the darling of the English-speaking world, won the riches of the Congo for Belgium and its energetic King Leopold II. How this came to pass is a textbook study of missed opportunity.

The shy and withdrawn King Leopold was nevertheless one shrewd operator. For most of the first 40 years of his life, he dreamed and schemed for Belgium to win glory via African conquest. In 1876, the time had come to put his plan into action.

Leopold invited distinguished delegates from the European powers, geographic society luminaries in particular (no government officials were allowed), to an International Conference on Africa in Brussels to discuss, purportedly, the future exploration and civilizing of Africa, as well as eradication of the slave trade. The ostensibly noble purpose of this conference concealed its true intent, that of serving as a sanctioning body for a series of Belgian thrusts into the scramble for Africa.

The Conference was a big success, and Leopold and other European contributors were soon sponsoring African expeditions. However, after two years, little of note was accomplished and both the moral and economic force of the Conference was running out of steam.

The timing was perfect for a savior to appear. One year earlier, Stanley had emerged at the mouth of the Congo to widespread acclaim from the world public. Britain, however, was blind to his real achievement. The British regarded Stanley as having achieved an incredible feat of endurance. The potential implications of what he had done for the future of Britain eluded them. This despite Stanley's lobbying, upon his arrival in England, for Britain to send him back to claim the whole Congo region for Great Britain. He wrote:

> "I could prove to you that the Power possessing
> the Congo, despite the cataracts, would absorb to

itself the trade of the whole of the enormous basin behind. This river is and will be the grand highway of commerce to West Central Africa."

Prescient words. But no one in British governing circles took him seriously.

Stanley stayed around for several months, showered by a cascade of geographical medals and honors. But Britain never made a move to exploit Stanley's explorations. And so the brass ring passed it by. While the sun did not finally set on the British Empire for another 70 years, Britain's failure to avail itself of the riches offered her on a silver platter by Henry Morton Stanley might have been the beginning of her long decline.

In November, 1878, Stanley went to continental Europe and met with Leopold's representatives, made up of financiers and wealthy merchants from five European powers, who called themselves, unashamedly, the *Comite d'Etudes du Haut Congo*.

The King had attempted to recruit him for the Association (the outgrowth of the International Conference) when the explorer first emerged from the Congo, but Stanley was too tired, physically and emotionally, to consider it. Now he was ready.

The *Comite* was out for one thing only: money. While paying lip service to the public goals of the Association, their bottom line was . . . the bottom line. The plan was for Stanley to buy or lease river bank sites for manufacturing establishments and trading stations from the native rulers. Each member was prepared to put up £20,000, and the *Comite* appointed Stanley commander of the expedition.

As honorary president, Leopold housed the *Comite* in the same building as the Association and appointed his right-hand man executive director. Thus, he was able to use the Association and its "good works" goals as the smokescreen for both Belgian political aspirations in the Congo and the commercial exploitation of the region by Belgian companies. Stanley was able to function under the blue and yellow

Association flag to hide his true activities on behalf of Belgium and its King.

Despite one million gold francs from the *Comite*, Stanley confronted a daunting prospect; wrenching open the impenetrable Congo and its riches to exploitation by "civilized" man." Impenetrable" is a word easily bandied about when discussing African exploration. However, when speaking of the Congo in the late 1870s, the use of the term is completely appropriate.

The Lower Congo is the most inaccessible riverine system in the world, bar none. A series of thirty-two dangerous and extremely difficult rapids faces any upstream traveler. The hardy vessel *Lady Alice* met her demise on the Lower Congo. This was not a trek for the faint of heart, or even for the strong of heart. There was probably only one man who could have seriously contemplated such an impossible feat, the indomitable Henry Morton Stanley.

Stanley's solution to the problem of the Lower Congo was to build a road around the thirty-two rapids, transport steamboats in sections up the road, and put them together again once past the danger at Stanley Pool. The project was audacious, and every knowledgeable geographer, engineer, and Africanist who knew about Stanley's plans pronounced them wild and impossible.

Stanley shipped out in June, 1879 with a vast store of provisions and equipment, including four steamers. The stores and equipment were sent to the river mouth, while Stanley himself went to Zanzibar on the East Coast to recruit from among his old Africa hands. No less than three-quarters of the 68 *pagazis* who agreed to accompany him were veterans of his previous trek across the continent.

While Stanley sailed up the East African Coast and around the Mediterranean, then down the West Coast to the Congo mouth, the short-lived *Comite* went bankrupt while all Europe buzzed with rumors that the great expedition was, in actuality, for the sinister and base purpose of colonization, as opposed to its publicly-stated mercantilist mission. This happened to be true, and was soon publicly documented in a set of secret instructions sent to Stanley from the King.

In fact, things could not have gone better for Leopold since, with the *Comite* eliminated, he was the sole guiding force behind this now unabashedly political undertaking. Stanley, eternally naive about politics, deluded himself into thinking that nothing had changed and that he was actually pursuing the project for the benefit of the Congo natives. For two more years, he continued to address his reports to the defunct *Comite*.

Stanley arrived at *Banana*, the town at the mouth of the Congo, in mid-August, 1879. A week later, he was ready to proceed. His flotilla made good progress at first and soon left Boma—the same Boma that was the culmination of his great triumph two years earlier, and the last European outpost on the Congo—in its rear. Fifty miles upriver, in a place called Hell's Cauldron, the river became unnavigable. It was here that Stanley built his first station, at the base of the *Yellala* Falls, and named it *Vivi*. It was soon to become the most important settlement in the whole of Central Africa, the bottleneck through which all trade and soldiering had to pass, and the model for all subsequent Congo stations.

Vivi Station was completed in January, 1880. It was time to move on to the next and most important phase of the Congo project; the overland transport of two steamers around the lower falls and rapids and the establishment of stations up to and including Stanley Pool.

The labor involved in this ambitious undertaking was backbreaking, worthy of pharaonic, pyramid-building lore. It involved fifty-two miles of hauling and dragging up and down ravines, through snake-infested jungles, dawn-to-dusk, day-in and day-out, afflicted by horrible gastrointestinal diseases, incessant fevers, even a suicide, blasting through stubborn rocks when it was impossible to shunt them (the source of Stanley's famous African nickname, "*Bula Matari*," the "Breaker of Rocks").

To top it off, Stanley was barraged with anxious letters from King Leopold, urging him to move faster. The King had recently learned that a French expedition, under the command of Pierre Savorgnon de Brazza, was moving in Stanley's direction from the French colony of Gabon, and he feared that

Brazza would leapfrog Stanley and become the first to establish stations on the upper Congo, thus defeating his grand scheme.

On November 7, 1880, the bad news reached Stanley directly while he was still struggling with the cataracts. A native ran up to him and handed him a piece of paper upon which was written the following: 'Le Comte Savorgnon de Brazza, *Enseigne de Vaisseau.*' The native described the tall white man who had handed him the note as a 'Francess.'

One hour later, Brazza himself, along with 15 men, stepped out of the jungle and into Stanley's encampment, drawn and gaunt but impressive nonetheless in his blue navy coat.

The second great encounter of African exploration was about to take place.

Pierre Savorgnon de Brazza

Pierre Paul Francois Camil Savorgnon de Brazza was already France's greatest African explorer when he stepped out of the bush and into Stanley's life. How he arrived at that lofty status was improbable and worthy of a digression in our tale.

The son of an Italian aristocrat—thus the social and economic opposite of his rival—Brazza, like his fellow Italian Napoleon Bonaparte, grew up totally smitten with everything French. He was a strikingly handsome man whose physical appearance was said to make women faint when he appeared among them. His father's connections got him appointed a French naval cadet, which he quickly parlayed into French citizenship. Brazza reveled in fantasies of contributing mightily to *La Gloire de France* and pinpointed Africa as the land of opportunity where he would find the perfect synergy between both his adopted land's destiny and his own.

While Stanley was traversing Africa in 1875, Brazza went exploring up the *Oguwe* River in Gabon. While hardly the same magnitude stream, the upper tributaries of the Oguwe actually join with the tributaries of the middle Congo. It was this realization that fired his creative imagination about the economic potential of the Congo Basin. In fact, during one foray into the middle reaches of the Congo Basin, Brazza, completely exhausted, stopped roughly one hill short of discovering Stanley Pool before Stanley!

Back home, the Italian expatriate pestered the French government to send him back to Africa at the head of an expedition designed to do precisely what Leopold enlisted Stanley to accomplish. But the powers-that-be were not very interested. Eventually, he managed to persuade the French branch of Leopold's International Association—headed by Leon Gambetta, the future president of the Third Republic—to finance a modest-scale expedition. Brazza sailed for Gabon, having ceded Stanley a six-month head start. Stanley's lead would not last long.

Brazza, with a much smaller, more mobile entourage, moved rapidly southeast, stopping only long enough to establish the first of his interior stations, *Franceville* on the Oguwe. Soon he too was in the Congo basin. His simple and highly effective *modus operandi* was to make small gifts to local chiefs in exchange for acknowledgement of French authority in the area.

Thanks to his prior African experience and the information he was able to absorb after Stanley emerged from his great trek and dazzled the world, Brazza knew that the key to control of the Congo basin began and ended at Stanley Pool. That was where he headed and where he arrived first. The local chief, the *Makoko*, was heavily courted with pomp and ceremony until succumbing; he formally placed his tribal domains—nine miles of the right bank of the river—under French protection. Only then did Brazza go downriver to meet his rival.

Encounter at Stanley Pool

Unlike Stanley's first epic African encounter, which was marked by great joy and affection between the participants, the one with Brazza was humorless and tense, cool and competitive. It did not help that neither explorer was particularly fluent in the other's native language. But that was not really the issue, since any one of Stanley's Belgians could have translated easily. The hostility and misunderstanding ran much deeper.

Brazza knew that Stanley was his arch-rival. Stanley, on the other hand, full of hubris and intoxicated with Europe-wide adulation, simply assumed that he had a divine right to be where he was and do what he felt needed to be done. He had hardly heard of Brazza, and until meeting him at Stanley Pool, did not realize the magnitude of the threat he represented.

Brazza, in contrast, planned shrewdly for the two-day meeting. He never mentioned his treaty with the *Makoko*—which had yet to be ratified by the French government—and the two explorers maintained polite, if less-than-friendly, talks. Stanley, overwhelmed by his own tribulations, was, in present-day parlance, "very much into himself," and perhaps did not realize what was going on. For most of their sessions, the two discussed Stanley's labors. Brazza, on the other hand, revealed nothing.

It was only after they parted ways, Brazza toward Vivi and Stanley heading for the north shore of the Pool, that reality intervened in the form of two natives dressed in French navy shirts and carrying a tricolour on a staff, led by a Senegalese in a French navy sergeant's uniform. The sergeant marched right up to Stanley, who was talking with a village chief at the time, addressed him in perfect French, and handed him a note. When he unfolded the note, he received the shock of his life; formal notice from Brazza that the territory through which Stanley was progressing had already been claimed for France! The note went on to say that Sergeant Malamine was the local French authority in the region, invested with all the authority of *La Patrie*.

Despite his surprise and consternation, Stanley actually handled the devastating blow quite well. First he accurately assessed the military situation and saw that he was outgunned. Reacting calmly, he launched his steamers into the Pool, left the small village—which was to become Brazzaville—and headed south across the water to the opposing shore, where he founded the station that would soon become the much more important city of Leopoldville (now Kinshasa).

Aftermath

In the end, both France and Belgium "won." France, listening to Brazza, did not contest the rigors of nature or Henry Morton Stanley, satisfied to use the Oguwe as the route into the Congo Basin. Stanley, for his part, ceded the right bank and stayed on the left bank, which ultimately proved to be an economic bonanza for his patron that dwarfed anything France derived from its Central African holdings.

The French government ratified the treaty with the *Makoko*, thus turning the battle of the explorers into something much bigger, a scramble for Africa among all the European powers. The old, quaint, swashbuckling style of exploration as an end in itself or to increase the breadth of human knowledge and understanding was history. Now it became a power game, one that cost a great many lives and many more tears, and one that still continues today in the artificial boundaries and legacies bequeathed to the unhappy successors of the colonial powers.

As for relations between the two Congo explorers, they deteriorated until they sank into the gutter, with condemnations of double-dealing and underhandedness hurled at one another from Europe as well as Africa. The culmination came during their second and last encounter, this one in Paris on October 20, 1882 before a packed dinner crowd and sponsored by the Stanley Club. Stanley got up and spoke after dinner. He used the occasion to accuse Brazza of all sorts of crimes and deceptions, concluding that his rival had "introduced immoral diplomacy into a virgin continent." He, on the other hand, had no political ambitions whatsoever.

As he was speaking, Brazza walked in and took a seat next to the U.S. Minister. When Stanley finished, Brazza stood up, walked over, and took his rival's hand. His speech, which he had translated into English, praised Stanley's African endeavors and acknowledged his great example. He concluded by proclaiming his French nationality and toasting the civilizing influence of the inevitable European conquest of the continent. Then he left the hall.

The lives of both Brazza and Stanley, insofar as Africa was concerned, were over.

Denouement

Brazzaville became the capital of the French Congo and, after independence, the Republic of the Congo. It remains so to this day.

When Brazza returned home to Paris, he was a sensation. The press labeled him *"Conquerant Pacifique"* for his success in expanding France's colonial empire without firing a shot.

In the 1880s, Brazza was named governor-general of the French Congo. He was recalled in 1897 due to the colony's poor profitability and critical reports that he treated the natives too well, not something that colonial governor-generals were often accused of. Brazza left after condemning the manner in which concessionary companies repressed and exploited their native workers.

By 1905, stories reached Paris of how bad conditions had become for the natives under the colonial administration, the concessionary companies, and the Catholic Bishop of the Congo. Brazza was sent by the government to investigate and his report was devastating. It was so condemnatory, in fact, that when presented to the National Assembly, it was suppressed. Consequently, conditions never improved and oppression remained the order of the day until the end of French colonial rule many decades later.

Brazza married Thérèse de Chambrun and thus became the great-uncle by marriage of Vichy France Prime Minister Pierre Laval, who along with Marshal Petain was the most important collaborator with the Germans during World War II.

His last assignment, the investigation of conditions in the Congo, took a toll on him. He died of dysentery and fever during the return trip to Dakar, Senegal—rumor had it that he had been poisoned. He was given a state funeral at *L'Eglise de Sainte-Clotilde* in Paris and was buried in the famous *Père Lachaise* cemetery. However, his widow, Thérèse had his body exhumed and reinterred in Algiers. His fitting epitaph on his headstone reads: *"une mémoire pure de sang humain"* ("a memory untainted by human blood").

In 2005 the presidents of Congo, Gabon, and France laid the foundation stone for a memorial to Pierre de Brazza, a $10 million Italian marble mausoleum in Brazzaville. The next year, his remains, along with those of his wife and four children, were transferred there from Algiers. The mausoleum honors his humanitarian work against slavery and the native abuse.

Henry Morton Stanley, despite the influence of David Livingstone and his many interactions with native populations, was hardly a humanitarian. He had driven his native porters hard, sometimes to the point of death, during his African explorations, and harbored the attitude that they were dispensable. Forced labor was his preferred method of "employment."

Stanley led one more expedition to Africa following the encounter at Stanley Pool. In 1887, he was sent at the head of a military force to relieve Mehmed Emin Pasha, governor of the Equatorial Province of Egypt, cut off by the Mahdist revolt of 1882 in the neighborhood of Lake Albert. Stanley decided to move towards Lake Albert via the Congo River, counting on his old African ally, Tippu Tib, to supply porters. At *Yambuya* on the Congo, Stanley left a rear column with orders to await Tippu Tib's porters. The rear column failed to rejoin the expedition, likely because of foreknowledge of Stanley's brutality. Eventually the main body of the expedition assembled at Lake Albert, gathered up a reluctant Emin Pasha, and made for the East Coast, 1,500 people strong, arriving at Bagamoyo in December, 1889. During the journey, he discovered the Ruwenzori Range, Ptolemy's Mountains of the Moon, as well as the river linking Lakes Edward and Albert. This latter discovery cleared up the remaining mystery about the sources of the Nile which had vexed explorers and geographers for much of the nineteenth century. For that, Stanley received a Special Gold Medal from the Royal Geographic Society.

Stanley married Dorothy Tennant in July 12, 1890 and adopted a son, Denzil. He became a "renaturalized" British subject in 1892, renouncing his U.S. citizenship, and was elected to Parliament in 1895, serving until 1900. He was knighted by Queen Victoria in 1899, bought a small estate in Surrey, and lived there until his death in 1904. He is interred in a churchyard in Pirbright, Surrey, marked by a modest headstone, a stark contrast to the Brazza Memorial.

> *Author's Note: The stark contrast between Stanley's obscure headstone in a country churchyard vs. the splendid Brazza Memorial is paralleled by how the French and British have chosen to inter their country's greatest champion. Napoleon is buried in a spectacular setting in Paris in an elevated sarcophagus centered beneath the Dome des Invalides, an unmissable structure of grandiose proportions. In contrast, Winston Churchill is buried in his family's simple plot in St. Martin's parish churchyard at Bladon, a forgettable village just outside Oxford. Even upon arrival in Bladon, the burial site is hard to find. Not so Napoleon's.*

The Congo Free State became the private property of King Leopold of the Belgians and was run as a plantation, replete with tens of thousands of slaves. Its mines were among the most brutal on Earth. The later history of the Congo, down to the present day, has been one of civil war, unspeakable brutality, and dictators who raped their country of its resources and its people of their dignity.

Johann Wolfgang von Goethe
(As painted by Josef Raabe, 1814)

Brazza and Stanley were conquerors, but compared to one of the next encounter's participants, they were minor players. Brazza was not, of course, the first Italian for whom French was a second language to embark on a campaign of conquest on behalf of his adoptive country. A small, olive-skinned Corsican preceded him in that. He was not quite so benign. He was, however, intensely curious in all things, a trait he had in common with the other participant, a towering literary figure and humanist whose greatness led to his enshrinement in Walhalla (more on that later).

Stretching the theme of this book a bit, let's then examine the "meeting" between two of the greatest, most charismatic, and most destructive human wills imaginable.

Chapter 8 – Encounter at Erfurt

Napoleon and Goethe:
Clash of the Curious

Every step of life shows much caution is required.
                    Johann Wolfgang von Goethe

In politics stupidity is not a handicap.
                              Napoleon Bonaparte

It is difficult to zero in on only one of Napoleon's many great encounters—with Alexander I, Tsar of all the Russias; Arthur Wellesley—the Duke of Wellington—during the Battle of Waterloo; an astute, observant Colonel Carl von Clausewitz, also at Waterloo; the great Italian sculptor Antonio Canova, who loathed him; Danton and Robespierre during the Terror; Talleyrand, the ultimate political chameleon; the artist Jacques Louis David; the Marquis de Lafayette; Metternich, the Steve Bannon of his era, who later deconstructed all that Napoleon accomplished; and the crowned heads of virtually every European nation.

The decision, after much author deliberation, comes down to his brief meeting with Johann Wolfgang von Goethe, the greatest German humanist, literatus, and polymath, and the embodiment of German high culture, at the Governor's Palace in Erfurt, Germany on a late morning in 1808.

Johann Wolfgang von Goethe

Germany honors its greatest personages in a unique way: via 130 busts and 65 plaques inhabiting *Walhalla*, the Parthenon-like temple on a hilltop high above the Danube River just east of the ancient Roman city of Regensburg (Ratisbon). This hall of heroes is named after *Valhalla*, the heaven of Norse mythology. Walhalla's honorees span more than 2,000 years of German history. Its fewer than 200 commemorations render it a hall of fame that makes gaining entry to Cooperstown (baseball) or Canton (football) look like a piece of cake. Select honorees include:

- Arminius (Hermann), the victor of the decisive Battle of the Teutoberg Forest that decimated several Roman legions and forever stopped the advance of Rome into Germania;
- Alaric, who sacked Rome in 410, thus accelerating the imminent fall of the greatest empire in the world;
- Charlemagne, the Holy Roman Emperor;
- Frederick Barbarossa, the Holy Roman Empire's greatest medieval emperor who, even in his lifetime, rose to legendary status and to this day is believed by many Germans to be asleep with his knights in a cave under a Bavarian mountain. The legend says that when ravens cease to fly around the mountain, Barbarossa will awaken and restore Germany to greatness;
- Catherine the Great, the obscure German princess who became the autocrat of Russia;
- Count Albrecht von Wallenstein, the Bohemian leader of the Catholic armies in the Thirty Years' War that devastated the land for centuries to come;

- Artists such as Durer, Holbein, Memling, and van Dyck, van Eyck and Rubens (the curators of Walhalla harbor an expansive definition of who qualifies as "German");
- A slew of great composers, including Bach, Mozart, Haydn, Händel, Beethoven, Schubert, Wagner, Richard Strauss, Brahms, von Weber, Gluck, and the transcendent Hildegard of Bingen;
- A bevy of authors, poets, clergymen, inventors such as Gutenberg, and geniuses like Albert Einstein (grudgingly added late because he was a Jew); and . . .
- Johann Wolfgang von Goethe, whose Walhalla bust sits in a special place of honor reserved for the greatest German of them all (Adolf Hitler's description of himself notwithstanding).

Goethe was, in the best sense of the concept, the epitome of what it means to be German. This is a pretty high bar, given the number of luminaries the German-speaking lands have produced. Ask any German even today and his status at the top of the national pantheon is not subject to debate.

Goethe in his lifetime and from an early age was considered one of the greatest geniuses of his era, if not of all time. People graced with his presence treated a meeting with him as a great gift, a high point of their lives. Not so Napoleon, as we shall see.

Johann Wolfgang von Goethe was born in 1749 in Frankfurt am Main to a 39-year old father and 18-year old mother. He was blessed by a great education thanks to his father and a succession of able tutors and quickly became fluent in Latin, Greek, French, English, Italian, and Hebrew. As a child, he memorized large sections of the *Pentateuch* (the five books of Moses), the *Aeneid,* and Ovid's *Metamorphoses.* He was interested in and studied literally everything, the platform for his becoming perhaps the world's greatest ever polymath.

When he turned sixteen, he enrolled in the University of Leipzig and studied law, but hated its dryness and dullness, preferring instead to attend poetry lectures. He himself began to write poetry and, in 1770 published his first collection of poems. He also wrote prose feverishly, but discarded almost all of his early attempts except for a verse comedy, *Die Mitschuldigen* (Partners in Guilt). In 1768, he was forced to return to Frankfurt, his studies having stalled.

Returning home, he became quite ill. Two years later, he left once again, this time to study at the University of Strasbourg. In contrast to his prior academic experience in Leipzig, the Strasbourg curriculum entranced him. There, he met Johann Gottfried Herder, the great German philosopher (Herder's bust also resides in Walhalla). They became close friends and Herder kindled Geothe's passion for literature, especially Shakespeare.

In 1771, Goethe acquired his law degree and opened a law office in Frankfurt. He proved an abysmal attorney, however, losing most of his cases, and decided to close his practice after only a few months.

This proved to be the tipping point that began his transformation from mediocre lawyer to literary giant. He read a biography of a noble highwayman from the sixteenth century German Peasants' War and, in only a few weeks, turned it into a dramatic work—*Götz von Berlichingen*, which ever since has been considered one of his greatest works.

Götz was not an immediate financial success, so Goethe once again began to practice law, this time at Wetzlar. But his heart was not in it and he spent most of his time writing the book that skyrocketed him to worldwide fame, *The Sorrows of Young Werther*. *Werther* is the poster child for classical German romanticism summed up by the not easily translated concept of "*herz schmerz*."

Although it was an instant success, Goethe did not earn very much from Werther due to the casual nature of copyright law at the time. However, it did win him an invitation in 1775 to the court of 18-year old Duke Carl August of Saxe-Weimar-Eisenach. Goethe went to live in Weimar, where he remained for the rest of his life, serving as the Duke's best friend and advisor. The Duke's patronage also provided him with the financial independence necessary to pursue his literary career without distraction. He held a series of official posts in the Duke's government, including Commissioner of War, Commissioner of Mines and Highways, and Chancellor of the Exchequer (in essence prime minister). In 1782, the Duke made him a noble, enabling him to add "von" to his name.

As War Commissioner, Goethe became a human trafficker, clearly at odds with our image of him as a leading figure of the Enlightenment. He sold vagabonds, criminals, and political dissidents into both the Prussian and British armies that fought the colonials during the American Revolution. Somehow, his humanist literary reputation managed to prevail over this seamy interlude.

A high point in his literary development was his two-year trip through Italy and Sicily from 1786 to 1788, motivated by a similar journey of his father when he was a young man. This Italian interruption was also stimulated by a general renewed interest on the part of European intellectuals in classical Greece and Rome. For Goethe, it became a pilgrimage. He was overcome by the profusion of great art and architecture he encountered there. His diaries formed the basis for his *Italian Journey*, which subsequently inspired thousands of German youths to replicate his trip.

He returned to Weimar fired with enthusiasm. In 1792, he participated in the battle of Valmy against revolutionary France and was also a military observer during the siege of Mainz, writing about both.

From 1793, Goethe devoted himself exclusively to literature. In 1794, he received a letter from the other great German writer of the era, Friedrich von Schiller, who offered him friendship. They had first become acquainted six years before, but remained rivals until Schiller's peace offering. Goethe eagerly accepted and they developed a warm relationship that lasted until Schiller's death in 1805. Upon becoming director of the Weimar theater, Goethe premiered Schiller's plays. When Schiller died, no one dared inform Goethe of his great friend's passing.

In 1806, Goethe was living in Weimar with his mistress and their son Julius August Walter von Goethe. In October, Napoleon's army invaded the town and a group of poorly disciplined French soldiers took up residence in his house, where they consumed all his food and wine and threatened to kill him. He was terrified, but his mistress Christiane organized the defense of the house, barricading the kitchen and cellar, and saved the day. A few days afterward, Goethe married Christiane. She died in 1816.

In 1823, he fell in love with Ulrike von Levetzow whom he wanted to marry, but, because of her mother's opposition, he never proposed. Their last meeting in Carlsbad inspired him to write his *Marienbad Elegy,* another of his finest romantic works.

Goethe died in Weimar in 1832 at age eighty-three, probably of heart failure. He is buried alongside his great friend and rival, Schiller, in the Ducal Vault at Weimar's Historical Cemetery. He lived a rich, full, and prolific life and, unlike his namesake Wolfgang Mozart, was showered with honors and riches while alive.

His influence over contemporary and succeeding German generations to this day was and is enormous and extends beyond his native land. His immense body of work encompassed epic and lyric poetry, prose, verse dramas, memoirs, autobiography, literary and art criticism, four novels, his great drama *Faust* (1808), and treatises on botany (his *Metamorphosis of Plants*, published upon his return from Italy, was a major influence on Darwin), anatomy, and color, as well as countless literary and scientific observations, more than 10,000 letters, and nearly 3,000 drawings. His novel, *Wilhelm Meister's Apprenticeship*, is considered by literary scholars one of the greatest ever written.

Napoleon Bonaparte

The life of Napoleon does not require the same detailed rendition as that of Goethe. The highlights of the French emperor's existence are well-known to most Americans.

Napoleon Bonaparte was born in Ajaccio on the French-controlled island of Corsica in 1769 (France had purchased Corsica from the Genoese Republic just two years before) to an Italian family. Like his fellow Corsican, Comte de Brazza, Napoleon Bonaparte realized early on that his fortune and colossal ambition could only be achieved on the mainland in France. In 1779, at the ripe old age of ten, his father enrolled him in the French Royal Military School at Brienne-le-Chateau, where the scrawny, undersized, Italian-speaking boy on full scholarship learned French, history, geography, mathematics, and other required courses necessary to advance to the Ecole Militaire in Paris, which he entered in 1784, having finished 42nd out of a class of 56 students at Brienne.

He was distinguished at Brienne because of his rich Corsican accent and his very vocal hatred of France for being the overlord and occupier of his home island (he dreamed of returning home to launch a revolt against French rule). He also excelled at history, geography, and mathematics. His low class standing is attributable to his loathing of German and consequent terrible grades in that subject.

At both military schools, he was never part of the in-crowd, suffering the taunts of his peers because of his small stature, his alien-sounding name, and his imperious attitude. His standard retort to the cascade of abuses: "One day I'll make you French pay!"

He did, but not in any predictable way.

He graduated from the Ecole Militaire in 1785 with the rank of second lieutenant of the artillery, and reported to his first posting at Valence in southeastern France. But for the cancellation of the naval gunnery exams that year, Napoleon would have been billeted to the French Navy and European history would have proceeded in a much different direction.

He spent the next five years as a contrarian. His drive, curiosity, interests, intelligence, and unquenchable thirst for knowledge were comparable to Goethe's. While his fellow students spent their limited off-hours boozing, whoring, and gambling, Napoleon remained closeted in his miserable monk's cell of a room reading voraciously about every conceivable subject and taking voluminous notes about what he read and jotting down the ideas he derived from his studies. However, his writing was so illegible that he himself often could not decipher what he had written. What he could still discern often became the basis for policies he would implement when he came to supreme power.

He was forced by economic circumstances to lead an extremely frugal existence. His thirteen-year-old brother Louis was now living with him, making his tiny room even more cramped. He sent a portion of his pay to his mother in Ajaccio, subsisting on small amounts of bread and cheese, and looked emaciated.

On July 14, 1789, the Paris mob stormed the Bastille and launched the French Revolution. This seminal event had no impact on Napoleon, stationed in a backwater hundreds of miles from Paris.

In June 1791, he was promoted to First Lieutenant. The tumult surrounding the monarchy over the next several years (he witnessed the storming of the Tuileries Palace and dethroning of King Louis XVI) appear to have made little or no impression on Napoleon, who was still raging against France's oppressive rule over Corsica. His only lasting impression from the chaos surrounding him was a lifelong fear and loathing of "the masses."

His unit was relocated to Paris following the revolution. His regimental years in Paris were interrupted by six long leaves in Corsica, during which he agitated against French rule, going so far as to rig his own election as a lieutenant colonel of a battalion of Corsican volunteers. As such, he and his troops attempted to seize the Ajaccio citadel from the French garrison. At the same time, having neglected to request a leave extension, he was declared AWOL by the War Ministry and was struck from the list of serving officers.

He returned to Paris several months later and, despite his outrageous rebellious activities on Corsica, managed to have all of the charges against him dropped and was, to his own amazement, allowed to rejoin his artillery regiment with promotion to captain!

Upon his return from this particular Corsican adventure and the resumption of his French military career, he began to cultivate political ties while frequently attending sessions of the new Legislative Assembly. Always impatient, he now felt compelled to do whatever was necessary to obtain higher rank and accelerate his career. This may have been prompted in part by his father's early death at age 39.

This lowly artillery captain demonstrated his nerve and boldness by barging in unannounced on the new naval minister and requesting an appointment as lieutenant colonel of the artillery in the French navy! Amazingly, Navy chief Gaspard Monge was favorably disposed to grant Napoleon's audacious request.

Events, however, intervened. Shortly after this brazen attempt at self-advancement, he requested and was granted yet another extended leave to take his young sister Elisa back to Corsica, where he immediately invoked his former commission as lieutenant colonel in the rebel volunteer army and took part in an attempted Corsican invasion of nearby Sardinia! Now all hell broke loose and Napoleon found himself not only at odds with France but also with his Corsican countrymen who, bizarrely, accused him and his family of being pro-French. The Bonapartes were forced into hiding for a year until June, 1793, when they secretly sailed for Toulon. The France to which Napoleon returned was a nation in chaos, consumed by the terror wrought by Maximilien Robespierre and his Committee of Public Safety. Louis and his queen, Marie Antoinette, had been executed six months before.

Stunningly, Napoleon's brother Joseph who, upon arriving back in France had gone to Paris to lobby influential friends, returned to Marseilles (where the family had taken up residence) three months later armed with the exalted title of *Commissaire de Guerre* (akin to quartermaster) and a lucrative salary supplemented by bribes from merchants seeking to do business with the army. The Bonapartes were now, for the first time, no longer in desperate economic straits.

Napoleon returned to a country at war with Austria, England, Spain, and Holland, while also coping with numerous internal pro-royalist revolts and food riots. This provided a lot of work and opportunity for the twenty-four-year-old artillery major (he had been recently promoted).

Napoleon took on the recapture of Toulon from the combined British/royalist forces that had seized the city. His indefatigable energy, creativity, and military success dazzled his superiors. The Hero of Toulon was immediately jumped in rank to brigadier general at age twenty-five.

The remaining few years of the eighteenth century were full of *sturm und drang* for Napoleon. He was briefly imprisoned in 1794, suspected of being a Jacobin and supporter of the abruptly disgraced and recently beheaded Robespierre. A few months later, he was promoted to General of the Army of the West and assigned the task of suppressing civil unrest and rebellion against the Republic. Within weeks, he won promotion to Commander of the Army of the Interior, and five months later was given command of the French army in Italy. In 1796, he married Josephine and immediately took off to battle against Austria, emerging victorious and returning to Paris at the end of 1797 a national hero.

In May, 1798, Napoleon launched his Egyptian campaign, taking Alexandria, winning the Battle of the Pyramids, and conquering Cairo at the same time that this French adventure was coming to an end when the British fleet under Admiral Horatio Nelson destroyed the French navy at Aboukir Bay.

In August 1799, Napoleon returned to a Paris in turmoil and, three months later, staged a *coup d'etat*, emerging as First Consul of the new French government. He established his household in the Tuileries Palace and soon took off on a second successful Italian campaign against Austria. He returned to Paris the supreme power in France. In December, 1804, he crowned himself emperor in Notre-Dame Cathedral.

Napoleon spent the next four years campaigning throughout Europe and, by the time he arrived in Erfurt in 1808, was the undisputed ruler of much of the continent.

The Meeting with Goethe

Napoleon in 1808 was at the height of his power and glory. He was in Erfurt to meet with Tsar Alexander I of All the

Russias, and in his free time decided to satisfy his curiosity about the enigmatic Goethe.

The only account we have of this meeting comes directly from Goethe himself. He writes that he was summoned by the emperor to meet with him at 11:00 AM on October 2, 1808 and that when he arrived at the Governor's Palace he was greeted by a "fat chamberlain," Monsieur Pole, who told him to wait. After a brief interlude, he was introduced to General Savary, one of the heroes of the battles of Austerlitz and Jena, and to the foreign minister, Talleyrand. They accompanied him into the emperor's study.

Napoleon sat at a large circular table eating a late breakfast. Talleyrand took a seat to his right alongside Daru, one of the emperor's "household generals" and confidantes, with whom he was discussing taxes.

Goethe waited by the door until Napoleon signaled him to approach. He remained standing in front of him at a "suitable distance." Napoleon looked at him for an uncomfortable, long moment, then said: "You are a *man*," a high compliment coming from the macho emperor. Goethe bowed his head, not knowing how to respond to such an unusual observation. Napoleon's next question was: "How old are you?" "Sixty," replied Goethe. "You are well preserved. You have written some tragedies." Goethe nodded his head in agreement. Then Daru began to speak, flattering Geothe by saying that he had read some of his works along with other German literature. He also stated that he was versed in Latin literature and had even translated Horace. He added that he was aware that Goethe had translated some French works, among them Voltaire's *Mahomet*. At which point the emperor interjected: "That is not a good work," adding that it was very unfitting for the conqueror of the world to paint such an unfavorable portrait of himself.

Napoleon then brought the conversation to Geothe's *The Sufferings of Young Werther*, the book that was a sensation in Europe (while also driving many young men to suicide), which it was apparent he had studied in detail. After several perfectly pertinent observations, he mentioned a specific part of the book (Geothe does not tell us which part) and said: "Why did you do that? It is not natural." Goethe said that Napoleon "spoke at length on this and with great perspicacity."

Goethe listened, "my face calm," and replied "with a satisfied smile" that he was unaware whether anyone had ever made the same criticism, but that he found it perfectly justified and agreed that one could find fault with this passage's lack of verity. "But", he added, "a poet can be excused for taking refuge in an artifice which is hard to spot, when he wants to produce specific effects which cannot be created simply and naturally."

Geothe noted that the emperor seemed to agree with him. Napoleon turned the conversation to drama and "made some very sensible remarks, remarks which could only have come from someone who had observed the tragic stage with a great deal of attention—such as a criminal judge might do—someone who felt very deeply how far French theatre had strayed from the natural and true."

The topic then turned to destiny plays, which Napoleon criticized as belonging to the dark ages. "Why these days do they keep giving us destiny?" he said. "There's no destiny, only politics."

An odd thing happened at this point. Without skipping a beat, Napoleon turned once again to Daru and spoke to him some more about taxes. Geothe, unnerved, stepped a few paces back, and noticed that Berthier, another of Napoleon's fawning generals, stood behind him with Savary and someone else he did not recognize. There was no sign of Talleyrand.

Next, Marshal Soult was announced. Goethe noted that he was a tall man with a "fine head of hair." Ignoring Goethe completely, the emperor questioned Soult "teasingly" about some unpleasant events in Poland. Goethe said that this gave him time to look around the room, one that he remembered fondly from having visited thirty years before. He reflected on the past: "The old tapestries were still there. But the old portraits had gone."

While musing about the portraits, the emperor rose, came straight towards him and, "by a sort of maneuver, separated me from all the other people in the line in which I found myself. He turned his back to those people and spoke to me lowering his voice. He asked me whether I was married, whether I had children and other personal matters. He also questioned me on my relations with the house of the princes, on the Duchess Amalia, on the prince and on the princess. I replied in a natural manner. He seemed satisfied and translated for himself these replies into his tongue, but in slightly more forceful terms than I had managed."

"I must also remark that, in the whole of our conversation, I had admired the variety of his affirmative replies and gestures, in that he was rarely immobile when he listened. Sometimes he made a meditative gesture with his head and said 'Yes' or 'That's right' or something similar; or if he had stated an idea, he most often added; 'And what would Monsieur Goethe say to that?'"

"I took the opportunity to make a sign to the chamberlain to see if I could retire. On his signaling yes, I immediately took my leave."

Two weeks later, Goethe received in the mail the Grand Cross of the *Légion d'Honneur*, the highest award of merit for both military and civil accomplishments. The award came unaccompanied by any words.

The impression left with the modern reader is one of a deferential, somewhat intimidated and obsequious literary genius and an only casually interested, self-absorbed, towering egotist who, by this stage in his tumultuous life, had trouble concentrating on more than one thing at a time.

Aftermath

Following the Erfurt encounter, Goethe returned to Weimar and his writing career while Napoleon resumed warring against the growing alliance of nations threatened by him, supplemented by countries that did not appreciate French rule. Meanwhile, his equally tumultuous personal life began to take its toll on him and his seven siblings, whom he had ensconced in positions of power throughout conquered Europe in a display of naked nepotism that makes Donald Trump look like an amateur:

- Brother Joseph became King of Spain and Naples.
- Brother Lucien was named Prince of Canino.
- Brother Louis was appointed King of Holland.
- Brother Jerome was designated King of Westphalia.
- Sister Elisa was made Princess of Lucca and Piombino and Grand Duchess of Tuscany.
- Sister Pauline was anointed Duchess of Guastalla.
- Sister Caroline became Grand Duchess of Berg and later Queen of Naples.

Napoleon divorced the habitually unfaithful Josephine in December, 1809 and, several months later married Archduchess Marie-Louise of Austria, who bore him a son a year later, and whom Napoleon designated "King of Rome."

In June, 1812, Napoleon's downfall began when his *Grand Armée* of somewhere between 650,000 and 900,000 troops, the largest army ever assembled up to that time, crossed the Niemen River and invaded Russia. His goal was a quick victory that would force the Tsar to the negotiating table. Six months later, on December 5th, Napoleon left the army in Russia and returned to Paris. Nine days later, the few (estimated at 9,000) *Grand Armée* stragglers still alive crossed the Niemen in retreat, the army having been decimated by a combination of the brutal Russian winter, guerilla attacks, disease, an unsustainably long supply chain, and starvation caused by the Russian people's scorched-earth resistance.

Emboldened by Napoleon's devastating defeat, Prussia declared war on France and an anti-French coalition of virtually all of the other European powers began to cut away at French hegemony. In January, 1814, the coalition army entered France. Two months later, it took Paris. Napoleon abdicated and was exiled to the island of Elba off the Tuscany coast.

Ten months later, he escaped and landed in the south of France, where he rallied the French army and began his "Hundred Days" campaign which ended with his defeat at Waterloo, Belgium. He abdicated for the second time and was permanently exiled to the island of St. Helena in the South Atlantic, where he died five years later.

Commonalities

Goethe and Napoleon would never be considered birds of a feather. The German literary genius is universally viewed as one of the most peaceful of men while the Corsican military genius comes across to us over the two hundred years that intervene as one of the most warlike. However, a deeper, more nuanced examination of these two remarkable, world-changing lives reveals that they shared a number of very important traits that contributed to their success:

- They were blessed in being born to fathers who understood the core importance of education at a time when very few parents did. This led them to push their sons to learn and to love learning. Both men were blessed with unusually good educations that prepared them for the lives they would lead.
- They were voracious readers—literate omnivores—for whom no subject (including foreign languages other than German in Napoleon's case) was uninteresting or off-limits.
- They were insatiably curious, continually questioning what the writers and scholars whom they read were telling them.
- They were "information sponges," constantly soaking up knowledge of incredibly diverse subjects.
- They were both able to apply what they learned, an extremely rare talent in any age.

- They were precocious. By age 25, they had already risen to heights within their professions unattainable by others: Goethe a literary lion; Napoleon a general.
- They were both incredibly lucky. Napoleon missed becoming a naval officer by the skin of his teeth. Had the 1785 naval gunnery exams not been cancelled, we might never have heard of him. Goethe was a disinterested lawyer with an avocation that he quickly turned into a vocation, an example for thousands of today's attorneys who seek a way out of the strictures of their often poorly-chosen profession. While luck played a role in their lives, in both cases fortune favored the prepared. It always does.

Author's Note: The Other "Encounter"

The meeting with Goethe was not the only one between Napoleon and a monumental ego of legendary proportions. Another "encounter"—the strangest in this book—occurred over a temporal separation of eighty-four years and was not a face-to-face confrontation. Such a meeting would have been impossible since Napoleon, the butcher of more people than anyone else in his century died almost 70 years before the birth of the undersized Austrian who competed strenuously (with Stalin and Mao) to murder more people than anyone else in the twentieth century.

Nevertheless, Napoleon Bonaparte and Adolph Hitler have much more in common than (1) mass murder and (2) coming to grief 132 winters apart in the unforgiving snow, sleet, ice, cold, mud, and expanse of Russia. They actually "met" in something of a New Age sense.

On October 23, 1805, the 36,000 man army of Russia's greatest general, Prince Mikhail Kutuzov, immortalized by Tolstoy in War and Peace, arrived in the tiny, backwater Austrian frontier town of Braunau-am-Inn in order to link up with 22,000 Austrian troops. Kutuzov's now-60,000-strong

army gathered in Branau to defend the "Third Coalition"—
consisting of the Russian Tsar, the Hapsburg Emperor, and
the King of Prussia—against Napoleon's Grande Armée.

Braunau had had one prior flirtation with fame. In 1706, it
was the headquarters of a short-lived peasant rebellion
against the Hapsburgs.

However, Branau did not recede completely into the mists
of history, soon to be forever forgotten following Kutuzov's
overnight stay. The small city on the south bank of the raging
River Inn, which has demarcated the border between Austria
and Germany since Roman times, soon thereafter provided
the platform for what became an incredible coincidence.

Three weeks after Kutuzov left Branau, Napoleon himself
arrived and made the village his own overnight
headquarters. There, he refined the strategy that resulted in
his great victory at Austerlitz in nearby Moravia two weeks
later.

Napoleon billeted in the second story rooms of a local
gasthaus, the Haus Schudl. There in a small cramped
bedroom, he and his generals and aides laid maps out on a
table and plotted the likely tracks of the enemy armies before
they went to sleep. The next morning, his forces provisioned
and rested, Napoleon mounted his horse and rode off to the
northeast and glory.

Braunau withdrew into temporary obscurity. Five years
later it experienced yet another historical footnote: it
provided the location for the transfer of Austrian
Archduchess Marie Louise from her Austrian handlers to the
French, who escorted her from there to Paris and her
bridegroom, the Emperor Napoleon.

For the next 80 years, Braunau was not heard from. In
1871, a red-faced, hard-drinking, corpulent, minor Austrian
civil servant and all-around martinet, Alois Schickelgruber,
was posted to Braunau. In 1874, Braunau's largely wooden
buildings were destroyed by a fire. Only the stone houses
survived, including the Haus Schudl. In 1876, Alois legally
adopted the surname "Hiedler," divesting himself of the taint
of his illegitimate birth which had haunted him for the first 39
years of his life. By 1889, Alois and Klara, his wife, were

living on the second floor of the Gasthaus zum Pommer, formerly the Hotel Schudl.

At 6:30 PM on a dark April day, the thick clouds suspended low in the sky, Klara gave birth to a small son in their bedroom. By this time Alois had "Austrianized" the spelling of his last name to "Hitler." Two days later, baby Adolf was baptized.

The bedroom where Adolf Hitler was born was the same room in which Napoleon planned the strategy for the coming Battle of Austerlitz eighty-four years before. Perhaps there was something in the air . . . ?

Adolf Hitler believed that disabled children were untermenschen (subhumans) unworthy of life. He did his utmost to eliminate as many of them as possible. Today, part of the former Gasthaus zum Pommer serves as a home for disabled children.

Abdul Aziz Ibn Saud and Franklin Delano Roosevelt

Many of the encounters in this history, as in ordinary lives, are about power. Certainly Napoleon and Hitler, and Stanley and Brazza, meet that standard. In a more complex way, the same holds true for Francis, Dominic, and Pope Innocent. Perhaps even Beethoven and Mozart, in a more personal way, are also about power.

The next encounter is no exception. It is also the first of two almost-contemporary encounters we will examine. Being so close to our own time, they require less explication in order for modern readers to grasp their significance, but perhaps merit more elaboration so that the oceanic differences between the protagonists can be placed in perspective.

Chapter 9 – The Great Bitter Lake

FDR and Ibn Saud
Grease the American Century

The oil can is mightier than the sword.
Sen. Everett McKinley Dirksen

This is not just a story about the only meeting between two charismatic giants of the twentieth century, one an American President from the heart of the Northeastern establishment; the other the King of Saudi Arabia from the desolate wastes of the Empty Quarter. It is also tightly interwoven with the story of oil, the most valuable substance on Earth, the feedstock that fueled the American Century.

First, we need to examine the lively and colorful history of oil.

Oil was first discovered in the Middle East 5,000 years ago in Mesopotamia. It was first used in the service of man as caulking for boats and binding for bricks, as well as, intermittently, as a light source. Its first recorded appearance in the annals of ancient times was in the form of *bitumen*, first observed seeping to the surface from underground near Baghdad.

That was the last interesting fact about the nexus between oil and the Middle East until the first year of the twentieth century.

Not much changed regarding oil and its usefulness until the late nineteenth century when the invention of the automobile dragged oil front-and-center and made it the most important resource on Earth. While that stunning development occurred in North America and Europe, history's oil stage shortly returned to its roots in the Middle East, thanks to a concession granted by the Persian government to a flamboyant English entrepreneur, William Knox D'Arcy.

D'Arcy's *coup* soon attracted other adventurers, and the Middle Eastern oil boom was on. At first, the rulers of the remote, desert wastes sitting on top of unbelievable riches did not know what to make of their serendipitous good fortune. Legend has it that, in the early days, Emirate chieftains would sit in their tents on the shores of the Persian Gulf on cold desert nights and burn millions of dollars worth of paper money received for oil concessions in order to keep warm!

Nevertheless, they soon learned. And furthest ahead on the learning curve was Abdul Aziz Ibn Saud.

The events that culminated in Desert Storm and the ensuing 2003 invasion of Iraq began very quietly 58 years before in a meeting of Occident and Orient that was incredibly bizarre, but also so significant for the history of the latter half of the twentieth century that it is surprising that historians have not paid much attention researching and writing about it. Probably, the timing of the event allowed it to get lost in the shuffle of more immediately momentous happenings. The epic meeting coincided with the end of the war in Europe and occurred just days after the much better known and much more infamous Yalta Conference in the Crimea, which historians have concluded was a victory for Joseph Stalin and the Soviet Union.

I would argue that the most important meeting to take place in April, 1945 did not occur at Yalta. Rather, it was this encounter, the subject of this chapter, because it did more to shape the post-war world in the long run than Yalta, which essentially blessed a *fait accompli*, one that would have become a political reality regardless of whether the dying President Roosevelt ever went to the Crimea at all.

Today the Yalta Agreement is no longer of much relevance. A relatively free and market-oriented Eastern Europe has come so far in just a quarter century that their status as "captive nations" is everyday a more distant memory. Most are members of the European Union and also of NATO. This was victory for the west that rivals Rome's over Carthage.

Today, too, the focal point of world attention is still on the Middle East, that supremely unstable collection of countries always at each others' throats, warring constantly over a few acres of sand and blood-feuding about events that may or may not have taken place 1,500 and 2,000 years ago. While sitting atop the greatest riches and most vital resource on the planet, the lifeblood of the world economy, they export their oil and their violence to the rest of it.

Communism proved to be a relatively brief, historical anomaly. In the end, the "rubbish heap of history" claimed its inventor. Islam and oil, however, keep on going, becoming more and more the obsession of the West.

The two principals with whom Roosevelt met in those weeks in April were very much contemporaries of each other. Both Joseph Stalin and Ibn Saud were of fairly humble origin, rose through dint of will to great power, and died in the same year, 1953, after which they were succeeded by nonentities— Georgi Malenkov and Ibn Saud's oldest son—who did not survive long in power at all. But while we have dissected Stalin's life and career from every conceivable angle in an effort to understand the monster, very few people have even heard of Ibn Saud, who strode the Middle East like a larger-than-life figure for 50 years, and whose "aura" is palpable today, more than 100 years after his birth. It is arguable that it was Ibn Saud whom history will prove to have been the more influential and more important to the West.

Western economies, especially that of the United States, became addicted to their daily oil fix much earlier in the twentieth century. Their addiction increased markedly during the unprecedented economic boom after World War II. Not even the "oil shocks" of 1973-74 and 1979, when first the Arabs and then the Iranians turned off the oil spigot, could sober us up. We were, and to a lesser extent still are, hooked. Desert

Storm was about oil. More specifically, about guaranteeing the free and unfettered access to oil vital to the West.

What gave this yearning for more and more oil its greatest impetus was a meeting aboard the *U.S.S. Quincy* in the middle of Egypt's Great Bitter Lake in the Suez Canal on April 14, 1945, a meeting between the triumphant but ailing leader of the cultured West—Franklin Delano Roosevelt—and his presumably uncultured counterpart from the desert, King Ibn Saud of Saudi Arabia. The meeting was momentous for many reasons and on many levels. Most Americans in 1945 had never even seen an Arab before (unless you count the silent films of 1920s). The newsreels of this meeting were a first, and were a source of considerable intrigue to the American movie-going public.

The center of attention of this interest was not just any Arab. It was the supreme Arab, Abdul Aziz Ibn Abdul Rahman Al Faysal Al Saud, who has come down to us foreshortened as Abdul Aziz Ibn Saud, or simply Ibn Saud, the founder of Saudi Arabia and the father of his country in more ways than one.

Before we address the meeting and its implications, let's examine the two major players who set the scene for the oil question for the rest of the twentieth century.

To the Manor Born

A visit to Hyde Park, New York tells you all you need to know about the patrician origins and upper crust lifestyle of the thirty-third president of the United States. There is a tape tour by his wife, the redoubtable Eleanor, where she quite matter-of-factly relates a visit by King George of England and his Queen, in the same tone you and I might use to describe the visit of a run-of-the-mill relative.

If anyone were ever born to rule, it was FDR. It was as natural to him as the Divine Right of Kings must have been to Louis XIV. Ruling was part of the natural order of things if you were born a Roosevelt.

FDR had all the advantages, and was having himself a nice, gentle skate through life when polio struck him down in his late thirties. However, aided by a tremendous support system of family and aides, one that was surely unique in America and the world, and bolstered by his own unquenchable optimism and ambition, he fought back. The rest is history.

He made such a mark on his world that he is still a center of attention today, more than 70 years after his death. As I write, both Democrats and Republicans, even as the latter attempt to undo the philosophy and some of the achievements of the New Deal, claim portions of his legacy.

There is no need to go into detail about this most scrutinized of men and dissected of presidencies. If every schoolchild does not know about FDR and his times, that is his or her loss as well as a sad commentary on the state of education in these United States.

To the *Wadi* Born

While FDR was born to wealth and a life of ease, Ibn Saud was not exactly born to abject poverty, at least by the standards of the desert. His family did not have blue Ford *Phaetons* with special hand controls in which to ride around (like Roosevelt), but they had plenty of camels, a sign of significant riches among the inhabitants of the Arabian peninsula.

The personal history of Abdul Aziz Ibn Saud is so shrouded by the desert mists and so steeped in the legends that have grown up around this complicated, contradictory soul that even his birth date is a point of contention. So much so that students of his life cannot pinpoint it within twenty years! No other modern historical figure or national leader can claim that kind of ambiguity. For our purposes, we will opt for 1876.

Moreover, while virtually every day of Franklin Roosevelt's life is documented, virtually no documentation at all exists with respect to the life of Ibn Saud. Disputes and contradictory accounts of his achievements and of key events in his life are the norm. There is almost nothing written about him in Arabic, and the closest thing to a primary source is quite distant indeed: British official documents dating from approximately 1910, plus the diaries and memoirs of Englishmen who came into contact with him beginning in the 1930s.

The corner of the world into which Ibn Saud was born was— and is today—one of the most remote and desolate on the planet. It is also the largest expanse of continuous desert outside the Sahara, extending east-to-west a distance equivalent to that separating New York City from Des Moines, Iowa and north-to-south the equivalent of the distance between Madison, Wisconsin and New Orleans. In other words, an enormous vastness.

The largest component of this desert is the famous *Rub' Al-Khali*, the Empty Quarter, 250,000 square miles of nothing. On the surface, anyway. Below lies one of the largest oil fields on Earth. Other than a handful of oil workers, the Empty Quarter today is still virtually uninhabited. The Empty Quarter, however, was good to Ibn Saud, providing him a much-needed refuge at several points in his storied career of conquest.

Perhaps this remoteness and vast emptiness contribute to the paucity of material about Saudi Arabia, at least in the historical sense. As epic a work as the *New Cambridge Modern History* volume covering the first 45 years of the twentieth century not only never mentions Ibn Saud, but also omits any reference whatsoever to Saudi Arabia!

Abdul Aziz Ibn Saud, scion of the family *Al Saud*, was so much a son of the desert that, until the end of his life, he maintained the Bedouin nomadic tradition, moving with his retinue from oasis to oasis during the course of the year. Only two generations prior to his emergence, the Al Saud lived in a totally closed society in its *Nejd* homeland, isolated by climate, topography, and attitude. Contact with the outside world even within the Arabian peninsula was virtually non-existent, but for a bit of camel-trading with the Persian Gulf coast and Damascus, as well as occasional religious contact with Mecca in order to perform the *Hajj*, the pilgrimage every Muslim must undertake once in his life.

The history of the *Al Saud* family is one of constant warfare spurred by religious fervor. Like the Mongol hordes and their

Hunnish successors, it is also one of accordion-like expansion and contraction. In short, a tumultuous history, full of sword and crescent. Ibn Saud himself killed many men, most with either a sword or a rifle. Most of these were, from a political and survival standpoint, necessary deaths. In contrast, Franklin D. Roosevelt never personally lifted a weapon in anger in his life.

The theocratic state that rules absolutely the Arabian peninsula today got its start almost 250 years ago, when Ibn Saud's direct ancestor offered a safe haven to one Sheik Muhammad bin-Abdul Wahab, a fundamentalist Muslim fleeing his hometown after insisting that a local adulteress be stoned to death in accordance with the law of the *Shari'a*, the strict Koranic legal system that still governs Saudi Arabia today and has even become a rallying cry for American xenophobes. The adoption of the extremely simple *Wahabi* creed (its power lay precisely in its simplicity) was the defining moment of the development of the House of Saud. Overnight, the whole relationship between leader and people in Dar'iya, the Saudi capital, was radically altered.

The melding of the religious and the secular fired the ambitions of the *Al Saud*. It is virtually impossible for a modern Western reader to believe, much less understand, that a whole people could do something like this, particularly since this total cultural makeover required the renunciation of virtually all of the old ways of doing things and the adoption of rigorous new standards insinuating themselves into every facet of daily life: no more shrines, alcohol, tobacco, dancing gaudy garments, gold jewelry, *jinns* (demons), evil eyes, music or laughing. Harsh? Yes. But the most positive and salutary principle espoused by *Wahabism* more than counterbalanced these proscriptions: the concept of a universal Islamic community, which wiped out tribalism at one fell swoop. Somehow, it gained traction, quickly took hold, and worked.

Infused with the strict law and new fervor of the desert Muslims, the armies of the *Al Saud* fanned out from their desert redoubt in the *Nejd* to such lengths that they soon occupied Mecca and Medina, and even extended beyond the Arabian peninsula, exacting tribute from as far away as Aleppo in Northern Syria. This latter incursion was a big mistake. Aleppo is disturbingly close to Turkey, the homeland of the Ottoman Empire.

When the Sultan in Constantinople heard about the *Al Saud's* military venture, his retribution was swift and terrible: the first Saudi state disappeared, its capital was razed, and its leader, Amir Abdullah bin Saud, was taken to Constantinople and beheaded.

The Sultan's retribution did not stop there. Through his Egyptian surrogates, he managed to totally destroy Dar'iya, the *al Saud* capital. To this day, if you drive the short stretch from modern Riyadh to Dar'iya, all you see are ruins, left as a memorial to the legacy of the *al Saud*.

For the remainder of the nineteenth century, the fortunes of the *al Saud* went alternately up and down. In 1865, competition for power between two sons of the long-time ruler, Amir Feisal bin Turki, temporarily brought down the dynasty. Their bitter competition eventually caused the family to go into exile in 1891. They abandoned Riyadh, including the (probably) 15-year old Abdul Aziz Ibn Saud, and set out across the desert northeast to Kuwait, an arduous trip that took two years.

The trek across the sands proved to be an invaluable training ground for the future king. Not only did he learn, by direct contact, the ways of the Bedouin; he also picked up the skills necessary to survive in the desert: camel riding; horsemanship; tracking; where to find water and food; and how to use the sword, dagger, and rifle.

The Kuwaiti exile put the capstone on Ibn Saud's education. Its strategic location on the Persian Gulf made Kuwait City a gathering point for adventurers and government functionaries from all over the world. Ibn Saud was able to observe international geopolitics first-hand. Moreover, he became a favorite of the local Sheik Mubarak and learned much, thanks both to the formal education in mathematics, history, geography, and English he received at Mubarak's *majlis*, as well as being able to observe his mentor play off the interests of the British, French, Russians, Germans, and Turks.

Eight years after Ibn Saud arrived in Kuwait, there occurred a confluence of events that determined his destiny. Sheik Mubarak concluded a secret protection treaty with Great Britain and thereby gained some wiggle room vis-a-vis the Ottoman Turks. He employed his new freedom to harass the *al Rashidi* family, who had supplanted the *al Saud* in Riyadh. In 1901, Mubarak led a raid against the *al Rashidi* across the *Nejd*, attacking them in *Hail*, their ancestral capital, while Ibn Saud led a small commando group against Riyadh. The raid failed and both contingents retreated back to Kuwait.

Now it was the *al Rashidis'* turn to seek revenge. Soon, raiding parties approached Kuwait. The British treaty was invoked and a British fleet stood off Kuwait in the Gulf ready for action. The raiding party, impressed and intimidated, withdrew.

The moment had arrived. Ibn Saud, manifesting his strategic brilliance, asked Mubarak and his father for permission to attack Riyadh while the enemy raiders were preoccupied far away from their capital. He knew that Riyadh was defended by only a tiny force and, from his observations during his own earlier raid, knew that the walls lacked proper fortifications.

Permission was granted and he rode off across the desert with 40-50 relatives, hoping to pick up tribal supporters along the route. However, the Bedouin are not known for sticking with a particular project very long, and by the time Ibn Saud reached the environs of Riyadh, his force was back to its original size. In early morning darkness of January 16, 1902, he led them through the palm groves adjacent to the city walls. They used palm trunks to scale the walls and surprise the small garrison. By first light, Abdul Aziz Ibn Saud was ruler of Riyadh. But he had bigger plans.

At the beginning of his quest to carve out of the desert a nation-state for his family, Ibn Saud owned nary a patch of sand. By the end of his life, he and his family were undisputed rulers of 865,000 square miles, making their realm the 13th largest country on Earth.

Getting around in this huge sandy expanse was slow (25 miles per day by camel on average). It was not until 1935 that Ibn Saud himself abandoned the camel for the motor car.

The Run-Up

The meeting aboard ship between East and West was a startling clash of cultures. For one thing, an area that, only two generations before, had been considered impossibly remote, would be sending a representative to meet with the head of the greatest military, political, and economic power in the world. For another, this representative was a man only a few years removed from nomadism and a way of life that had marked desert existence for thousands of years, back to biblical times and beyond. Ibn Saud, for example, made it a political point throughout his life to move from one settlement to another every year in order to honor the *Al Saud's* historical links to both the settled Arabs (the *Hadar*) and the Bedouin.

FDR, on the other hand, was considered by many to be one of the most "civilized" human beings on the planet, an epitome of the end product of many millennia of evolution, cultivation, and breeding. Any movements he made were between Hyde Park, Washington, DC, Campobello Island, and Warm Springs, Georgia, and had nothing to do with anything other than business or seeking refuge therefrom.

Ibn Saud traveled to the meeting, one of his few journeys outside of Saudi Arabia, on the U.S. destroyer *Murphy*, which he boarded in Jeddah on the Red Sea in 120-degree heat. To the amazement of his American sailor hosts, he and his 49-person entourage promptly pitched their Bedouin tents on deck, proceeded to sleep and pray in them, and slaughtered goats for food during the two-day journey into Egypt!

The American Century was about to begin in earnest. The British and French colonial empires were on the way out, and it was time for the new kid on the block to flex its considerable muscles as it tried to determine what to do with its legacy.

It was the last meeting Franklin Delano Roosevelt would have in his life with a head of state. Upon his return home, he went to Warm Springs Georgia and died the next week.

Five years before, Roosevelt had replied, when confronted with advice to develop the American presence on the Arabian peninsula: " . . . tell the British I hope they can take care of the King . . . This is a little far afield for us."

Circumstances change rapidly in modern times. By 1945, Roosevelt's thinking had done a 180-degree turnabout. Jewish emigration into Palestine after the Holocaust, and the enormous importance of oil to the allied victory in the war, dramatically altered the geopolitical equation. America was equated in the eyes of the Third World (that peculiar Cold War term had not yet, of course, come into existence) with nationalistic aspirations, thanks in large part to the memory of Woodrow Wilson and his policies at the end of the previous global conflagration less than a generation before. America, in short, represented the future, and its exports of movies, big shiny automobiles, industrial might, popular culture, and overall modernity were supremely seductive.

If ever there was a meeting of opposites, this was it. Franklin D. Roosevelt was the ultimate exemplar of the American aristocracy evolving out of meritocracy, cosmopolitan, well-read, highly-educated, representing the world's most powerful nation, and exuding a sophistication that was much more than skin deep. His transport of choice was his beloved, custom-designed Ford Phaeton, which he kept at Hyde Park. Ibn Saud, on the other hand, was a marginally literate desert warrior who represented almost 900,000 square miles of little more than sand dunes and wadis (although what went on underneath this vast expanse of sand was something to behold!). He was most at home on the back of a camel.

Their meeting was secret. It had to be for several very good reasons. First, the Great Bitter Lake was within range of German bombers. Although the war was rapidly winding down and Adolph Hitler would be dead in less than three weeks, there were no security guarantees. The other major reason for secrecy was the rather grand U.S. plan for Saudi Arabia after the war, which had been formulated since 1941 and which would effectively render the U.S. the major power in the Middle East, taking over from Britain and France and locking in the newly crafted "special relationship" between the U.S. and the Kingdom.

Departure

At 3:00 p.m. on February 12th, Ibn Saud ordered his entourage, temporarily installed at Jeddah, to decamp into their trucks and limousines for Mecca. Not until he was in his car did he alert his driver to head for the harbor instead. Less than two hours later, he was aboard the *Murphy*, steaming out of the harbor and leaving behind him the wails of his harem.

The departure would have gone much more smoothly and quickly had it not been for the loading of more than 100 sheep and goats, which were vigorously resisted by the ship's captain who argued his point with a copy of the U.S. Navy's livestock regulations in hand. Since a proper Muslim must eat only freshly-slaughtered meat, things were at an impasse until the president's liaison, one Col. Eddy, suggested a compromise. Seven animals were permitted to board. At the moment the compromise was reached, the negotiators looked up and saw, to their amazement (especially that of the American side), that the King's retainers had wasted no time and were slaughtering and skinning a goat on the fantail of the destroyer as it prepared to steam away from Jeddah into the Red Sea.

The other issue delaying the departure was a dispute over the number of Saudis allowed on board. Ibn Saud never travelled anywhere without hundreds of servants and retainers, and this trip was no exception. Fortunately for future relations between the richest oil reserve on the planet and the hungriest oil-consuming nation, another compromise limited to 48 the number of Saudis who could sail with the King. The man who once boasted that he had never slept one night of his adult life alone without a woman by his side now had to leave his whole harem in Jeddah.

The lack of cabin space for all of these desert warriors was not a problem. They enthusiastically made do with gun turrets in which they brewed coffee and either slept open on deck or in pitched tents. Ibn Saud, in fact, quickly abandoned the captain's cabin in order to join his entourage, and slept on rugs underneath a canvas stretched taut across the fo'c'sle.

While the ship sailed, the King faced Mecca five times a day and prayed.

Only one incident marred the voyage. Ibn Saud's sons and other members of the Saudi party saw their first-ever films, part of the ship's store of such entertainments. The viewing began tamely enough with a documentary about American sea power during the war in the Pacific. However, the American sailors soon brought out more interesting material depicting various young Hollywood starlets cavorting in intriguing garb (or no garb at all!). The Wahabi fundamentalist King never discovered the precise nature of what his sons were watching.

The Meeting

However, all of these cultural clashes were peanuts compared to what lay ahead at the Great Bitter Lake. On February 14, Franklin D. Roosevelt set eyes on Abdul Aziz Ibn Saud for the first time on board the USS *Quincy*. It must have been quite a sight, the tall son of the desert with the intense, charismatic eyes, his long robes billowing in the sea breeze.

FDR was Ibn Saud's first meeting with an infidel head of state. Unfortunately, we have no record of his impressions of the American president.

The President wasted no time bringing up the most controversial issue on the two nations' platters: the Palestine problem. Roosevelt criticized British handling of the situation, and he hinted that, at the same time, he was coming under severe pressure from the Jewish lobby back home.

Roosevelt described in detail the sufferings of the Jews of Europe at the hands of Hitler and the Nazis, in an effort to get the King to understand the U.S. position on the issue of a Jewish homeland. Then he asked the King if he had any suggestions. This most opinionated of twentieth century leaders jumped in with both feet:

"Give them and their descendants the choicest lands and homes of the Germans who oppressed them."

It was a startling and eminently logical response, and one that threw the President totally off his guard, accustomed as he was to the usual diplomatic doublespeak of Yalta, Teheran, and 12 years of daily dealings with politicians, bureaucrats, sycophants, and foreign representatives. But Franklin Roosevelt was nothing if not quick on his feet (figuratively, anyway). He explained that the Jews had an understandable aversion to remaining in Germany, as well as a palpable fear of their oppressors, and had in addition a 2,000-year old unrequited urge to return to their ancient homelands in the Middle East.

Ibn Saud pressed the point about a German homeland for the Jews, much to Roosevelt's discomfort, which was heightened by the failure of his legendary charm to work its usual magic on his counterpart. Roosevelt tried another angle: the equally legendary hospitality of the Arabs.

Ibn Saud ignored this plea and asked pointedly why Roosevelt was eager to save Germany from the consequences of its transgressions. Nevertheless, the King presented an alternative suggestion, one based on the traditional custom of the Bedouin to allocate the survivors and victims of war among the victorious tribes. Why not do the same with the Jews, and distribute them among the wartime allies?

Roosevelt realized he was being backed into a corner, so he did what politicians perfect to a high art form early in their careers: he changed the subject. The rest of the 5-hour meeting was rather general, but cemented the extraordinary relationship between Saudi Arabia and the United States that has endured for 70 years and made both nations immensely wealthy.

Ibn Saud did wring a major concession from the president: FDR promised that he would not assist the Jews against the Arabs and would make no move hostile to the Arab people. Perhaps it was this remarkable statement that cemented the Saudi-American alliance, doubtless one of the most important ones to which the U.S. has been a party in the second half of the twentieth century and beyond.

In addition, Roosevelt lavished his guest with grandiose gifts, including a wheelchair and a DC-3 airplane.

Roosevelt was not being frivolous with his concessions. On April 5th, he penned a letter to Ibn Saud memorializing his oral commitments. Ibn Saud was so impressed he could not stop talking to his courtiers and subjects about his warm relationship to the president.

A week later the president was dead. His successor chose to ignore FDR's commitments to Ibn Saud. Instead, President Truman became the rock upon which the State of Israel was built. Amazingly (and fortunately for the United States), the impression that the former president made on the king was so positive that it outweighed, and to a great extent, outlasted Truman's policy reversal. Saudi Arabia continued to pour its oil down the insatiable gullet of its Western ally at the same time that the U.S. was unabashed in its support of and largesse to the beleaguered Jewish state. It was as if the Saudis had no intention of being bound by any linkage between the issues of Israel and oil. If they had, the world and the place of the United States in it would have been very different.

Aftermath

Three days after meeting FDR, Ibn Saud met his second Western infidel chief, the irrepressible Winston Churchill. Despite Roosevelt's glowing endorsement of his wartime ally and friend, Ibn Saud took an immediate dislike to the British prime minister. One reason was Churchill's overt insensitivity to the Muslim proscription on alcohol and tobacco. The prime minister not only smoked and drank while at table with the Arab chieftain, but rubbed it in unapologetically. Moreover, due to his vast comprehension of the nuances of Middle Eastern politics and culture, he was considerably less naive and thus far less forthcoming than Roosevelt when it came to respecting and catering to Ibn Saud's point of view on the Jewish problem.

To top it off, Churchill gave the king a grand total of $100 worth of perfumes! The contrast, in Ibn Saud's eyes, between Roosevelt and Churchill could not have been more profound.

FDR was prolific by American standards, fathering five children. Ibn Saud, however, left him in the dust, leaving 34 sons and countless daughters. During his encounter with the American president, he shocked Roosevelt, who was no prude, by claiming that he had slept with a different woman every night of his adult life! His last son was born in 1947, two years after the meeting on the *Quincy*, when Ibn Saud was officially at least 60 and probably actually pushing 80.

They could not have led more different lives, these two powerful men. FDR "warriored" at a distance, commanding armies of millions of soldiers, and often had to give orders for men to march to certain death. Ibn Saud, by his own hand, killed hundreds of his enemies. Roosevelt was born to rule a nation already great and expansive. Ibn Saud created his nation, literally out of nothing.

No one could have predicted that these supremely different individuals, representing cultures utterly incomprehensible to one another, would hit it off so wonderfully well and that their personal attraction for each other would result in an oil hegemony for the remainder of the twentieth century and beyond.

There is no doubt World War II made the next 50 years the American Century. There is also no doubt that it could not have been achieved without the beneficence of the nation that was constructed out of sand, literally, by Abdul Aziz Ibn Saud.

First impressions count.

Nikita Khruschev and John F. Kennedy

For our final encounter, we return to Austria for the third and last time. Instead of musical and mystical encounters, however, the next appointment with history, between the two most powerful men in the world, was ultimately about survival. Not merely survival of a country. Rather, survival of mankind and of life on Earth.

Going into the meeting, no one knew exactly what was at stake. Coming out of it, however, the collision course was fixed and both protagonists proceeded down the road to the edge of the cliff and almost over it into an abyss that could have signified the end of the world.

Chapter 10 – Vienna II

Kennedy and Khrushchev Miscalculate

The only summit meeting that can succeed is the one that does not take place.

Sen. Barry Goldwater

Picture this scenario:

Newly-elected playboy president, bankrolled and pushed by outrageously ambitious, robber-baron daddy meets shrewd, rough-hewn peasant who just survived thirty years of indiscriminate terror and war, often going to work not knowing if he would live through the night, surviving only because of his incredibly nimble wits, and who has spent the last seven years consolidating his power over all of the other survivors of the daily Darwinian circus that was Josef Stalin's inner circle. These two opposites and opponents are about to engage in the highest-stakes poker game in history.

Compounding the obvious disparities between the players, the president is befogged by powerful drugs designed to mask excruciating back pain as well as a life-threatening illness, attended and ministered to by a notorious quack physician.

Now add the following high-risk miscalculation: the shrewd peasant leader grossly underestimates his opponent, who is hardly able to function, let alone bargain for the fate of the world, so doped up and intimidated is he.

Three horrific consequences result:

1. The Iron Curtain, until now a psychological barrier, becomes an actual one, imprisoning tens of millions of Eastern Europeans.
2. The world comes within a hair-trigger of ending.
3. The delusion of victory on the part of the American president's team that results from the crisis spawned by the Soviet leader's miscalculation inflates their hubris to such an extent that they foolishly believe they are invincible and thus blunder into a disastrous, unwinnable war which tears their country apart and opens wounds that do not heal for more than a generation.

Background

The Cuban Missile Crisis (the Russians call it "The Caribbean Crisis") was an object lesson in how *not* to manage the world. While both contemporary commenters and historians give President John F. Kennedy a great deal of credit for pulling the planet back from the brink of destruction, there has been far too little analysis of the run-up to the crisis and Kennedy's role in creating the circumstances for Nikita Khrushchev's gross miscalculation that put offensive nuclear missiles 90 miles from the U.S. mainland. Neither has there been adequate discussion of the role of the two world leaders' fateful summit meeting the year before in Vienna in bringing about the first and third consequences.

The story of the Missile Crisis and what led up to it should be required reading for any presidential aspirant and his or her advisors. Prior to being permitted to throw their hats in the ring, they should be subject to a rigorous examination about the event. If they cannot pass it, *they* should be history.

Five decades have passed since the day the world went to the edge of the precipice, looked over the edge and, although tempted to jump, blinked and stepped back. The intervening time period has revealed much about the crisis and its management that should shock the daylights out of any rational person. Thanks to the declassification of much material on the American side and the collapse of the Soviet Union and subsequent opening of archives by its Russian successors, we now can sift through revelations that are almost biblical in scope and implication. At least if your focus is the Book of Revelation.

The Setting

The single most dangerous event of the second half of the twentieth century originated a year earlier in the more refined and *gemütlich* setting of Schönbrunn Palace in the capital of Central European culture, the home of Mozart and Beethoven, of Strauss waltzes, of *Sachertorte* and *Lippizaner* stallions, of Habsburg decadence and modern psychiatry, and generally of people who really knew (and still know) how to *live*: Vienna.

Vienna was selected as the site for the momentous summit between Nikita Sergeyevich Khrushchev, General Secretary of the Presidium of the Central Committee of the Communist Party of the Union of Soviet Socialist Republics and Premier of the Soviet Union, and John Fitzgerald Kennedy, recently elected President of the United States (evidence of the reason Russians and Americans will never understand each other is manifest in the job titles we give our leaders: in Russia the length of the job title is directly proportional to the power inherent in the position; in America, it is just the opposite.). Since pre-Roman times, it has been the meeting ground between East and West, the place where the Asiatic hordes and supposedly civilized Europeans invariably collided and clashed.

The Romans established the garrison of *Vindobona* on the Danubian frontier 2,000 years ago because it was the fulcrum of one of the great East-West trade routes of ancient times. From Vindobona they could keep an eye on the brooding Slavic and Hunnish barbarians who smoldered in the dark forests and fog-encrusted mountains of the mysterious borderlands of Central Europe and points east (as well as in the imagination). The *Watch on the Rhine* extended east and was paralleled by the Watch on the Danube.

The Asiatic tidal waves of Alaric, Attila and the Mongol hordes consumed the European consciousness when they suddenly exploded out of the mists of the Hungarian plain and overwhelmed Vindobona. In more recent times, the furthest Western advance of the Ottoman Empire ran out of steam at the gates of Vienna, thanks to the heroism of Prince Eugene of Savoy and his troops massed on the *Kahlenberg* redoubt, overlooking the city and the Danube plain stretching east to Hungary.

A century-and-a-half later, the great Congress of Vienna conjoined East and West in settling the map of Europe for five decades, according the continent a half-century of relative peace. And almost exactly 100 years after Prince Metternich convened his Congress, another Austrian, the aged and lonely Kaiser Franz Josef, virtually imprisoned in his Vienna palaces, agonized over terrible events several hundred miles to the south in the roiling Balkans, and made a fateful decision that engulfed both East and West in "The War to End All Wars."

Not long before the Kaiser's fateful ultimatum to Serbia in July, 1914, a young social misfit and failed architecture student from the Austrian provinces seethed in the back alleys of Vienna, shunned by all, with only his deepening rage for solace. Adolf Hitler's war, a quarter century on, would make the Great War look not so great in comparison.

After this second global conflagration in only twenty years, Vienna was split between the great Eastern power—the Soviet Union—and its wartime Western allies. The city weathered the schism for ten years until both sides, recognizing the historical utility of a neutral meeting ground and spy shop, pulled their troops out of town. Even today, Vienna maintains its status as a meeting ground for East and West, headquartering two of the more important organizations that mediate East-West conflicts that, from time-to-time threaten to erupt into hostilities of global import—the International Atomic Energy Agency and the Organization of Petroleum Exporting Countries (OPEC).

The Peasant

Nikita Khrushchev was a shrewd, earthy, stocky son of the soil from a small farming village in the Ukraine. He rose from something worse than abject poverty to command enough firepower to annihilate all of civilization. Along with his counterpart, John Fitzgerald Kennedy, he came closer than any man in history to actually achieving that frightful possibility.

By the time Khrushchev arrived in Vienna for his summit meeting with Kennedy, he had been on something of a roll for four years, ever since the first week of October, 1957 when a tiny, 28-lb. sphere with a few antennae and a cute beeper signal called *Sputnik* was hurled into the first-ever artificial Earth orbit by a Soviet intercontinental ballistic missile from the *Baikonur* launch site in Kazakhstan.

It is difficult over 50 years later to describe the overwhelming impact *Sputnik* had on the American psyche. My family used to watch the evening news every night while we ate dinner, and the report this particular evening was one of the more electrifying any of us had ever experienced. I was so overwhelmed that I could not finish dinner. Viscerally, I could sense that the world I thought was so predictable and which I believed I knew so well had changed forever. (There would be many such defining moments in the rush of the next several years, but more on that later.)

I dropped everything and picked up the phone to call my best friend, the only other kid I knew who was remotely interested in world affairs. We spent the next few hours mulling over the implications of the launch for America and for ourselves. Our conversation kept returning to civil defense, and we debated what one would want in a fall-out shelter and how much to stock. We both decided to save up for pairs of high-power binoculars in order to enhance our civil air defense capabilities, patriots that we were.

If my friend and I suffered a crisis of confidence, it was as nothing compared to our country and its leaders. "End-of-civilization-as-we-know-it" language was rampant in the halls of Congress and in the Executive Branch. Blame was posited everywhere, and a sense of "second-rateness" pervaded the body politic. That, combined with the desperation among the military services' respective space programs, caused a national panic reaction.

By the beginning of the next school year, thirty of us were in special, accelerated science programs designed to play catch-up with the Russians. It was tremendously exciting. We felt that we were the vanguard of a new generation of Americans who would one day go forth to reclaim the mountaintop so suddenly wrested away by the Soviet space achievement.

On top of that, I became an annoying, pesky family advocate of building a bomb shelter, convinced that such an extreme measure was the only way out of the nuclear terror under which we all lived in those days, especially those of us at the most impressionable ages. I nagged my parents incessantly about excavating in the backyard, buying canned goods, and all the other appurtenances that would guarantee our survival when the Russians decided to rain a couple of ICBMs down on our rural, remote, upstate New York heads.

I discovered years later when, through my Army job I became privy to a lot of information about both our and the Soviet nuclear programs, that I was not far off-base in worrying about my tiny little community. We were only 20 miles west of Seneca Army Depot, where the U.S. at one time stored several thousand nuclear warheads, and only 25 miles east of Rochester, where the presence of Kodak, Xerox, Bausch and Lomb, and Stromberg Carlson, among others, made it a rather juicy target. An attack on either one would have left my little burg an incinerated memory.

Little did any of us realize at the time that the Russians had next to no delivery system for any hydrogen or atomic weapons they may have cobbled together with the secrets they stole from us. Remember the "Missile Gap," the fictional imbalance that many historians credit with boosting John F. Kennedy to victory in the 1960 presidential race (along with Richard Nixon's five o'clock shadow, Chicago Mayor Daley's frequent Democratic voters in Cook County, and Lyndon

Johnson's dead Mexican ballot casters)? Well, at the time of the presidential campaign, the Soviet Union, we now know, probably had all of *four* ballistic missiles capable of reaching the United States. When Jack Kennedy took office on a bitterly cold, wintry day in January, 1961, the actual missile gap was so much in favor of the U.S. that our advantage stood at more than 100 to 1!

In 1960, Khrushchev gained even more political capital when a Soviet surface-to-air missile (SAM) shot down an American U-2 spy plane 80,000 feet over Soviet airspace. President Eisenhower's inept handling of the incident made matters worse, and the wily peasant on the other side more than made the most of America's bungling and bumbling. The display of weakness by the American side, and the self-serving assertions of the Central Intelligence Agency's absurd overestimates of Soviet power and ability to project that power, painted the Republicans into a corner from which it would take a long time to extricate themselves.

Nikita Khrushchev was the best booster the Democrats had, and he himself, buoyed by the confidence he had gained as a result of the U-2 downing, even took credit for Kennedy's razor-thin victory in the 1960 election when he dictated his memoirs. The Kennedy victory, Khrushchev believed, put the Americans exactly where he wanted them.

Khrushchev was a "wild hair," unpredictable, crude, and given to bizarre (but probably calculated) outbursts, sometimes in public. Witness, for example, his 1960 performance at the United Nations when he took off his shoe and pounded it on the desk during a debate. Or his comment after the Vienna summit, when he boasted to colleagues: "Berlin is the balls of the West, and every time I squeeze them, they cry out!"

I don't know if CIA psychologists agree, but I suspect that this bluster and bravado was the result of a career spent cowering in fearful silence while at Stalin's side. Once Khrushchev got his chance to be himself, all those years of repression and sycophancy peeled away and the wily peasant-survivor was transformed from anonymous caterpillar to something of an overweight butterfly on the world stage.

The Patrician

John F. Kennedy was one of the least prepared human beings ever to serve as President of the United States (at least up to 2016). His working life consisted of World War II service and 14 years in Congress during which virtually all he accomplished was to position himself to run for president.

Despite my youth, I was very aware politically. I followed campaign developments obsessively. And I was absolutely smitten—nay, enamored—of John F. Kennedy. He made my pulse race with excitement. I put him right up there with Mickey Mantle and Jim Brown, my other two heroes of the day who could do no wrong.

As you read this chapter, you will find that I have altered my youthful, idealized opinion of President Kennedy. Today, I think he may have been the most reckless, dangerous, and unethical person ever to serve in that distinguished position (again at least up to 2016). When I say unethical, I am not referring to his obsession with adultery. That was his own business, enabled by his Secret Service handlers and cronies in the media who, on occasion, pimped for him.

What I mean by unethical is worse. He had no compunctions whatever about using the vast and intimidating machinery of government—and even of the mafia—for his own ends, whether it meant attempted assassinations of foreign leaders such as Fidel Castro, Rafael Trujillo, or Ngo Dinh Diem, or pulling the tax records of political opponents in order to harass them into doing his will. You may recall that Richard Nixon, Kennedy's 1960 opponent for the presidency and successor-once-removed, was quite rightly hounded out of office for stuff like this.

Kennedy got off to a rocky start, to put it mildly. The fiasco, nay, the patent absurdity, of the Bay of Pigs adventure boggles the mind to this day. How anyone with a modicum of common sense could possibly be gulled into believing that a handful of ill-trained Cuban exiles could land on the island and overthrow the third most powerful military force in the hemisphere is beyond comprehension. The fact that the President of the United States, the Director of Central Intelligence, and the Secretary of Defense either actually bought into that hokum or were too weak of character to question it speaks volumes about what was wrong with America in the 1960s. It should also have been grounds for impeachment or resignation, at the least. But that is another story. American presidents are quite willing to go on national television and spout meaningless phrases about "taking full responsibility" when something goes wrong, but unlike many of their foreign counterparts, they never fall on their swords, which would be too much like real accountability.

In any event, the sorry rag-tag Bay of Pigs invasion force, such as it was, was annihilated on the beach and the United States looked woefully inept. The nation was completely shamed on the world stage—a hell of a way to begin a presidency.

After 100 days in office, John F. Kennedy looked like what he had rightly been accused of being, a pampered rich boy totally out of his element; the picture of ineptitude and inexperience. Unfortunately, he saw the same reflection when he looked in the mirror and decided he had to do something about it.

This was Kennedy at his most dangerous and reckless. He needed to hit a home run in order to turn things around. Desperately.

To do that, he chose to meet with his powerful counterpart, Nikita Khrushchev, at the summit in Vienna.

Kennedy and Khrushchev had actually met once before, when the Russian visited the United States in the late 1950s and made a visit to Capitol Hill before setting out for Iowa and Roswell Garst's farm. Kennedy was a young and exceedingly undistinguished Senator, and the two shook hands and smiled at each other. That was all.

It is not an exaggeration to assert that the Vienna Summit set the scene for that gut-wrenching, painful decade, the Sixties. The assessments that the leaders of the only two superpowers on the planet made of each other, based on their interchange, influenced events not only during the next several years, but also far beyond their few remaining years at the apex of world power. In many respects, we are still experiencing the "fallout" of that encounter.

To wit, America's five-decade obsession with a piddling, penny-ante, third-rate island to our south—Cuba—is a direct result of the Vienna Summit and the terrifying and terrible events that derived therefrom and pushed the world to the brink of destruction. Similarly, the disaster of Vietnam directly resulted from the two leaders' assessment of each other and their actions and reactions in Berlin, Laos, and other hot spots. Every American president since JFK has felt, in one way or another, the sting of Vietnam and the constraints imposed on American policy as a consequence.

JFK was severely ill for most of his short life. He was in terrible physical pain in the early months of his presidency, even more pain than this extremely sick and sickly man was accustomed to, and he was accustomed to more than his fair share, to be sure. A litany of his ailments and his clandestine medical history, revealed only after his death, is instructive when put into the proper political context:

Addison's Disease. This was a cruel fate when, as a child, John F. Kennedy was diagnosed with it in the 1920s. Addison's Disease is a failure of the adrenal glands and, until quite recently, was often terminal.

As a candidate for president, Kennedy blatantly lied about having the disease when confronted by reporters. His doctors backed him up. The campaign was such an overwhelming strain on him that, when it was over, it was a month before he was even able to think coherently.

Massive cortisone injections, cortisone pills, and cortisone implants in the thighs were the only way to control the disease. This may have been a classic case of the treatment being almost as bad as the illness.

Both the Addison's Disease and its treatment wreaked havoc with Kennedy's immune system, rendering him all the more vulnerable to other ailments, many of which, such as fevers spiking to an unbelievable 106 degrees, were a constant in his life.

Three other interesting facts about this disease:

1. Addisonians often develop thick shocks of brown hair, which enhances their physical appearance.
2. Addisonians often take on a ruddy complexion, which contributes to the same.
3. The treatment regimen often causes elevated levels of testosterone, which in turn makes male Addisonians more interested in sex then the average Joe.

The Bad Back. Anyone who suffers from chronic back pain caused by degenerative discs can attest to the intense pain and immobility afflicting the sufferer. Contrary to the family mythology and the furtherance of the same by sycophants like Arthur Schlesinger and Theodore Sorenson, Kennedy's back trouble began long before his PT-109 days.

In private, he used crutches and canes to get around, this man who was falsely portrayed as brimming with "vigor."

His back doctor, Janet Travell, yet another in the long line of White House physicians who lied to the public who paid their salaries about presidential disability, putting the good of the politician far above the good of her country, was injecting Kennedy with novocaine concoctions sometimes as frequently as six times per day, according to Richard Reeves, a Kennedy biographer. Naturally, as is the case with such drugs, they lose their effect quickly as patient tolerance builds, and the dosage levels skyrocket accordingly, never a positive development.

In 1954, Kennedy had spinal fusion surgery in New York Hospital in an attempt to alleviate the pain. It was not successful and might have left him worse off then before.

Venereal Disease. It is hardly a surprise that Kennedy suffered from persistent VD, given his lifestyle. Newsworthy would have been a clean bill of health on this score. As we have learned since, thanks to HIV and the AIDS epidemic, a lifestyle marked by prolific licentiousness likely reduces the ability of the immune system to fend off disease. An already severely disabled individual was further weakened.

The Bad Stomach. Kennedy's stomach was so sensitive that his diet had to be kept purposely bland. State dinners were absolute hell for him. He spent a good portion of his time wracked by stomach aches and related gastrointestinal difficulties.

Allergies. These were so bad that they often debilitated him completely, causing him to take to bed for days at a time.

Deafness. The President was partially deaf in his right ear, probably the result of firing weapons in the Navy without using earplugs. Sometimes, in an attempt to hide his hearing loss, he would answer questions that he misunderstood, not answer them at all, or disrupt conversations to mask his inability to follow. Thus was policy made.

In addition to so-called legitimate doctors (although anyone who studies Dr. Travell's treatment regimens categorizes her in this group advisedly), Kennedy was most partial to quacks, understandable for a man suffering constant pain and daily debilitation. The chief quack was a New York eccentric, one Dr. Max Jacobson, who prescribed methamphetamine-based injection "cocktails" in order to give the president the delusion of a "high." Jacobson treated the President several times a week on occasion, and accompanied him to the Vienna Summit where he did some of his "magic"—and damage—immediately before Kennedy's initial meeting with Khrushchev.

Dr. Jacobson had been recommended to Kennedy by a host of his celebrity patients to whom he also provided similar cocktails. They swore to the president about the magical effects of Jacobson's concoctions. Jacobson's patient records included the following *selected prominenti*: Alan Jay Lerner, Anais Nin, Andy Warhol, Andy Williams, Anthony Quinn, Billy Wilder, Bob Cummings, Bob Fosse, Burgess Meredith, Cary Grant, Cecil B. DeMille, Eddie Fisher, Elizabeth Taylor, Elvis Presley, The Everly Brothers, Frank Sinatra, Gypsy Rose Lee, Howard Cosell, Igor Stravinsky, Ingrid Bergman, Jerry Lewis,

Johnny Mathis, Judy Garland, Lee Radziwill, Leonard Bernstein, Louis Nizer, Marilyn Monroe, Marlene Dietrich, Mickey Mantle, Nelson Rockefeller, Otto Preminger, Paul Robeson, Peter Lawford, Peter Lorre, Rex Harrison, Richard Burton, Rita Moreno, Rosemary Clooney, Roy Cohn, Sharon Tate, Tennessee Williams, Tony Curtis, Truman Capote, Van Cliburn, Yul Brynner, and Zero Mostel. There were many others. JFK either knew, was friends with, or related to a large number of Jacobson's patients, any of whom could have made the recommendation.

According to Richard Reeves and other chroniclers, the side effects of Jacobson's treatment were very dangerous: a heightened sense of power and dazzling capabilities; paranoid schizophrenia; confusion; and eventually death by poisoning.

Consequently, as the Vienna summit approached, the U.S. side was represented by a man who was virtually an invalid, in constant excruciating pain, and so doped up and near-psychotic that he was in no condition to perform the role for which he had been elected; representing his nation at the highest levels, not to mention at one of the most sensitive times in its history. Any condemnation of Roosevelt's conduct at Yalta when, terribly sick and within eight weeks of his death from a cerebral hemorrhage, he, Churchill and Stalin divided up the postwar map of Europe, needs to be considered from the perspective of the Vienna Summit 16 years later.

When Kennedy finally met Khrushchev, *mano-a-mano*, he was probably unable "to preserve, protect, and defend the Constitution of the United States." It is no exaggeration to say that we are lucky to be alive today to write and read this account.

The Meeting

JFK wanted Vienna not only as a way out of the Bay of Pigs (and Laotian) morass into which he had sunk. He also wanted to make sure Nikita Khrushchev understood that the US was committed to its role in the world, resolved to contain Communist expansion, and that he—John Fitzgerald

Kennedy—was the manifestation of such American determination. In short, he wanted to draw a line in the sand and make sure that Khrushchev recognized it and took it seriously.

Worthy thoughts. But pain, drugs, and their attendant fatigue can overwhelm even the most noble of geopolitical ideals.

Moreover, instead of a total focus by the American side on the concern that Khrushchev would underestimate Kennedy, there should have been some concern that Kennedy might underestimate Khrushchev. There was none. In fact, Kennedy and his "handlers" assumed that this would be a repeat of the famous Kennedy-Nixon debates of the previous year, when the younger, more telegenic candidate triumphed and easily at that, at least among the visually inclined (Americans who listened to the first debate on the radio were certain that Nixon had won).

Only minutes before the initial confrontation with the mortal enemy of the United States and the capitalist system, Kennedy called in Dr. Jacobson and received a megadose injection of his by-now customary and highly addicting methamphetamine cocktail.

At 12:45 p.m. Central European time on June 3, 1961, the *Chaika* limousine transporting Nikita Khrushchev pulled up in front of the residence of the U.S. Ambassador to Austria for their first of two meetings (the second one was at the Habsburg Palace of *Schönbrun*). Kennedy, sky high on methamphetamines and the other substances in Jacobson's cocktail, bounced out of the front door and bounded down the steps as Khrushchev emerged from the car.

The Soviet leader maintained his stolid expression in the face of the president's exuberant greeting. He was preoccupied with putting JFK "in his place," as he confided to his advisor Fedor Burlatsky. His objective was to wring concessions concerning Berlin out of his young rival.

The stenographic record of the two-day meeting shows that an inordinate amount of time was spent discussing ideological matters, an area in which a lifelong Marxist used to arguing about obscurantist claptrap and humbug was sure to prevail against the lightly liberal-arts-educated Harvard man. Charles Bohlen says that Kennedy damaged himself by permitting the dialogue to sink into ideological discussions of Marxism and colonialism and that, shaken, Kennedy left Vienna in "a high state of alarm."

Khrushchev put on his customary act, from time to time going off the rails, stomping and pounding on furniture in order to intimidate the drugged president. He wanted diplomatic recognition of East Germany in order to legitimize and make permanent the division of the country, and he wanted the Western powers out of Berlin. He was so confident that he even threatened the meek-seeming president with war. According to Burlatsky, Khrushchev came away from Vienna saying that JFK was "too refined," Politburo-speak for being a wimp, a tongue-tied lightweight not capable of making firm decisions in crisis situations. It is reported that he told his aides that Kennedy was so intimidated by him that he sat in front of him, mute, unable to respond. From what we know, that was accurate, but not because JFK was terrified by Khrushchev; rather, because he was narcoleptic and unable to focus due to the illegal drugs coursing through his system. When he should have been acutely alert, he was in a vegetative state.

Kennedy's inability to concentrate and articulate caused Khrushchev to make a serious miscalculation. The drugged, almost somnambulistic Kennedy was not the real Kennedy in a crisis. The Vienna summit is deemed by most scholars to have been a "disaster" for JFK and the United States. It was, for three reasons:

1. Emboldened by Kennedy's lackluster performance at the summit, Khrushchev naturally underestimated his adversary and went home to Politburo acclaim. Several months later, he ordered the Soviet Union's East German puppets to construct what became known as the Berlin Wall, a 155 kilometer concrete barrier surrounding West Berlin, designed to halt the flood of East Germans seeking to escape the

Communist bloc. In the 16 years between the end of World War II and the construction of the wall, 3.5 million East Germans had voted with their feet and left the Socialist paradise for life in the West. In the almost 30 years thereafter, until the wall was torn down in 1990, only 5,000 managed to escape. At least 300 East Germans died trying. The West's leaden response confirmed Khrushchev's conclusion reached at Vienna that Kennedy was a weak leader totally out of his element.

2. The Wall's success further inspired Khrushchev to test Kennedy's mettle, this time in a much riskier and orders of magnitude more dangerous endeavor—placing offensive, nuclear-armed missiles in Cuba and pointing them at the United States. Over the 13 days between the discovery of the missiles by American U-2 spy plane overflights of Cuba and the resolution of the crisis, thanks in large part to Kennedy's brilliant measured response to the crisis, the world was poised on the brink of annihilation. Both the U.S. and Soviet armed forces went on high alert. The U.S. military declared Defense Condition (DefCon) 2, one small step from imminent nuclear war. Khrushchev had badly miscalculated, again based on his assessment of Kennedy in Vienna 18 months earlier. This time, it was the Soviet leader who had to eat crow. At the time, the prevailing opinion was that Khrushchev blinked first. It was revealed much later that Kennedy had traded removal of our offensive missiles from Turkey on the U.S.S.R.'s southern border in return for removal of the Cuban missiles.

3. Now, infused with hubris as a result of his "victory" over Khrushchev, Kennedy blundered into what would become the quagmire of Vietnam, a military, political, and economic

disaster of epic proportions for the U.S. and major implications for the future of American military involvement on foreign soil, ones that are still influencing U.S. foreign and military policy to this day.

On a personal level, the Vienna summit was ultimately even more of a disaster for Nikita Khrushchev. The Cuban Missile Crisis was the first step in his undoing. From late 1962 until he was deposed in 1964, Khrushchev's political career was on a downhill slide.

Two conclusions emerge from the Vienna debacle:

1. The American public needs full disclosure of its presidential candidates' medical histories and current condition before they occupy the White House.
2. It is the height of irresponsibility for a president to put him/herself in a position to make decisions when *non compos mentis*. Absent Kennedy's drug-impaired performance at Vienna, there might not have been a Berlin Wall, could never have been a Cuban Missile Crisis pushing the world to the brink of extinction, and perhaps even no American intervention in Vietnam.

President Kennedy became addicted to Jacobson's magic potions for the rest of his short life. The American people and the rest of humanity deserved better than this.

****

This last encounter made for sweaty palms. While writing about these appointments with history has been enormously entertaining, this last one was not all that much fun to write. It certainly was no fun to have lived through those thirteen days in October, 1962 that changed the world. I was a high school student just returning home from an evening French Club meeting at school. My mom and dad had the TV on and, as I walked into the house, President Kennedy was just beginning to talk to the American people from the Oval Office. What he had to say was bone-chilling. I was convinced that the end of the world was imminent.

Epilogue

I don't like to write conclusions to my books. For one thing, I hate for them to end, particularly this one, because I so enjoyed researching and writing it. For another, I never quite know what to say, or even why a conclusion is necessary. I much prefer that readers draw their own conclusions.

Despite these reservations, this book seems to demand some kind of closure. Perhaps that is because the last great encounter, between the first two individuals in the history of the world to have the power to obliterate humanity, is one hell of a somber way to end a book.

For all the miscommunication and miscalculation that came out of the Vienna Summit, making it also the most dangerous encounter in history, I hope there is at least a little bit of a counterbalance in this book. Maybe Marathon provides that. Or Theodora's epiphany with Timothy. Or the afternoon in Vienna when the two greatest musical geniuses of all time met briefly, leaving us with an intense feeling of "what might have been."

History is not only about people. For me it has also been very much about place. The people are evanescent. They die and are gone. The places where they encountered one another are still here, open to the fortunate among us who can afford to make the journey.

The places where the encounters documented in this book occurred are magical ones. Some are special because they are beautiful or profoundly inspiring. All are magical because of what happened there. It is what the extraordinary human beings who passed though these places accomplished that makes them that way. I have not been to all of them. But the ones I have visited set my pulse racing and my emotions raging.

I have seen the shores of Lake Trasimene, the dense olive groves on the hillside leading down to the lake where Hannibal's ambush army lay in wait for Rome's legions, the morning mist lying low along the shoreline that hid the bloody onslaught about to abruptly end the lives, hopes, and dreams of 20,000 young Romans, the placid waters that once turned red with their blood. The passage of two millennia did nothing to temper my sadness as I looked down at the lake.

I have walked the narrow, hilly cobblestone streets of Assisi, gaped in awe at the basilica only a few weeks before the earthquake that destroyed many of its priceless frescoes, and walked the paths traipsed by the sandaled, sackclothed St. Francis atop Mount Subiaco, where the mystery of an alien faith gripped even a non-believer like me.

I have been to Rome and felt a tug at the crumbled ruins of secular empire and the gross ostentation of religious excess. The Rome of Scipio is gone. The Rome of Innocent III is going strong.

I have been to Lisbon, albeit briefly at the airport, where my strongest images were of the total dependence of this narrow country on the sea, and of machine-gun toting guards staving off modernity during the dying days of the Portuguese dictatorship.

I have been in the Bahamas, tantalizingly close to Columbus' landfall, the precise location of which is in hot dispute. I have gazed out over the reefs at the azure ocean and tried to imagine what it must have been like for the indigenous people to have seen the sails of the caravel *Santa Maria* and two naos, *Nina* and *Pinta,* inching up over the horizon.

I have been to Vienna, Salzburg, and Bonn and have explored the houses of Mozart and Beethoven, trying to imagine the sublime noises created therein and that cling oh so quietly to the walls and furniture.

I have been to Braunau-am-Inn and have felt nothing but a heavy sadness and a heavier contempt.

Finally, when in Vienna, I went to the Schönbrunn Palace, the first time not in order to marvel at this gigantic structure and its spectacular gardens, but rather to stand in the room where Kennedy sat with Khrushchev during their second meeting at the Vienna Summit and played dice with the fate of the world.

In August 2010, I desperately wanted to visit Greece and walk the beach at Marathon, traipsing over the hallowed ground where the West beat back the East exactly 2,500 years before. I wanted to climb the burial mound where the 192 Athenians who died there still reside, to put my foot on the same terrain on which Philippides ran, and visualize Miltiades leading the charge that flummoxed Darius' army and shocked the world. But it was not to be. The anniversary ceremony was cancelled due to the Greek financial crisis.

Bibliography

Chapter 1: Marathon

Aeschylus. *Agamemnon*, in *Eleven Plays of the Greek Dramatists*. New York: Grosset & Dunlap, 1946.

Botsford, George Willis and Robinson, Jr., Charles. *Hellenic History*. New York: The MacMillan Company, 1956.

Cooper, Lane. *The Greek Genius and its Influence: Select Essays and Extracts*. Ithaca, NY: Cornell University Press, 1952.

Fornara, Charles W. *Herodotus: An Interpretive Essay*. Oxford: Clarendon Press, 1971.

Grant, Michael. *The Classical Greeks*. New York: Charles Scribner's Sons, 1989.

Hammond, N.G.L. A *History of Greece to 322 B.C., Third Edition*. Oxford, UK: Clarendon Press, 1986.

Herodotus. *History*. New York: Tudor Publishing Company, 1928.

Herodotus. *The Persian Wars*. New York: The Modern Library, 1942.

Lacey, Jim. *The First Clash: The Miraculous Greek Victory at Marathon and Its Impact on Western Civilization*. New York: Bantam Books, 2011.

Lloyd, Alan. *Marathon: The Story of Civilizations on a Collision Course*. New York: Random House, 1973.

Pantreath, Guy. *Hellenic Traveler: A Guide to the Ancient Sites of Greece*. New York: Crowell, 1964.

Parker, Godfrey, Ed., *The Cambridge Illustrated History of Warfare*. Cambridge, UK: Cambridge University Press, 1995.

Plutarch. *Lives*. London: F. Warne, 1883.

Smith, Morton. *The Ancient Greeks*. Ithaca, NY: Cornell University Press, 1965, 1970.

Stephenson, Michael. *The Last Full Measure: How Soldiers Die in Battle*. New York: Crown Publishers, 2012.

Chapter 2: Hannibal and Scipio

Charles-Picard, Gilbert. *Daily Life in Carthage at the Time of Hannibal*. New York: MacMillan, 1961.

Cappo, Robert S. *Hannibal's Lieutenant: A Unique Biography of Hannibal*. Alexandria, VA: Manor House Publishers, 1994.

Connolly, Peter. *The Roman Army*. London: MacDonald Educational; Morristown, NJ: Silver Burdett, 1975, 1979.

Cornell, Tim. *Atlas of the Roman World*. New York: Facts on File, 1982.

Cottrell, Leonard. *Hannibal: Enemy of Rome*. New York: Holt, Rinehart & Winston, 1961.

Dodge, Theodore A. *Hannibal*. New York: Da Capo Press, 1891, 1995.

Dudley, Donald R. *The Romans, 850 B.C.-A.D. 337*, in J.H. Plumb, Ed. *The History of Human Society*. New York: Alfred A. Knopf, 1970.

Grant, Michael. *The Army of the Caesars*. New York: Scribner, 1974.

Jacobs, William J. *Hannibal: An African Hero*. New York: McGraw-Hill, 1973.

Lamb, Harold. *Hannibal: One Man Against Rome*. Garden City, NY: Doubleday, 1958.

Levin, Bernard. *Hannibal's Footsteps*. New York: Crown Publishers, 1985.

Liddell Hart, B.H. *Strategy*. Washington: Praeger Publishers, 1954, 1972.

Livy (Titus Livius). *A History of Rome, Selections*. New York: The Modern Library, 1962.

Nardo, Don. *The Punic Wars*. San Diego: Lucent Books, 1996.

Parkinson, Roger. *The Legions of Rome*. London: Wayland, 1973.

Polybius. *The Histories*. Oxford, UK. Oxford University Press, 2010.

Proctor, Dennis. *Hannibal's March in History*. Oxford, UK: Clarendon Press, 1971.

Simkins, Michael. *Warriors of Rome: An Illustrated History of the Roman Legions*. London: Blandford, 1988.

Windrow, Martin. *The Roman Legionary*. London, New York: F. Watts, 1984.

Chapter 3: Theodora and Timothy

Ash, John. *A Byzantine Journey*. New York: Random House, 1995.

Bradshaw, Gillian. *The Bearkeeper's Daughter*. Boston: Houghton & Mifflin, 1987.

Bridge, Anthony. *Theodora: Portrait in a Byzantine Landscape*. Chicago: Academy Chicago Publishers, 1978, 1984.

Browning, Robert. *Justinian and Theodora*. London: Thames & Hudson, 1987.

Gibbon, Edward. *History of the Decline and Fall of the Roman Empire*. London: Claxton, 1880.

Lamb, Harold. *Constantinople: Birth of an Empire*. New York: Knopf, 1957.

Maclagan, Michael. *The City of Constantinople*. New York: Praeger, 1968.

Norwich, John J. *Byzantium: The Early Centuries*. New York: Knopf, 1989.

Ostrogorski, Georgije. *History of the Byzantine State*. New Brunswick, NJ: Rutgers University Press, 1957.

Procopius. *The Secret History*. London: Penguin Books, 1966.

Veyne, Paul, ed. *A History of Private Life from Pagan Rome to Byzantium*. Cambridge, MA and London: Harvard University Press, 1987.

Wace, Henry and William C. Piercy. *Dictionary of Christian Biography and Literature to the End of the Sixth Century A.D., with an Account of the Principal Sects and Heresies*. Peabody, MA: Hendrickson Publishers. 1999.

Chapter 4: Innocent III, Saint Francis, and Saint Dominic

Barraclough, Geoffrey. *The Medieval Papacy.* New York: Harcourt, Brace & World, Inc., 1988.

Bishop, Morris. *St. Francis of Assisi.* Boston, Toronto: Little, Brown & Company, 1974.

De Rosa, Peter. *Vicars of Christ: The Dark Side of the Papacy.* New York: Crown Publishers, Inc., 1988.

Erikson, Joan Mowat. *St. Francis and His Four Ladies.* New York: W.W. Norton & Company, Inc., 1970.

Gontard, Friedrich. *The Chair of Peter: A History of the Papacy.* New York: Holt, Rinehart & Winston, 1964.

Goudge, Elizabeth. *My God and My All: The Life of St. Francis of Assisi.* New York: Coward-McCann, Inc., 1959.

Murray, Wendy. *A Mended and Broken Heart: The Life and Love of Francis of Assisi.* New York: Basic Books, 2008

O'Brien, Isidore, O.F.M. *Mirror of Christ: Francis of Assisi.* Paterson, NJ: St. Anthony Guild Press, 1944.

Synan, Edward A. *The Popes and the Jews in the Middle Ages.* New York: The Macmillan Company; London: Collier-Macmillan Limited, 1965, 1967.

Vicaire, M.H., O.P. *St. Dominic and His Times.* New York, Toronto, London: McGraw-Hill Book Company, 1964.

Walsh, Michael J. *The Illustrated History of the Popes.* New York: St. Martin's Press, 1980.

Chapter 5: Dias, Columbus, and King John

Bradford, Ernle D.S. *A Wind from the North: The Life of Henry the Navigator.* New York: Harcourt, Brace, 1960.

Buehr, Walter. *The Portuguese Explorers.* New York: G.P. Putnam's Sons, 1966.

Chrisp, Peter. *The Search for the East.* New York: Thomson Learning, 1993.

Dos Passos, John. *The Portugal Story: Three Centuries of Exploration and Discovery.* Garden City, NY: Doubleday & Company, Inc., 1969.

Fernandez-Armesto, Felipe. *Columbus and the Conquest of the Impossible*. New York: Saturday Review Press, 1974.

Fisher, Leonard Everett. *Prince Henry The Navigator*. New York: Macmillan; London: Collier Macmillan, 1990.

Granzotto, Gianni. *Christopher Columbus: The Dream and the Obsession*. Garden City, NY: Doubleday & Company, Inc., 1985.

Hale, John R. *Age of Exploration*. New York: Time, Incorporated, 1966, 1970.

Hauben, H.H. *Christopher Columbus: The Tragedy of a Discoverer*. New York: E.P. Dutton & Co., Inc., 1936.

Jacobs, William Jay. *Prince Henry, The Navigator*. New York: F. Watts, 1973.

Morison, Samuel Eliot. *Admiral of the Ocean Sea: A Life of Christopher Columbus*. Boston: Little, Brown & Company, 1942.

Morison, Samuel Eliot. *Christopher Columbus, Mariner*. Boston: Little, Brown & Company, 1955.

Morison, Samuel Eliot. *Portuguese Voyages to America in the Fifteenth Century*. New York: Octagon Books, 1968.

Morison, Samuel Eliot. *The European Discovery of America: The Southern Voyages, A.D. 1492-1616*. New York: Oxford University Press, 1974.

Outhwaite, Leonard. *Unrolling the Map: Exploration of the Earth from 2750 B.C. to the Space Age*. New York: The John Day Company, 1938, 1963, 1972.

Rienits, Rex and Thea. *The Voyages of Columbus*. New York: Crescent Books, 1970, 1989.

Chapter 6: Beethoven and Mozart

Arnold, Dennis and Fortune, Nigel. *The Beethoven Companion*. London: Omnibus Press, 1971.

Baker, Richard. *Mozart*. New York: Thames and Hudson, 1982.

Braunbehrens, Volkmar. *Mozart in Vienna*. New York: Grove Weidenfeld, 1989, 1990.

Carr, Francis. *Mozart & Constanze*. New York: Franklin Watts, 1984.

Cooper, Martin. *Beethoven: The Last Decade*. London: Omnibus Press, 1970.

Deutsch, Otto Erich. *Mozart: A Documentary Biography*. Stanford, CA: Stanford University Press, 1965.

Gal, Hans. *The Golden Age of Vienna*. London: Omnibus Press, 1948.

Harris, Robert. *What to Listen For in Mozart*. New York: Simon & Schuster, 1991.

Hildesheimer, Wolfgang. *Mozart*. New York: Farrar, Straus, Giroux, 1982.

Komroff, Manuel. *Mozart*. New York: Knopf, 1956.

Marek, George R. *Beethoven*. New York: Omnibus Press, 1969; London: Omnibus Press, 1948.

Melleus, Wilfred. *Beethoven and the Voice of God*. New York: Oxford University Press, 1982, 1983.

Orga, Ates. *Beethoven*. London: Omnibus Press, 1983.

Robbins, Howard C. *The Mozart Companion*. New York: W.W. Norton, 1956, 1969.

Solomon, Maynard. *Beethoven Essays*. Cambridge, MA: Harvard University Press, 1988.

_____. *Mozart: A Life*. New York: Harper Collins Publishers, 1995.

Rushton, Julian. *Coffee with Mozart*. London: Duncan Baird Publishers, 2007.

Spaeth, Sigmund. *A Guide to Great Orchestral Music*. New York: The Modern Library, 1943.

Stafford, William. *The Mozart Myths: A Critical Reassessment*. Stanford, CA: Stanford University Press, 1991.

Turner, William J. *Mozart: The Man and His Works*. Garden City, NY: Doubleday & Company, Inc., 1954.

Chapter 7: Stanley and Brazza

Cameron, Ian. *To the Farthest Ends of the Earth: 150 Years of World Exploration by the Royal Geographic Society*. New York: E.P. Dutton, 1980.

Forbath, Peter. *The River Congo: The Discovery, Exploration and Exploitation of the World's Most Dramatic River*. New York: Harper & Row, 1977.

Hanbury-Tenison, Robin. *The Oxford Book of Exploration*. Oxford, UK and New York: Oxford University Press, 1993.

Hills, Denis. "Fatal Africa," in *Into the Unknown: The Story of Exploration*. Washington, DC: National Geographic Society, 1987.

Hibbert, Christopher. *Africa Explored: Europeans in the Dark Continent, 1769-1889*. New York and London: W.W. Norton & Company, 1982.

Josephy, Alvin M. *The Horizon History of Africa*. New York: American Heritage Publishing Co., Inc., 1971.

Leithauser, Joachim G. "Secrets of the Dark Continent," in *Worlds Beyond the Horizon*. New York: Alfred A. Knopf, 1955.

McDonald, Gordon, Bernier, Donald W., Brenneman, Lyle E. et al. *Area Handbook for People's Republic of the Congo (Congo Brazzaville)*. Washington, DC: U.S. Government Printing Office, 1971.

Pakenham, Thomas. *The Scramble for Africa, 1876-1912*. 1st U.S. Edition. New York: Random House, 1991.

Stanley, Henry Morton. *Autobiography*. Boston: Houghton Mifflin, 1911.

Stanley, Henry Morton. *In Darkest Africa, or the Quest, Rescue, and Retreat of Emin Governor of Equatoria, in Two Volumes*. New York: Charles Scribner's Sons, 1890.

Stanley, Henry Morton. *Through the Dark Continent*. London: Sampson, Low, Marston, Searle, & Rivington, 1890.

Stanley, Richard and Neame, Alan. *The Exploration Diaries of H.M. Stanley*. New York: The Vanguard Press, 1961.

Wasserman, Jacob. *Bula Matari: Stanley, Conqueror of a Continent*. New York: Liveright, Inc., 1933.

West, Richard. *Brazza of the Congo: European Exploration and Exploitation in French Equatorial Africa*. London: Cape, 1972.

Chapter 8: Goethe and Napoleon (and Hitler)

Arnold, James R. *Crisis on the Danube: Napoleon's Austrian Campaign of 1809*. Ist Edition. New York: Paragon House, 1990.

Boerner, Peter. *Goethe*. Translated by Nancy Boerner. London: Haus Publishing, 2015. Kindle Edition.

Goethe, Johann Wolfgang von. *The Sorrows of Young Werther*. Devon, UK: Dover Publications, Inc., 2002.

_____. *Autobiography*. Translated by John Oxenford. Hamburg, Germany: Classic Books Publishing, 2008.

Haythornthwaite, Philip J. *The Napoleonic Source Book*. New York: Facts on File, 1990.

Hitler, Adolph. *Mein Kampf*. Boston: Houghton Mifflin Company; Cambridge, MA: The Riverside Press, 1925, 1962.

Schom, Alan. *Napoleon Bonaparte*. New York: HarperCollins Publishers, 1997.

Shirer, William. *The Nightmare Years, 1930-1940 (Vol. II of 20th Century Journey: A Memoir of a Life and the Times)*. Boston, Toronto: Little, Brown and Company, 1984.

Shirer, William. *The Rise and Fall of the Third Reich*. New York: Simon and Schuster, 1960.

Snyder, Louis L. *Hitler and Nazism*. New York: Bantam Books, 1967.

Speer, Albert. *Inside the Third Reich*. New York: Avon Books, 1970.

Walter, Jacob. *The Diary of a Napoleonic Foot Soldier*. New York: Penguin Books, 1991, 1993.

Chapter 9: FDR and Ibn Saud

Aramco and Its World: Arabia and the Middle East. Dhahran, Saudi Arabia: Aramco, 1980.

Aburish, Said K. *The Rise, Corruption, and Coming Fall of the House of Saud*. New York: St. Martin's Press, 1995.

Bishop, Jim. *FDR's Last Year*: April 1944-April 1945. New York: William Morrow & Company, Inc., 1974.

Blair, John M. *The Control of Oil*. New York: Pantheon Books, 1976.

Emerson, Steven. *The American House of Saud: The Secret Petrodollar Connection*. New York: F. Watts, 1985.

Halberstam, David. *The Reckoning*. New York: Avon Books, 1986.

Holden, David. *The House of Saud: The Rise and Rule of the Most Powerful Dynasty in the Arab World*. New York: Holt, Rinehart, & Winston, 1981.

Johnson, Paul. *Modern Times: The World from the Twenties to the Nineties*. New York: Harper Collins Publishers, 1983, 1991.

Lacey, Robert. *The Kingdom*. New York: Harcourt Brace Jovanovich, 1981, 1982.

Lindsey, Gene. *Saudi Arabia*. New York: Hippocrene Books, 1991.

McLoughlin, Leslie J. *Ibn Saud: Founder of a Kingdom*. New York: St. Martin's Press, 1993.

Mosely, Leonard. *Power Play: Oil in the Middle East*. New York: Random House, 1973.

Safran, Nadav. *Saudi Arabia: The Ceaseless Quest for Security*. Cambridge, MA: Belknap Press of Harvard University Press, 1985.

Sampson, Anthony. *The Seven Sisters: The Great Oil Companies and the World They Shaped*. New York: The Viking Press, 1975.

Stobaugh, Robert and Yergin, Daniel, eds. *Energy Future*. New York: Random House, 1979.

van der Meulen, Daniel. *The Wells of Ibn Saud*. New York: Praeger, 1957.

Yergin, Daniel. *The Prize: The Epic Quest for Oil, Money and Power*. New York: Simon and Schuster, 1991, 1992.

Chapter 10: Kennedy and Khrushchev

Beschloss, Michael R. *The Crisis Years: Kennedy and Khrushchev, 1960-1963*. New York: Edward Burlingame Books, 1991.

Brumberg, Abraham. *Russia Under Khrushchev*. New York: Frederick A. Praeger, 1962, 1963.

Clinch, Nancy Gager. *The Kennedy Neurosis: A Psychological Portrait of an American Dynasty*. New York: Grosset & Dunlap, 1973.

Gallois, Pierre. *The Balance of Terror: Strategy for the Nuclear Age*. Boston: Houghton Mifflin Company, 1961.

Hamilton, Nigel. *JFK, Reckless Youth*. New York: Random House, 1992.

Lertzman, Richard A. and William J. Birnes. *Dr. Feelgood: The Shocking Story of the Doctor Who May Have Changed History by Treating and Drugging JFK, Marilyn, Elvis, and Other Prominent Figures*. New York: Skyhorse Publishing, 2013.

O'Donnell, Kenneth P. and Powers, David F. with Joe McCarthy. *"Johnny, We Hardly Knew Ye."* Boston and Toronto: Little, Brown and Company, 1970.

Reeves, Richard. *President Kennedy: Profile of Power*. New York: Simon and Schuster, 1993.

Salisbury, Harrison. *The 900 Days: The Siege of Leningrad*. New York: Avon Books, 1969, 1970.

Talbott, Strobe, ed. *Khrushchev Remembers*. Boston and Toronto: Little, Brown and Company, 1970.

Talbott, Strobe, ed. *Khrushchev Remembers: The Last Testament*. Boston and Toronto: Little, Brown and Company, 1974.

Whalen, Richard J. *The Founding Father: The Story of Joseph P. Kennedy*. New York: New American Library, 1964.

About the Author

Richard Hermann is the author of ten books, a former law professor and entrepreneur, the founder and president of Federal Reports, Inc., a legal information and consulting firm. He writes a weekly op-ed column, a legal blog, and is a regular contributor to *National Jurist* magazine. He has degrees from Yale University, the New School University, Cornell Law School, and the U.S. Army Judge Advocate General's School.

He has always been interested in history and is an avid consumer of histories and biographies.

He lives with his wife in Arlington, Virginia and Canandaigua, New York.

www.ingramcontent.com/pod-product-compliance
Lightning Source LLC
Chambersburg PA
CBHW060258100426
42742CB00011B/1798